TRAUMA TO THE,
AND DISSOCIATION

D1521412

TRAUMA, TORTURE, AND DISSOCIATION

A Psychoanalytic View

Aida Alayarian

KARNAC

First published in 2011 by
Karnac Books Ltd
118 Finchley Road, London NW3 5HT

Copyright © 2011 to Aida Alayarian.

The right of Aida Alayarian to be identified as the author of this work has been asserted in accordance with §§ 77 and 78 of the Copyright Design and Patents Act 1988.

British Library Cataloguing in Publication Data

A C.I.P. for this book is available from the British Library

ISBN: 978 1 85575 876 6

Edited, designed and produced by The Studio Publishing Services Ltd,
www.publishingservicesuk.co.uk
e-mail: studio@publishingservicesuk.co.uk

www.karnacbooks.com

CONTENTS

ACKNOWLEDGEMENTS

It is a long-awaited privilege to be able to publish this book. I began gathering clinical data about fifteen years ago, and started writing the beginning of this book about six years ago. I have been discussing these ideas with my colleagues, in particular, Josephine Klein, since the early 1990s. Josephine and I were frustrated by the lack of resources available that would enable us to learn more about the clinical material we had been discussing and, in one of our meetings in the late 1990s, Josephine said, "Why don't you write about it?"

I began writing without a clear plan, unsure as to whether it would come to anything more than reflecting my thoughts, or whether a publisher would be interested in the idea. As time passed and I revisited my clinical data, I began to realize that there were positive dissociations presented by the more resilient patients with whom I was working.

In 2005, I decided to start systematically thinking about what I was observing, which had been raising unanswered questions in my mind for more than two decades. I thought I could make this the subject of a clinical research doctorate, so I wrote a proposal, and submitted it to Bob Hinshelwood. We then discussed it, and, as a result, I registered for a PhD study at the Centre of Psycho-analytical Study at Essex University.

I acknowledge the intellectual debt I owe to Professor Hinshel-wood for his objective and constructive criticism, which greatly aided my work over the past few years. I also express my appreci-ation to Professor Karl Figlio as the Chair of my supervisory board, whose constructive questions and critiques have been the source of important ideas and good advice. My deep gratitude goes to Dr Josephine Klein and Dr John Denford for reading my draft and sharing my views on resilience and dissociation. I also thank many other friends and colleagues whose valuable contributions have helped me to broaden my views and knowledge and have guided the development of this work.

Finally, my gratitude is mostly to my patients. I feel indebted to the people I have worked with, who have been instrumental in making this work possible. They introduced me to their inner world and took me to the most private corners of that world, help-ing me to understand the nature of their psychic function and teaching me how to relate to them usefully. I thank them for trust-ing me and for allowing me to collect clinical material as necessary data for this study. Without them, this study would not have been possible.

ABOUT THE AUTHOR

Aida Alayarian, BSc, MSc, DocSc, PhD, is a consultant clinical psychologist, child psychotherapist since 1986, and adult psychoanalytic psychotherapist since 1998. She studied, and has a Masters in, Medical Anthropology and Intercultural Psychotherapy, with a background in Medicine. She is the founder and currently Clinical Director of the Refugee Therapy Centre. She developed and is the Director of a four-year training and MA course, run in collaboration and partnership with the University of East London (UEL) and the Refugee Therapy Centre.

FOREWORD

Why are some people who are subjected to cruel and inhuman treatment, even prolonged torture, both of body and mind, able to emerge relatively unscathed from their experiences and go on to rebuild their lives, while others are completely shattered by the same experiences, and remain broken and ineffectual all their lives after?

Using the psychoanalytic concept of object relations, Dr Alayarian argues convincingly that the differences are explained by early family life having allowed the establishment of good loving and secure figures in the psyches of the resilient ones, and the absence or insufficiency of such presences is responsible for the vulnerability of the others.

Aida Alayarian should know, if only from her own experience. Exiled from her home country many years ago, she has established herself securely in the UK and, in helping to establish, and now directing successfully, The Refugee Therapy Centre, in North London, which cares for and provides psychotherapy for asylum seekers and refugees, and running training courses for those doing similar work, she has shown the very resilience she analyses in this book.

The ideas explored are also valuable for defining the aims of therapists in this field. That is, to try to establish, via the therapeutic relationship (both with the individual therapist and the institution that cares for the client) an equivalent caring, but individual, internalized presence of the welcoming host country, which will be a source of strength and reassurance for the person trying to adjust to the new life and come to terms with all the hurts and losses that have occurred before.

John Denford
Psychoanalyst and Chairman of Trustees,
The Refugee Therapy Centre

PREFACE

Ordinary daily life in times of relative peace depends on a series of theories about the world and about ourselves. Of particular relevance to trauma are three assumptions. First, regardless of knowledge of personal vulnerability and mortality, we operate on an assumption of personal invulnerability. Indeed, in the West, illness and death are often called "life" events in the hope that by singling them out we will see them as a part of life. If they truly were what we experienced as part of life, we would not need to call them "life events". Second, we operate on an assumption that the world and our experiences within it can be experienced as meaningful. Finally, regardless of unconscious doubts, we largely have a consciously benign view of our place in the world. Trauma calls into question all these ways of viewing the self and the world.

Lerner's (1980) "Just world theory" underlines the sense of a fair world in which people get what they deserve. A trauma causes a problem here. There are religious, political, and social doubts activated after natural and man-made disasters. Disasters are not fair. They destroy the innocent as well as the guilty. Therefore, they disturb the assumption that there is a simple concept of justice at work. Indeed, this emphasizes the need for justice and fairness in working with victims and perpetrators alike to minimize post traumatic stress disorders. Additionally, positive assumptions about the individual's place in the world are also eroded by trauma.

Trauma comes from the Greek, meaning, "wound", from an earlier derivation meaning "to pierce". It has long been used in medicine and surgery as meaning both an injury where the skin is broken as a result of external violence and as the consequences on the organism as a whole. In using the term "trauma", psychiatry, psychology, and psychoanalysis includes all of the following components.

A person has experienced an event that is outside the range of usual human experience that would be markedly distressing to almost anyone, such as: a serious threat or harm to one's life or physical integrity; serious threat or harm to one's children, spouse, or other close relatives and friends; sudden destruction of one's home or community; seeing another person who has recently been, or is being, injured or killed as a result of an accident or physical violence.

These break down into:

1. An external stressor that comes suddenly and therefore cannot be prepared for.
2. A stressor that is strong enough to break through the protective shield of skin and mind (Freud, 1920g), which cannot be adequately mentally processed and affects the whole organism.
3. The stressor that interacts with the individual's internal world, including unconscious guilt and phantasy.

In addition to psychoanalytic theories on trauma, we can add the knowledge, from Spitz (1945) onwards, on how childhood attachment is a prerequisite for safety. Spitz showed how children in an orphanage who were physically cared for but who had no attachment figures were more vulnerable to dying. Attachment to one or more adults protects children from danger while they develop the maturational skills to care for themselves. The contemporary refugee experience, however, of dispossession, abuse of human rights, torture, racism, legal and ethical betrayals, lead to an impossibility for some parents to protect their young. The common refugee experience, that a parent is unable to screen a child from danger or is part of a dangerous experience for a child, altering or destroying a young child's perception of safety and of adult pro- tectiveness, makes Alayarian's question even more important— what then makes for resilience?

Dr Aida Alayarian, BSc, MSc, Doc.Sc, PhD, is the co-founder and Clinical Director of the Refugee Therapy Centre, a charity in North London. As both a consultant clinical psychologist and child psy- chotherapist and an adult psychoanalytic psychotherapist, she is aware of the impact of trauma and torture experiences across the lifespan, with no false divisions marked by chronological age. She knows only too well the experiences of dispossession and human rights violations. Additionally, she has taken care to ensure that the majority of the Centre's therapists have a refugee or immigrant background and bring with them the requisite linguistic, cultural, and shared experiences. She is also a member of the International Rehabilitation Council for Torture Victims.

As a result of all that lived experience, this is a significant clini- cal, conceptual, and theoretical book which also provides realistic, non-delusional hope.

While psychoanalytical approaches have largely not been seen as the most helpful when dealing with chronic PTSD and dissocia- tion, Alayarian provides a full theoretical review of analytic think- ing on trauma that will enrich practitioners from all approaches, as well as looking into the specific features that might identify those who would respond to such treatment or find alternative methods for those who do not.

Additionally, she chooses to undertake a qualitative research project to show the meaning of resilience as a factor in working with trauma. Indeed, the whole concept of this book comes from a research question: "What is the unconscious aspect of the personal- ity that enables some people to be resilient to traumatic experi- ences?" To aid her with this question, she uses a theoretical review, powerful clinical anecdotes, and a conceptual hypothesis that being listened to by a therapist, a listening other, in itself creates psychic space and a sense of self.

In insecure times we care more about bottle-feeding than breast- feeding, in knowing and measuring rather than trusting in the intersubjective connections. It is perhaps due to the empiricism of the scientific revolution that "fact" components are seen as more valued than concept components. Indeed, the psychoanalyst André Green (2000) attempts to console the psychoanalytic researcher by claiming, "the scientific method till the present has proved to be sterile in psychoanalysis".

Finding that a piece of theory is substantiated in clinical practice is open to all sorts of scientific research questions. Fonagy aptly notes, "Data is, of course, not the plural of anecdote . . . but is a crucial issue for the psychoanalyst" (2001, p. 4). However, Alayarian has found a gap in the theory, an oubliette, from which comes the need first to properly validate the old historic concept of dissociation, with which I heartily concur (Sinason, 2004, 2010), and then radically to explore the difference between healthy and unhealthy dissociation.

Those of us working with the extreme limits of dissociation, including dissociative identity disorder and mind control, find that in the end the most precious thing we can offer, and sometimes the only thing, together with transparency, respect, and our psychoanalytic tools there to aid and resource us, is the act of bearing witness. Being alongside and listening allows a space to open up, a small green shoot to come through, even where the level of early and ongoing damage means recovery does not exist.

Valerie Sinason
Director of the Clinic for Dissociative Studies

This study aims to explore the resilient factor and its relation to dissociation (both healthy and unhealthy) in people who have endured trauma. It is hypothesized that such dissociative activity involves the "deconstruction" of otherwise symbolically integrated self/other constellations, evoked independently or in response to, but always in interaction with, the patient's own unique organization of multiple centres of psychic awareness and unconscious accessibility. Understanding trauma is a central aspect for both practical and theoretical challenges in this study. Treatment of trauma will be from a relational perspective, with the view that childhood trauma of a patient is a dual narration. Throughout the study, the theoretical material is presented in close conjunction with clinical data. Clinical vignettes and extended case studies are used to illustrate the key points and to illustrate the theoretical conceptualization. The importance of patients' early experiences will be emphasized, along with the developmental processes as a factor in creating resilient qualities.

The term dissociation used is distinct from other current meanings; looking at psychoanalytical ideasm this study aims to address three main issues:

- the characteristics commonly associated with trauma and with resilience;
- the creation of an intrapsychic and secure state of mind with reference to Freud and contemporary psychoanalytic thinking, specifically object relations theory;
- the relationshp between being resilient and psychological health, or lack of it.

The main research question is: "What are the traits in the unconscious of the personality which enable some people to be resilient to the experience of trauma and lead fulfilling lives and cause others to collapse psychologically?"

It is hypothesized that resilient people can manage their traumatic experience by successfully dissociating as and when necessary, in order to pursue the business of their lives, while vulnerable people have certain unconscious mechanisms that interrupt and disable that necessary dissociation. This will be linked with the "sense of self" and idea of an inner "psychic space", which can be fostered by having a "listening other" in therapy. To test the research question and establish the foundations of resilience and vulnerability, discussion centres on dissociation (healthy and unhealthy). The listening other, psychic space, and the sense of self are referred to throughout the thesis as an element of the overall hypothesis on resilience and healthy dissociation, or lack of it. Methodology used in this study is psychoanalytic therapy, which has informed the author's practice. The centrality of transference and countertransference, the unconscious, and dreams are emphasized throughout, while taking into consideration the need for a creative and flexible intercultural approach to therapy and reconstruction. Qualitative analysis of qualitative content will be used in the form of literature review, vignettes, and in-depth clinical case studies in order to identify patterns of symptoms; in particular, relationships between current and previous defences and coping mechanisms and the pattern of dissociation (healthy and unhealthy) and its relation to resilience and vulnerability.

Consciousness and the sense of self are provided by memory, perception, social narratives, and possibilities. I suggest, therefore, that

- consciousness and sense of self come from the sense of inner world;
- resilience is an inner psychic process providing a sense of containing oneself and one's experience (even traumatic ones), and the existence of psychic space;
- clear memory, thinking, and narrative of events contribute to the sense of inner psychic space to reflect and process the experiences, traumatic or not;
- the ability to have a listening other is the mechanism for relating to an other in a containing manner and comprises resilience.

Vignettes and case studies are refracted through the integrative perspective of elusive theoretical concepts and between normal and pathological identifications, presenting the terms resilience *vs.* vulnerability and healthy dissociation *vs.* unhealthy dissociation to characterize the sense of self that is integral to ego function and intrapsychic space.

Resilience is considered as being an effective model of assessment of the quality of the sense of self and understanding the possible breakdown of inner psychic space and how this might be reversed as analytical therapy progresses, bringing an insightful component of one's experience which leads the self to become a single, simple, continuing, and accessible mental substance. Resilience is considered the measure of treatment outcome in the treatment of anxiety, depression, and stress reactions, and people diagnosed with post traumatic stress disorder, with improved resilience increasing the positive outcome.

The formulation of this research question contrasts with a more didactic approach to other aspects of the therapy: for example, resilience in the therapist, which is not the subject of this thesis.

Introduction

The theme of this study, and its specific hypotheses about what it is that makes people resilient, comes out of my clinical experience. Over the decades, I have been enthralled and fascinated by people who have been traumatized. Too often, those who have survived atrocities are unable to shake off their unbearable memories and this continues to disrupt their attempts to make a life for themselves. Psychotherapists and other professionals in the field, seeking to alleviate the suffering of people who have experienced external trauma, frequently face stress and frustration. It is distressing for therapists for a number of reasons, and, in my view, one of them is related to understanding of psychoanalysis, that is, the unconscious effects of trauma, dreams, and transferential behaviour.

This led me to consider the following as a research question: "What is it in the unconscious aspects of the personality that enables some people to be resilient to traumatic experiences, and to lead subsequently fulfilling lives? Why is it that some people respond to trauma with a successful act of dissociation, leaving the organization of their world reasonably intact, while others experience fragmentation (ego weakness) of the self and of their perception of the world?"

I divided the study into two parts. In the first part, I begin with a literature review, examining the psychoanalytic and psychological literature on trauma, resilience, and the conceptualization of dissociation in psychoanalysis to date, as well as considering other related concepts in psychoanalysis such as the sense of self; the relevance of inner psychic space and the therapist as the patient's listening other. The literature will be discussed in terms of (a) the core ideas, (b) the pros and cons, (c) a critique of how convincing the texts are and why, and (d) the relevance for this study. The main aim is to find out these ideas, rather than starting with ready-made conclusions. Therefore, the literature review is used to create a potential theoretical base to the research question in response to the idea of resilience being created, and enhanced by being attended to, or listened to (in therapy the therapist is the listening other) that results in the development of psychic space and a good sense of self.

In the first part, I use clinical material and data from several short vignettes and, in the second part, two more detailed cases as evidence. Data used throughout the study are clinical material from psychoanalytic therapy, which has informed the author's practice. The centrality of transference–countertransference, the unconscious, and dreams is emphasized, as well as the need for a creative intercultural and flexible approach to therapy and reconstruction when working with traumatized patients. This flexibility also runs alongside the empirical testing of hypotheses for further understanding and progression. The importance of patients' early experiences is emphasized, along with developmental processes as a factor in creating resilient qualities.

One chapter is devoted to methodology used in research questions involving the testing of hypotheses and supporting theories in an empirical way. Following the methodology, the first part covers the three main areas implicated in the research question: psychological trauma, resilience, and dissociation. The chapter on psychological trauma opens with an introduction to the term "trauma" and a comprehensive description of the phenomenon, including the differences between internal and external trauma, between trauma and stress, indeed, the effects of a single traumatic event and repeated or ongoing trauma. Following this, there is a discussion of the potential causes of trauma, various mechanisms, individualized dynamics, and multiple implications for psychological well-being. Emphasis is placed on the trauma experienced by individuals, paying specific attention to the creation of psychic space and the sense of self as linked with past and present resilience (or lack of it) and "dissociation", both healthy and unhealthy. Then there is a discussion of trauma and post traumatic stress disorder (PTSD). PTSD is considered to be an outcome of vulnerability and ego fragmentation because it represents an intrapsychic and world dissolution. Although the notions and hypotheses in this study are general and not specifically about "refugee trauma", clinical data are from work with traumatized refugee patients. For this reason, a specific section in this chapter is devoted to issues particular to refugees in relation to trauma. Emphasis throughout is given to the fact that people have subjective reactions to objective events, and that no two people will experience, or respond to, a stressor in the same way. This leads to a discussion on the principles of psychoanalysis and trauma (as perceived by Freud and, indeed, contemporary psychoanalysts) in relation to the ways individuals typically cope with trauma. A vignette of a traumatized patient is presented, with emphasis on transference as a psychoanalytic instrument. Transference, as the unconscious redirection of feelings from one person to another in a relationship, and its meanings is a crucial aspect of psychotherapeutic work, and will be discussed throughout this study. The powerful and often overwhelming feelings that the psychotherapist may have in the psychotherapeutic relationship is what makes psychoanalytical psychotherapy dynamic and effective, while simultaneously making it challenging to practice. The contemporary object relations psychoanalysis determines that as a therapist, it is through our own feelings, enactments, fantasies, and imagination that we become the subject who knows what the patient needs to convey. So, transference is not just the result of the patient's past but is the product of an intersubjective field created in the therapist–patient dyad, where transference and countertransference are reciprocal. In this relationship, the therapist's responses are sensitive detectors of the patient's object-relational expectations and the co-created result of the living relationship with the therapist.

The next chapter is on resilience as a concept and a means of illustrating why two people can have different responses to the same potentially traumatic occurrences. This chapter begins with a definition of resilience, with reference to the psychological perspectives on the concept, and the longstanding psychological research of Emmy Werner (1984, 1994; Werner & Smith, 1992) and Norman Garmezy (1970, 1981, 1991, 1993; Garmezy, Masten, & Tellegen, 1984), which has been briefly referred to in the literature review. A list of factors typically found in resilient people is presented and psychoanalytic concepts that can be viewed as equivalent to resilience are listed. Psychoanalytic theories are applied to vignettes presented in this chapter, which are specifically chosen to illustrate one individual who demonstrates resilience and one who lacks resilience, with emphasis on transference and countertransference. It is possible to replicate Werner's conclusions about the presence of a significant other (listening other) as a protective factor. Accordingly, the first vignette is of a prisoner who, with some of her fellow prisoners, had each other as their listening other for support, and in the second vignette, the boy had his therapist as his listening other. The listening other, sense of self, psychic space, and dissociation, both healthy and unhealthy, is referred to in this chapter and throughout the study to explore a literature-based research question alongside the main hypothesis.

It is important to note that at times the tone of the discussion in this chapter may seem didactic, specifically when referring to resilience and psychoanalytic treatment. This is due to the fact that resilience has been and remains missing from the psychoanalytic vocabulary. I see resilience as part of specific character formation, which I hypothesize to be relational. In my view, in psychoanalytical treatment the creation of resilience is certainly a background experience; presented in different terminology, it informs the analysis of transference and countertransference. The emphasis in this chapter, however, remains on using the academic analytical format to develop an argument based on relevant data from the research, rather than moving towards personal opinion-based arguments that are based on intuitive experience. It is based on the contributions of psychoanalysis to clinical understanding of psychological development, its disruptions, and various forms of psychopathology deriving from disruptions of normal developmental processes and the consequences.

The next chapter is devoted to dissociation, and starts with a literature review with particular attention to the history of psychoanalysis, with three brief clinical vignettes, and expands this to a non-clinical encounter with a traumatized person in power . This chapter focuses on the previously wider discussion on resilience, relating this process directly to dissociation, both conscious and unconscious processes.

The history of Freud's (1895a) and Janet's (1892–1907) concepts of dissociation is briefly outlined. This is necessary, as the term "dissociation", as it is used in this study, is distinct from those uses which appear infrequently and inconsistently in psychoanalysis at large (both contemporary and historical). Identification of a gap in the psychoanalytic literature in relation to dissociation and my formulation is the main part of my research question, that is, a new conception of "healthy dissociation". The notions of healthy and unhealthy dissociation will be examined in more detail, as these relate to resilience and vulnerability, respectively. There is emphasis on what unhealthy dissociation is distinct from (i.e., repression and splitting). The clinical relevance of dissociation to resilience is presented using vignettes which illustrate both forms of dissociation. The nature of dissociation will be discussed to examine the main hypothesis of the study, which states that healthy dissociation engenders resilience, but unhealthy dissociation creates ego fragmentation and vulnerability, preventing the development of resilience. Care is taken to delineate the concept of dissociation as it is used in this study, which comes with positive connotations and is considered as distinctively independent. It is distinct from the deficit disorder or problem-orientated paradigm that is used in other clinical researches; it is also distinct from dissociation as defined in the *Diagnostic and Statistical Manual of Mental Disorders* (*DSM-IV*). In contrast to a medical view, consideration will be given to the social suffering and its effect on a traumatized person; this is in line with what Kleinman (1985) elaborates in a meaningful manner, allowing a humanistic understanding of the challenges that we all face in our lives. He and his colleagues (Kleinman, Das, & Lock, 1997) describe suffering as a social experience that connects the moral, political, medical, health, and social policies.

The dissociation (healthy and unhealthy) is further discussed in relation to the twofold nature of trauma; that is, in a situation where the traumatized person may retain a clear attachment to the knowledge of the experience of traumatic memories, but chooses not to recall this in order to survive. This is when the person decides not to give attention to the particular traumatic memories and to redirect the attention to something else. There is always an unconscious element involved in this process; however, at the conscious level, the different emergent mental processes bring a degree of the person's vulnerability (i.e., patients such as Daniel, one of the main cases in Part II), or resilience and mutual independence (i.e., patients like Farina, the other case in Part II). The mental processes of both conscious and unconscious perception of the individual are considered to be related to the level of conscious understanding of the external reality and unconscious effects.

The second part of the study comprises clinical evidence in the form of detailed case studies. Two patients are presented, a female I call Farina, and a male whom I call Daniel. The clinical material is used to explore and present evidence of how the human mind develops resilience and shows how, in therapy, a patient's resilience can be enhanced. This is an enormous area, and I address it in a limited way. Patients' vulnerability and resilience are tested through the transference and dream interpretations. I hypothesize that patients who are seeking therapeutic help may have resilient aspects in their personality, but usually approach therapy with the vulnerable or fragmented part of themselves, the part affected by trauma.

The clinical data here aims to:

- demonstrate how the transference is experienced in phantasies, in particular in idealization and aggression, which can be conveyed through the ambience patients have built up;
- focus on how these are linked with the patient's past history, present behaviour (conscious and unconscious), and the way in which the patient dissociates in the transference;
- look into and analyse how primitive aspects of the patient's early object relationships and defences emerge and are lived out in the transference;
- examine whether a patient, by an act of dissociation, attempts to draw the therapist into the acting out.

The therapist's countertransference is monitored and analysed as data to establish how the therapist is able to work with these, and

whether therapist is able to facilitate a reasonably safe enough therapeutic environment by being a listening other to the patient and
whether this can lead to some change in the patient's internal
objects and creation of psychic space and a sense of self, thus transforming the unhealthy dissociation to healthy dissociation and
resilience. The clinical data focus on two patients as examples of
resilience and vulnerability: Farina as resilient, and Daniel as vulnerable, with the characteristics they bring to the treatment in the
transference relationship, their ways of surviving the trauma they
endured, and what this means to them. Specific attention is given
to gathering data on their ability to dissociate healthily or unhealthily, and what drives this ability, or lack of it, specifically at an
unconscious level. In this part, the psychoanalytic theory and its
implications are blended with clinical presentation, which will
serve to bring together the main data, leading to the discussion of
the usefulness of psychoanalytic treatment for traumatized people.
It is aimed to present theories and concepts alongside corresponding methodological implications and recommendations, serving to
iterate and focus on the four key characteristics of resilience identified: the psychic space, the sense of self, a listening other, and
healthy dissociation.

PART I
LITERATURE REVIEW

CHAPTER ONE

Introduction to literature review

T he literature review is intended as a means of examining the psychoanalytic and psychological literature on resilience, as well as other related key concepts in psychoanalysis, with the aim of drawing out a possible theoretical response to the research question. This part lays the foundations for the discussions on trauma, resilience, and dissociation in the following three chapters. It starts with a brief discussion of two enduring pieces of psychological research into resilience, and goes on to assert the importance of certain psychoanalytical conceptualizations in working with people who have endured trauma. The significance of unconscious processes and states in driving human behaviour is a central tenet emphasized here and throughout this study. Specific attention is given to object relations theory as a way of understanding how internal and external realities are structured in the mind, as well as intrapsychic relationships. In this context, a perception of "psychic space", the "sense of self" and its relation to the external world, and the distinction between secure and insecure attachment in early development are discussed. The self (true and false) and disruption of the self in relation to trauma, vulnerability, retraumatization, and resilience as major tenets of an individual's personal characteristics are discussed. Some key defence mechanisms identified as specifically used by traumatized patients, and which are central to the hypothesis of resilience, are described, including dissociation. Dissociation is emphasized throughout this study as intrinsically linked with the concept of an inner psychic space or lack of it, relevant to having a "listening other", as therapeutic tools for the development or regaining of the sense of self which have been lost as the result of the trauma the patient has endured.

Resilience

Resilience in psychological literature

Two important contributors to the psychological study of resilience during the twentieth century were Werner (1984, 1989, 1990, 1992, 1994, 1995, 1996; Werner & Smith, 1982) and Garmezy (1970, 1981, 1991, 1993; Garmezy, Masten, & Tellegen, 1984). Werner's study of nearly 700 infants from the island of Kauai, Hawaii over a period of forty years (from the 1950s to the 1990s) from birth to adulthood identified protective factors that enabled some children to emerge healthily despite coming from an impoverished, high-risk background, and also allowed her to trace the long-term effects of negative early life experiences.

Due to multiple risk factors, such as chronic poverty, alcoholism, abusive or psychotic parents, one-third of the infants in her study were considered high risk at birth. By studying these children over a long period, Werner was able to begin to understand how the effects of trauma are passed down from one generation to the next. Her findings were that, somehow, one out of every three of the high-risk children grew into emotionally healthy, competent adults, while two-thirds of the high risk group did develop psychological and psycho-social problems. Over 80% of the original high risk group had bounced back and were doing well by their thirties. Werner was specifically interested in these children who, despite the presence of multiple risk factors in their early childhood, and despite the exposure to trauma and family risk factors such as those mentioned above, developed healthy personalities, stable careers, and strong interpersonal relationships. She discovered hope where she expected to find despair. She sought to identify the *protective factors* that contributed to the self-righting tendencies and resilience of these children, enabling them to overcome the adversities in their developmental process and achieve a successful transition into adulthood.

A caring connection with someone other than a family member (often a neighbour, teacher, social worker, or an official) was found to be a powerful protective factor, and was identified as a key contributor to developing resilience and self-righting competencies in these individuals. On reflection, many of the resilient group said that the reason they had been able to rebound from adversity had to do with someone—an adult or peer—who reached out to them. Many viewed their teachers as having had a more significant effect on them than their parents. Some remembered a teacher who had helped them with reading, or had encouraged them, and that good experience remained with them twenty or thirty years later when they were being interviewed by Werner.

Werner (1994) identified two clusters of personal protective factors: (1) those that elicit positive responses from a variety of caring people, and (2) skills and values that lead to resilience and efficient use of abilities. Her study suggests that protective factors have a more profound impact on the life of children growing up under adverse conditions than do specific risk factors or stressful life events. Her subjects showed an awareness of the self-righting tendencies that led them to healthy adult development even under the most persistent adverse circumstances, and those protective factors transcend ethnic, social class, geographical, and historic boundaries.

Norman Garmezy, a clinical psychologist, after a long process of working with children of schizophrenic parents in the 1940s and 1950s, also identified resilience in some of those children. He found that some of the children presented healthy development and competence despite living under the most chaotic and stressful circumstances (Garmezy, 1970). He began investigating different forms of schizophrenia and loosely categorized them as '*process*' and '*reactive*' schizophrenias. He observed that people with process schizophrenia tended to be chronically ill, while those with reactive schizophrenia progressed better and were able to improve with therapeutic intervention. He suggested (*ibid.*) that this was due to the different ways in which these patients handle stress. Garmezy emphasized that children whose parents have schizophrenia live in one of the most stressful situations imaginable; they have no control over what is happening to them and are angry at how their lives are being spoiled. Usually, such parents have no time for children, so these children have no childhood and feel lonely; it is impossible for them to ask friends home, and they dread that they might inherit their parent's illness. Garmezy, in his early research work on schizophrenia, studied how adversity in life affects mental health. He focused on resilience rather than on pathology, taking into consideration cognitive skills, motivation, and other protective factors that might hold clues to preventing mental illness. He later thought that if he could understand how some of these children developed healthily in spite of their genetic backgrounds and profound family difficulties, this might lead to an increased knowledge of mental illness (Garmezy, 1981).

Garmezy's recognized that understanding the origins of the competence and resilience of many children he studied might hold essential clues to preventing mental health problems and promoting life success in children at risk. Garmezy's studies (1971, 1981, 1991, 1993; Garmezy, Masten, & Tellegen, 1984) concluded that the quality of resilience plays a greater role in mental health than anyone had previously suspected. He cut across prevailing ideas and practices by suggesting that instead of trying to devise models of treating children when they became ill, it might be more useful to study the forces helping children to survive and adapt and avoid mental illness.

With Emmy Werner, Garmezy influenced much research on the processes that protect human development in perilous conditions and promote healthy development in children whose life is affected by poverty, family violence, war, and other disasters. Although he was known for his early work on schizophrenia, Garmezy's later work on resilience in the face of disadvantage is important in building a foundation for understanding the capacity to function adaptively.

One of Garmezy's examples is a nine-year-old child who became known as "the boy with the bread sandwich". This child's father had left home when he was baby, his mother was an alcoholic, and he grew up in severe poverty. He would bring a sandwich to school each day that he had carefully made himself from two pieces of dry bread without anything in between. He reported that he did this so that no one would feel pity for him and no one would know about his mother.

Werner's findings are also corroborated by further researches in education, which suggests that the support teachers can provide to students by listening to them and validating their feelings, demonstrating kindness, compassion, and respect, enhances resilience (Gordon 1995; Higgins, 1994, Meier, 1995). Teachers' high expectations can structure and guide students' behaviour; indeed, can challenge students to go beyond what they believe they can do (Delpit, 1996). Caring teachers, who treat students as responsible individuals, allowing them to participate in all aspects of the school's functioning, and to express their opinions and imagination, make choices, problem solve, work with and help others, create a physically and psychologically safe and structured environment (Kohn, 1993, Rutter, 1995; Rutter, Maughan, Mortimer, Ouston, & Smith, 1979; Seligman, 1995). In this context, students' strength and resilience can be recognized by: (1) not taking personally the adversity in their lives; (2) not seeing adversity as permanent; and (3) not seeing setbacks as pervasive.

Werner and Smith (1992, p. 202) indicate that resilience skills include the ability to form relationships (social competence), to problem solve (metacognition), to develop a sense of identity (autonomy), and to plan and hope (a sense of purpose and future). Werner emphasized the importance of social skills and intelligence, and of humour, this last enabling the individual to laugh when they would rather cry. She used the analogy of life as a lemon, and a resilient person knowing how to make lemonade out of it. Rutter (1995), in line with Werner (1994), emphasizes that promoting self-esteem and the opening up of positive opportunities is a method for fostering resilience. He (Rutter, 1995) lists several resilience fostering categories, such as: (1) reducing the personal impact of risk, (2) reducing negative chain reactions, (3) promoting self-esteem, (4) opening up positive opportunities, and (5) the positive cognitive processing of negative experiences.

A key implication of Werner's work and the other researchers after her is that in difficult circumstances, where a community member comes to a child's rescue, this is of benefit in helping the child overcome those circumstances. From a psychoanalytical viewpoint,

Lifton (1994) suggests that an innate self-righting mechanism that resilient individuals have is the capacity to transform and change the adverse life circumstances, regardless of what their risks are. Many factors discussed by Werner and Smith (1992, p. 202) are close to psychoanalytic thinking. They indicate that "resilience skills" include (1) social competence, which is the ability to form relationships—having a "listening other", (2) metacognition, which is the ability to solve the problem without falling apart—having enough "psychic space", (3) autonomy, which is development of the "sense of self", and (4) to plan and hope, which gives a sense of purpose and of a future.

The psychological research has identified resilience in children, and some of the external factors and personality differences that are involved in it, but the standpoint of this research is to consider resilience in psychoanalytic terms. From this perspective, the psychological literature is considered inadequate, as it fails to look at how resilience can be understood in terms of internal processes and relations between the self and other. In psychoanalytic terms, this protective factor can be understood as the internalization of a good object in the process of development, a concept that will be explored further in the discussion of object relations theory that follows. In this way, perhaps, we can hope to come to an understanding of what is missing in patients without resilience.

Object relations theory

The term "object relations" refers to the self-structure that a person internalizes from early childhood which functions as a foundation for establishing and maintaining prospective relationships. Object relations theory is primarily concerned with love, especially the need for parental or primary carer love. It developed from drive theory, which derived from the discharge mechanics of the libido. Psychopathology is an expression of traumatic self-object internalizations from childhood acted out in our present relationships. Laplanche and Pontalis (1973) say:

> We may speak of the object-relationships of a specific subject, but also of types of object-relationship by reference either to points in

development (e.g. an oral object-relationship) or else to psycho-pathology (e.g. a melancholic object relationship). [pp. 277–278]

As a relational model, object relations is the most useful theory in working with people who have endured trauma. The theory accounts for the distortion of objects by pointing to the inherent difficulty of the search for relatedness. An important aspect of object relations theory is that it looks not only at what others have been for us, but also what we wanted them to be. Although cognitive development is not independent of affective factors and psychodynamic struggles, early primitive forms of cognition are unavoidable and universal. Greenberg and Mitchell (1983) suggested that

> Early forms of perception and cognition, lacking a sense of time, space, and object constancy, contribute to the painful intensity of the struggles within early object relations. For the relational model theories one need not fall back on drives to account for distortions of interpersonal reality. [p. 406]

Object relations theory is relevant to people who have endured trauma, as it emphasizes the importance of relatedness and self-definition. Central to the theory is the idea of a struggle taking place in the interpersonal and intersubjective relational medium. In the first stage of object relationships, various defences are constructed in response to external demands. Thus, ego organization, or lack of it, which is in the service of adaptation to the environment, may be fragmented by the procurement of object relations. Repeated compliance with such demands, associated with a withdrawal from self-generated spontaneity, leads to an increased stifling of impulses for spontaneous expression, thereby culminating in a false self-development; hence, there will be no sense of self.

The concept of the sense of self and its relevance

The concept of false self that Winnicott (1965) discusses is usually adopted in vulnerable states of mind, as a defence against the unthinkable, and to the denigration of the true sense of self. It may be constructed in response to a fear of death, both of the self and of others. However, such fear is a form of existential anxiety, which people who have endured trauma in adult life have experienced in the past and/or present. However, it is possible that the unconscious displacement of the emerging false self is presented within the interpersonal conditions of the earliest object relations. In this context, the false self, as a collection of behaviours, thoughts, and feelings, is motivated by vulnerability and the need to cling to the object. In my view, this is not just a result of external trauma in the adult life of a patient, but must be rooted in earlier trauma. The false self can defensively function against separation anxiety, the fear of abandonment, the fear of death and annihilation—which signify and correspond to the vulnerability which impedes integration of the whole self-object representations—and that is the foundation of resilience. This will affect the ability to "dissociate healthily" as there is no psychic space and no integrated and cohesive sense of self to begin with. As a result, the capacity for spontaneity, autonomy, creativity, and resilience is blocked further and lost in a false-self created to survive the unresolved internal conflicts resulting from early life experiences and external traumata in adulthood. Mourning, for this type of patient therefore, may not be just about the loss of the object, but also be about the loss of the sense of self. It is about both fear of annihilation of the self and fear of the loss of the other, and, in cases where the false self is totally lost, there is neither a true nor false self existing.

Klein's emphasis (1935) on the different angles of loss is helpful in understanding psychical pain. It provides clarity on the difference between the paranoid–schizoid position (that is, fear of annihilation and total destruction of the self), and the depressive position (that is, fear of the loss of the other). There is clarity in terms of the loss of the object and the grief which the psyche, as an internal space, goes through; that is, to distinguish how other the lost other is. The concept of projective identification initiated by Freud's theory of mourning is also helpful in understanding that the loss of a loved m/other/object is equal to a temporary disruption of the self. So, if the sense of the self has not been totally fragmented, there may be a need for containing, restoring, and reclaiming part of the lost self, which, as a result of not being able to go through consolatory mourning, has been projected on to the lost other. This is necessary and can be done by having a therapist as the listening other for reclaiming the sense of self and an autonomous and resilient self. It is clear that if the good object becomes damaged and lost, it does affect the ego, and the ego becomes less organized and loses part of its identity. A persecutory feeling and dread of the superego may first replace part of the ego that has been lost if the person loses internal resources and no longer is able to identify with the good internalized object. The mourning of the lost ego and of the loved object creates persecutory anxiety: the ego loses its function and is gradually replaced with fear and guilt. As a result, the psyche is populated by, and presents with, circumstances which indicate an abnormality about internalizing the object—the inability to give or to identify good enough objects which may be available. This can be an indication of a total loss. So, what we may see is the failure of the system of defence and the modes of functioning: the loss of the sense of self.

Winnicott's contribution is of vital importance in working with patients who have endured trauma. Especially, his concepts of self (true and false), his conceptualization of psychic development of the child in relation to a real and influential parent, his idea of environmental impingement, his conceptualization of space (1947), which is quite close to psychic space, the concept I am using in this study, his idea of the 'holding environment', which facilitates the transition to being self-sufficient, and his conception of the 'transitional object' (1951) are all useful concepts in working with traumatized people. He defined trauma for the infant by linking it with the idea of impingement, and suggested that in the developmental stage, impingement occurs in the form of a parent intruding when the infant needs to be left alone, or the parent being absent when is needed (Winnicott, 1960).

His theory of normative development (Winnicott, 1958) links with the holding environment in the early stages of life, in which holding involves both physical and psychical aspects. These may or may not lead to ego integration and the capacity for object relating, and eventually the capacity for object usage, all of which are also useful concepts that can be applied in working with a traumatized person. Winnicott's (1960) model of the false self as an ego defence that arises in response to environmental demands, demonstrated in *Playing and Reality* (1971), is relevant to the characteristic identified in traumatized people, that of adopting a false self to deal with traumatic experience. In the context of object relations, Winnicott's (1971) notion of trauma as an impingement offers a way of understanding this process better by looking at a traumatized patient's relationship in all its complexity, which can involve a combination of feelings of love and affection with violent, aggressive, sexual, and envious states. It is not difficult to imagine that the external world of a person who has endured trauma has been impinged and intruded upon, resulting in the loss of "the sense of a continuity of being", which is an existential anxiety. So, the false self can be a replacement when the true self has been impinged upon and, in some cases, lost. The state of mind can be impinged upon further for traumatized people, such as those who are taken hostage, or who are refugees, due to lack of cultural and language barriers. This is very important, as it provides dimensions that are integral to a fuller understanding of the possible retraumatization of patients in the new environment; indeed, transmission of trauma between survivors of trauma and their offspring.

All of these are indications that personality development throughout life, from infancy to adulthood, occurs as the result of complex dialectical developmental forces that are important for the expansion of an increasingly differentiated, integrated, resilient, and mature sense of self, and that is contingent on establishing satisfying interpersonal relationships. Equally, the development of mature, reciprocal, and satisfying interpersonal relationships depends on the growth of a mature self-definition and resilience. Relatedness or attachment to the developmental line enables us to note more clearly the dialectical developmental transaction between relatedness and self-definition.

Because of an environmental impingement, the loss of the self prevents normative continuity or a true state of existence in a dangerous and dysfunctional environment. It is also true that if someone uses a false self, then they depend very much on complying with the external world, making it possible that they may be very lost if that familiar, although dysfunctional, external world is taken away from them. This raises the question of whether some traumatized people develop a false self because they have lost everything in their world that made up their true life, or whether they are people who have always, from childhood, developed and lived a false self because of environmental impingements and in compliance with their external world, or whether it can be a combination of these two possibilities. Even the latter group are retraumatized by the loss of their familiar, though dysfunctional, external world. This is important, as resilience characteristics distinguish those people who have it from those who do not.

The nature of the false self presented by a patient manifests itself in various forms and degrees, but a false self is constructed, mainly, to hide and protect the true self from danger. However, this self may not initially have been false at all, and the false self may be a defence mechanism to facilitate survival; nevertheless, its function is not based on true reality. In an attuned false self organization, a patient can present an amenable, submissive, compliant, and interpersonally polite attitude, seeking to behave in a socially acceptable manner. In such cases, a tendency towards falseness serves to allow relations and interpersonal involvement and encourage acceptance in the environment. In contrast, the conditions can significantly intensify in those who have presented an intrapsychic structural vulnerability of the self that stems from developmental process, but which, although intensified, is not a result of trauma in adulthood. For those whose personality formation is affected by early trauma, the secondary trauma in adulthood can result in a distorted self. This is different from the false self, the function of which is to hide the inner realities of the true self. Hence, if the true self flourishes in response to the good enough m/other: and the "facilitating and holding environment", a patient who has had a good early developmental process, although traumatized in adult life, with the help of a good-enough therapist, as a listening other, should be able to go back and make reparations, and thereby regain or redevelop resilience and a true sense of self.

For people who endured early trauma and as a result already have personality impairment, the false self system may consist of an organization of various part-selves, none of which is so fully developed as to have a comprehensive personality of its own, similar to that which Laing (1959) called the "divided self". With such people no single false self exists, but various complex and fragmented selves constitute the personality. The fragmented self, then, may experience unhealthy dissociation or splitting of its embodied and disembodied aspects of being. The sense of being is subjected to existential modalities already constitutive of its being, and the true self may be structurally deficient, hence false. This falseness is not owed just to self-deception; it can be due to the lack of developmental interactions that should have formed the psychological basis of a cohesive self: the foundations of resilience, the intrapsychic space, and a good sense of self.

In some cases, a traumatized person's intrapsychic structure is so deficient, for reasons of both developmental personality formation and, later, external trauma and persecutory feelings that the emergence of a false character organization is reflective of the social environment. So, there is no capacity to play, to begin with. Participation for such a patient is a basis for testing, in search of an opportunity for the exploration, recognition, and integration of disavowed or discarded aspects of one's personality, and for the affirmation of emergent parts. This is in line with Stern's (1985) "unformulated experience", Atwood and Stolorow's (1992) "pre-reflective unconsciousness", Bollas's (1987) "unthought known", and also the clinical phenomenon described under projective identification (Bion, 1967; Hinshelwood, 1983, 1994a, 1999; Joseph, 1987; Rosenfeld, 1971, 1983; Sandler; 1990; Segal 1973; Spillius, 1992) and enactment (Jacobs, 1986, 1991; McDougall 1985, 1986; McLaughlin, 1992), basic fault (Balint, 1968), and self as an object and the other (Cassimatis, 1984; Searles, 1959, 1965, 1986).

Conceptualization of dissociation as an active defence

Freud and Breuer's (1895a) and Janet's (1892–1907) explanatory theories of hysteria, dissociation, and the nature of the mind, although they had differences in their methods, are important for this study. Freud's ideas of unconscious reminiscences and the origin of the unconscious are different from Janet's idea of the subconscious. Janet (1892–1907) suggests that, under stress, parts of the conscious mind become disconnected and detached from the rest of consciousness, while Freud and Breuer (1895a) focus on the active process of repression of certain contents of the mind related to traumatic experiences which happened in the past, the effects of these, and the way one deals with them in the here and now. Freud's (1892) view on dissociation was that

> We can succeed in bringing such a memory entirely into normal consciousness; it ceases to be capable of producing attacks. During

an actual attack, the patient is partly or wholly in the second state of consciousness . . . and is aware of the change in his state and of his motor behaviour, but the physical events during his attack remain hidden from him. [p. 151]

Freud initially seems to go along with Charcot's (1878, 1879) and Janet's (1892–1907), suggestions that attacks of hysteria are the manifestations of traumatic memories, which belong to a second state of consciousness. Freud's position here is within the general perception of dissociation framework, but with Breuer (Breuer & Freud, 1895a) he formulated the essence of hysteria as a "splitting of consciousness which is so striking in the well-known classical cases under the form of 'double conscience'" (p. 63). However, there is an important difference between Janet and the French school, who thought of a passive process of coming apart under stress with dissociation as the function of a weak constitution, and Freud, who thought of an active process of a defence solution that weakens the personality.

According to Freud (1915d), repression is a normal part of human development: indeed, the analysis of dreams, literature, jokes, and slips of the tongue illustrates the route via which our desires continue to find an outlet. In the case of a person who is faced with obstacles due to external traumatic events, which may or may not be combined with fixation on earlier phases of development, the conflict between libido and the ego and/or between the ego and the superego may be unconstructively harmed. Freud (1920g) argued that affects owe their aetiological importance to the fact that they are accompanied by the production of large quantities of excitation, and that these excitations, in turn, call for discharge in accordance with the principle of constancy. In his view, traumatic experiences and pathogenic forces produce quantities of excitation too large to be dealt with. Treatment of traumatic memories by abreaction is, thus, based upon this more fundamental principle of constancy, that is, that the quantity of excitation must be kept constant. Breuer and Freud (1895a) suggest that all powerful affects restrict association. They say that active affects level out the increased excitation via motor discharge, but anxiety blocks the ability to bring about this reactive discharge and may paralyse the power of movement as well as that of association, and creates abreaction through facilitating verbal expression alongside emotional discharge through motor activities (Breuer & Freud, 1895a, p. 277). Later, in *Beyond the Pleasure Principle* (1920g), Freud formulates two principles of mental function: (1) to produce and represent to the psyche experiences that have resulted in pleasure in the past or are likely to result in pleasure in the present, and (2) to avoid or eliminate experiences that have resulted in unpleasure. One principle of pleasure-seeking is to avoid pain, and the reality principle defers gratification when needed. In a good enough environment, one learns to endure pain and defer gratification through reasonable ego, which no longer allows itself to be governed by the pleasure principle, but obeys the reality principle, which also seeks pleasure, but pleasure that is, although postponed, assured through taking account of reality. This is principle selection exercised either through hallucinatory wish fulfilment for pleasurable experiences, or through repression for unpleasure.

However, hallucination or repression are not satisfactory concepts to explain intrapsychic tensions that may develop and remain in the mind of a person as the result of external force and trauma that is existential and will not disappear, and with an organism limited to the pleasure–unpleasure principle the person could not survive it. As a consequence, when it comes into effect, the pleasure principle does not encounter the reality principle of pleasure as an effective remedy that reduces the tension of an external object. Taking into account the conditions of internal and external reality of a traumatized person, the reality principle is futile in reversing the pleasure principle in these types of external trauma and, therefore, cannot transform the mode of expression and action. This is because the constancy principle that governs pleasure may no longer exist in the person's intrapsychic tension. This is due to the loss or diminishing of the sense of self through a reduction relative to a certain constant and by submission to certain requirements of reality and its effects on personality. Therefore, the psychic space and the ability of a traumatized person to achieve an immediate reduction of sources of tension may be lost through lack of the capacity to think about the memory of trauma as the unpleasure principle. This forces the psyche to dissociate to a different level, due to the personality of the person prior to the trauma. So, the principles can be inscribed within the trajectory of the principle of pleasure–

unpleasure, but they are insipid and may integrate, to varying degrees, other characteristics of the psychic life of the traumatized person into their operations, without calling into question the primary and fundamental principle of the orientation of a person's psychic function in reality.

Freud (1920g) describes processes that seemingly contradict the pleasure–unpleasure principle, emphasizing the existence of mental impulses which reactivate experiences that had not produced any conscious or unconscious satisfaction either at the time or through deferred action due to the repetition compulsion. Therefore, the pleasure principle appears as a secondary principle; the primary or fundamental tendency is no longer the avoidance of unpleasure or the search for pleasure, but, rather, repetition of an earlier state, indeed, the tendency to return to an earlier state. Just as the plea-sure-ego can do nothing other than indulge in wishful thinking and the avoidance of pain, the reality-ego needs to strive towards pro-tection of the self. For a traumatized person, and specifically in reference to clinical examples presented in this study, a patient whose self or at least part-self has been lost, the proxy of both real-ity and pleasure principles are no longer signifiers that restrain or safeguard the self against pleasure and reality principles. In a severely traumatized person who needs to dissociate from the memory of trauma to survive, the mental energy will focus on dissociation and, therefore, a momentary pleasure or the will to gain an assured pleasure may not exist in the psyche. This is due to the effects of external trauma that can influence one's psyche very powerfully and enforce rejection of desire, in the form of projection and introjections; therefore, there is no psychic space and no sense of self to achieve pleasure.

Bion's (1967) very brief explanation of dissociation is close to the types of dissociation that I discuss in this study. In his paper that he presented to the British Psychoanalytical Society, he discussed the phenomenon and indicates that he observed severely disturbed patients are best described by the term "splitting", as it is used by Melanie Klein, leaving the term "dissociation" free to be employed where a more benign activity is being discussed. He further suggests that the origin of the splitting processes revealed by the patient he presented were violent, which was intended to produce minute fragmentation, deliberately aimed at effecting separations which run directly counter to any natural lines of demarcation between one part of the psyche, or one function of the psyche, and another. But he viewed dissociation as being a gentler force that has "respect for natural lines of demarcation between whole objects and indeed to follow those lines of demarcation to effect the separation" (*ibid.*, p. 342). He suggests that the patient who dissociates is capable of depression, and that dissociation "betrays dependence on the pre-existence of elementary verbal thought" (*ibid.*). He emphasizes that when he talks about the developmental aspect of the activity in the history of the patient's analysis, he uses the term "splitting" and when he talks about a benign process related to the non-psychotic part of the personality he refers to "dissociation".

The concept of inner psychic space

In examining the components in the development of the capacity to experience inner space, psychoanalysis overlooks the concept of resilience. The psychic space is referred to loosely in psychoanalytical literature, but it is presented differently from the resilience perspective as inner psychic space or lack of it—the emptiness and vulnerability. The lack of psychic space in a patient may be communicated to the therapist through the experience of transference and countertransference. Kernberg (1976) talked about extreme schizoid emptiness, which sooner or later culminates in the psychotic loss of the experience of inner emptiness. This is specifically the case when the patient has lost the experience of possessing a body. Hence, inner and outer emptiness fuse to become a void in which patient is not able to experience the self and the therapist as two persons together in a room: there is no sense of self, no psychic space and no listening other. It is possible for patients to experience that no one exists in the room and to have concrete phantasies of all sorts in a void. The psychic space or lack of it in relation to trauma is relevant to all cases presented in this study and is linked with dissociation (healthy and unhealthy) and resilience or lack of it. Not directly discussed, but relevant to resilience and vulnerability, Grotstein (1978) talked about psychic space. He believed

> the capacity to experience space is a primary apparatus of ego autonomy in Hartmann's terms, which seems to have emerged

from the inchoate sensations upon the foetal skin at birth, thereby 'awakening' the skin with its sense receptors into its functions as a surface, as a boundary between self and non-self, and as a container of self. [p. 56]

Grotstein's first inner space derives from the skin, and the second is the ability to separate from the mother. He suggests that the development of the awareness and toleration of the "gap", the space in distance and time between the going and coming of the primary object, constitutes the "baptism" of space. If the infant can "contain" this space in the absence of his object, he is able to initiate and expand his sense of space and is, therefore, able to be separate. Because of this he can perceive some separated aspects of his experience that he can then begin to represent (Grotstein, 1978, p. 56). His concept is similar to Milner's (1969) discussion referring to strength, but they are both different from the psychic space, which is considered an aspect of resilience in this study.

Dreams

The association and interpretation of dreams is one of the main techniques in the practice of psychoanalysis, and, indeed, an important analytical tool in this study. The rationale for dream analysis can be considered similar to that of free association and it is extremely important in working with people who have endured trauma. Working with dreams, linking their associations to the past and present in transference, helps the patient to gain insight and increased function. This is clearly illustrated in Farina's case (a resilient patient), which is presented in detail in the second part of this study. Her dream associations and interpretations helped us to handle and work with material that she had previously denied. Her case has implications for an evidence-based intervention, supporting the use of dream material in clinical interventions to enhance her sense of self and acquire knowledge that would aid her recovery by creating more psychic space that would lead to association and connectedness. For patients (specifically those involved in politics, such as Farina) who are well defended, dreams, as opposed to free association, are of particular importance. This is because this type of patient is usually motivated by a strong superego, which, of course, functions less effectively in sleep. However, it is important to note that there is a distinction between the manifest content of a dream (what the dream appeared to be about) and its latent content and the unconscious and repressed desires or wishes that are its real object. The interpretation of a patient's dreams and responses to carefully selected questions leads the analyst, as the patient's listening other, to the unconscious representations producing the neurotic symptoms and facilitates an environment for the patient to become conscious of unresolved conflicts buried in the unconscious mind. Where successful, this process leads to sublimation.

Understanding these concepts is helpful and relevant in working with traumatized people, since some traumatic events can involve a total loss of social environment, as well as loss of the self or part of the self.

Mourning

In response to trauma, people can go through a consolatory and inadequate model of mourning, in some cases enforced, as they have to acknowledge the socio-political morals and principles that are involved in their loss. Hence, a lot of introjections and projections are going on at the same time. Many who have lost their loved ones may fail, or may not be allowed, to grieve and therefore may suffer the pathology of melancholia, a less loving, ambivalent, distractive, and violent grief. Mourning is important to understand the private and public pain that some people may have been through. In an environment with an oppressive system, aggression may serve the purposes of mourning. Consolation and an understanding of the problem of bereaved aggression should, therefore, be considered as integral concepts in working with traumatized patients. Freud's (1916) changing ideas about mourning in the context of war stand in contrast to wartime mourning practices in which groups of people from communities represented their shared grief and found collective consolation through memorializing acts informed by classical, religious, and romantic traditions. Freud was writing about his own experience, indicating the trauma of the First World War, and mourning was, for him, about loss of object. He describes mourning as a mode of personal and social recovery, a process of reality-testing with which to soberly acknowledge that lost objects no longer exist. However, for a person who is not allowed to mourn, or is deprived of being in a community, or is forced to live in exile (clinical examples in this study), this might be something much more. It can be a total disruption of the core self due to the loss of a familiar environment, and loss of the sense of self. Freud (1914g), in his early mourning theory, indicated that when we reject the belief that everything has been lost, we are inspired by ourselves, and our libido becomes free. Then we are able to replace the lost objects with new ones that are as loving as the old ones, or sometimes even more precious. He later (Freud, 1917e) redefined the process of identification associated with melancholia as a fundamental part of both subject formation and mourning an object which was lost and set up again inside the ego: an "object-cathexis" that has been replaced by an identification. He acknowledged that he did not previously appreciate the full significance of this process and did not know how common it was. He suggested that the identification process he had previously linked to a pathological failure to mourn in fact makes available the only stipulation whereby the id abandons or relinquishes its objects. Later (Freud, 1926d), his view changed again and, in relation to his daughter's death nine years earlier, he came to believe that even though the intensity of mourning does eventually fade, substituting the loss is impossible. If we are able to find a substitute to close the gaping wound, it will never resemble the person we have lost and mourned for. But, he argued, only by such a process can one continue to feel the love felt for what, or who, is now lost. He disregards his earlier theory (Freud, 1917e) and describes the enduring bonds of love that remain long after the other's loss, elaborating the identification process as a positive incorporation of the lost other. Laplanche's (1999) critique of Freud's mourning theory addresses this affirmation of otherness in the self, of an enduring "voice" belonging to the other that is understood as "related to the superego, but which is not entirely merged with it" (Laplanche, 1999, p. 254).

Mourning involves a process of obsessive remembrance of the lost other in the space of the psyche, replacing an actual absence with an imaginary presence. This restoration of the lost other enables the mourner to assess the value of the relationship and comprehend what has been lost in losing the other. With a very specific task to perform, an ordinary mourning seeks to convert loving remembrances into a memory, and move on.

Conclusion

In summary, examination of the centrality of unconscious processes from the psychoanalytic perspective at large is important in working with people who have endured trauma in adult life. The notions of *resilience, dissociation,* inner *psychic space* and the *sense of self* are considered central to this work. Dream analysis is considered as an important therapeutic technique. Work on mourning, language, and dialogue in relating to others is thought to be important in feeding our understanding of the experience of those who have suffered trauma. In working with traumatized people, the work of mourning is considered relevant as a process of elaborating and integrating the reality of loss or traumatic shock by remembering and repeating it in a symbolic and dialogic manner. It is a process of converting and representing loss that may encompass a relation between language and silence that, in some sense, could have been ritualized.

Hypothesis

It is hypothesized that resilient people can manage their traumatic experience by successfully dissociating healthily as and when necessary, in order to pursue the business of their lives, while vulnerable people have certain unconscious mechanisms that interrupt and disable that necessary dissociation. This is linked with having a stable sense of self and idea of an inner psychic space, which can be fostered by having a reasonably healthy early development or a listening other in therapy. To test the research question, and establish the foundations of resilience and vulnerability, discussions mainly centre on dissociation (healthy and unhealthy). The listening other, psychic space, and the sense of self are referred to throughout as elements of the overall hypothesis on resilience and healthy dissociation, or lack of it. The formulation of this research question contrasts with an instructive approach to other aspects of the therapy: for example, resilience in the therapist, which deserves empirical investigation but is not the subject of this thesis.

CHAPTER TWO

Methodology

The methodology used is psychoanalytic as an evolutionarily science of the mind, taking into consideration patients' socio-cultural and intercultural characteristics, which have informed the author's practice. Within psychoanalysis, there are questions of the nature of science, and the nature and place of research by which science has attempted to add to its established knowledge base. The centrality of transference and countertransference and dreams is emphasized, as is the need for a creative and flexible approach to therapy and reconstruction when working with a traumatized person. This necessary flexibility runs alongside the need for the empirical testing of hypotheses, as a scientific method employed for further understanding and progression in the field of intercultural psychoanalytic approach, taking into consideration the nature of transference. Stekel (1939) indicates:

> ... Freud's discovery of the transference is undoubtedly one of the greatest of his scientific achievements. Yet it is strange that the displacement of affects upon some neighbouring object had never attracted notice before. (The transference can, perhaps, be best characterized as displacement from the far to the near.) For, as Freud

rightly declared, psychoanalysis did not create this phenomenon, but merely drew attention to its occurrences. It is something common to all sorts of human relationships, and not peculiar to the relationship between psychoanalyst and analysand . . . a general formula for transference can best run as follows: the patient substitutes the analyst for the most important person in his life, and makes the analyst the sustainer of the central idea around which all the parapathic symptoms are encampt. [p. 155]

By using a number of vignettes and two extensive case studies, the study aims to respond to the perceived weaknesses of the single clinical case study as a research method: that is, the problem of data, the analysis of data, and generalizing it in order to gain credibility for the research. Critics of psychoanalysis argue that psychoanalysis is not a unitary, coherent theory, and as such cannot be considered scientific. It has also been considered to be a decadent, expensive treatment.

The place of quantitative in comparison with qualitative research has overwhelmed social and behavioural science, and become debatable within increasing empirical research enterprises in psychoanalytic science. It may seem that all psychoanalytically informed psychotherapists, and, indeed, the critics of psychoanalysis, know the distinction between quantitative and qualitative research. Nevertheless, there are distinct definitional problems to begin with, when syntheses are made between the natural and the human sciences within which the research is conducted, and, indeed, the position of psychoanalysis within this spectrum of sciences. It is mainly for these reasons that the dominant treatment in the UK's National Health Service is cognitive–behaviour therapy.

The experimental potential of psychoanalysis, in focusing on a single case study, has been criticized and considered not to be a strong empirical tool. Some critics argue that a single case study does not offer grounds for establishing either reliability or generality of findings as an approach to research bias. Since the time of Freud, there has been great deal of debate about the most appropriate research methodology for investigating psychoanalytic psychotherapy. There have been tremendous advances in our psychological understanding that have resulted from the focus on the single case study, but psychoanalytic research has now moved beyond this approach.

Kernberg (1993) suggests that in psychoanalysis, to do justice to the richness of the psychoanalytic situation as in other areas of research, once a body of research has been produced, the results can be "woven together" to "restore complexity" to the research endeavour. He highlights two major concerns regarding empirical research in psychoanalysis: (1) research methods which "invade" the clinical situation would unavoidably, and destructively, alter and interfere with the psychoanalytic process (work already done has suggested this fear is groundless, and that this type of research has a positive influence on analytic technique); and (2) "operationalizing" key psychoanalytic concepts would not do justice to their complexity, and would produce a tendency to oversimplify definitions and dilute essential psychoanalytic concepts.

One of the major critics of psychoanalysis is Popper, a distinguished philosopher of science of the twentieth century. Popper (1974) presented the idea that the central problem in the philosophy of science is that of demarcation, that is, of distinguishing between science and non-science, under which heading he ranks, among others, logic, metaphysics, psychoanalysis, and Adler's individual psychology. He put forward his own way of distinguishing between science, of which the exemplar was the new physics, and pseudoscience, of which the exemplars he considered were Marxism and Freudianism. Popper also accepted the legitimacy of metaphysical statements, but denied they were any part of science. His view was that of a form of logical empiricism called "falsificationism", which, in its mature versions, held that something is scientific in so far as it is liable to be falsified by data, tested by observation and experiment, and to have predictions made about it. He believed the Falsification Principle could not be falsified and was openly metaphysical. In this context, he called Darwinism a metaphysical research programme. It was no more falsifiable (he thought) than the view that mathematics describes the world and it was just as basic to modern biology (Popper, 1974).

Grünbaum is also one of the major critics of psychoanalysis. His (1976, 1984) criticism of the philosophical bases of psychoanalysis encounters difficulties. His argument does not provide a useful basis for advancing psychoanalytic knowledge and particularly for promoting the search for applicable standards of validation within psychoanalysis. Grünbaum's approach to psychoanalysis imposes a standard of logical reductionism and methodological purity that not only violates the nature of psychoanalytic knowledge, but imposes an invalid standard of verification and scientific confirmation. Reasoning that Grünbaum offers for a standard of verification is impossible, and forces psychoanalytic propositions into artificial positions that do not reflect the actuality of analytic practice.

Edelson (1986), although another critic, holds a different view from Grünbaum, insisting that clinical studies must and should be performed, and that clinical data is a reliable and necessary source of evidence, as the theory of psychoanalysis would be impossible to test otherwise (p. 232). Edelson suggests that the core theory of psychoanalysis and the case study method can provide rational grounds for considering its clinical implications. He indicates that a clinical method must adhere to scientific standards if we are to believe one explanation or hypothesis over another. He emphasizes that any arguments suggesting exempting a clinical illustrative method from scientific principles of conjecture is both unjustifiable and unwise.

One scientific test of psychoanalytic theory and practice was carried out by Henry Ezriel (1950) in his group work. His group setting approach tended to be as if he was working with one patient, seeking unifying themes, assumptions, and trends in the interaction of the members. He restricts his activity as a therapist to two basic tenets: (1) everything the patients say or do is related to the therapist; (2) the only intervention of the group leader is to interpret, and with each interpretation to focus on and reinforce the view that all intrapsychic and interpersonal behaviour of all the patients is always therapist-orientated, and always transferential. He later (Ezriel, 1956) explained that in his group work he "refrained from making a reference to the past and used solely here and now interpretations" (p. 48). He emphasized that a strict "here and now approach" will allow the experimental study of the behaviour of an individual in the psychoanalytic intervention. He concludes that a here and now approach without reference to the patient's past, overcomes objections which are commonly brought against the possibility of using the psychoanalytic session as an experimental situation in which hypotheses about human behaviour can be tested.

Cases are presented in this study, facilitating an understanding of complex issues and extending what is already known. They provide contextual analysis of a limited number of events or conditions and the relations between them. The qualitative method is used to provide the basis for the application of ideas and extension of techniques, as an empirical enquiry. Vignettes and case studies as methods of enquiry are considered as data and applied to establish a firm research focus. Each patient presented complex and difficult life events, consciously or unconsciously, wanting to understand and resolve the effects of traumas that they had endured. Each patient's presentation brought many interrelated elements and factors connected to their political, social, historical, and personal issues, providing a range of possibilities for questions. Each case is considered as a contributing factor to the whole study, while remaining a single case study in itself. A key strength of this method involves using multiple sources and techniques in the data-gathering process, and providing evidence for the research questions without standardizing a uniform method for all patients. However, the method used represents a contribution towards the systematic and empirical investigation of psychoanalytic treatments, which allows the translation of clinical data into amenable qualitative form and empirical means for understanding psychoanalytic processes in working with people who have endured external trauma, theoretically and clinically. Case studies are used for data collection, transforming complex issues into implicit source material and conveying a vicarious experience, allowing readers to question and examine the study to reach an independent understanding. Case studies focus on generating data from multiple sources, while avoiding losing sight of individual presentation: indeed, the original research questions. In two main case studies, the treatment hours of five years of analysis for each were recorded, and blocks of ten sessions were selected at regular intervals throughout the course of the analysis. These descriptions of analytic hours are highly reliable, demonstrating the methods of addressing the problem presented by patients, clinical intervention, and result achievable at any given time. Results suggest that subjecting the traditional psychoanalytic case illustration to systematic and regular enquiry can establish empirical scientific methods for psychoanalytic intervention.

Data were collected and stored from multiple sources of evidence, comprehensively and systematically referenced in lines of enquiry to uncover patients' patterns of thought and dissociative behaviour. The cases are also observed to identify causal factors associated with the pragmatic phenomenon in a flexible but rigorous manner, and any changes made in patients are documented systematically. The evidence shown in the clinical process is the changes happening and the pattern of change, that is (1) whether the change comes immediately after an interpretation, or (2) in the form of a dream in the following sessions. Notes were taken on the content of sessions and used to categorize and reference data to be readily available for subsequent reinterpretation. Notes are specifically focused on recording the patients' feelings and intuitive hunches that pose questions as the clinical work is in progress. They record testimonies and stories, and illustrations are used to demonstrate and exemplify the patients' progress or lack of it. These notes assist in determining whether or not the enquiry needs to be reformulated or redefined based on what is being said and what is being observed in transference and countertransference. The full clinical notes were kept separate from the data being collected and are presented for analysis in this study.

Vignettes, as well as intensive review of the problematic aspects of two longer clinical cases examining the specific case history of two patients, Farina and Daniel, dominate the main discussion in this study. Contrary to the view of some critics, psychoanalysis is "characterised by a relentless deconstructive urge that allows no end points or perfect solutions" (Elliott & Frosh, 1995, p. 2). Deconstructing the psychopathology of a patient such as Daniel, by using a variety of methodologies in order to uncover the roots of his presenting symptoms while ratifying and validating empirical psychoanalysis, is an example of the insight that can be obtained into both clinical and research applications. To deepen the knowledge of psychoanalytic theory of treatment and relevant to scientific research, constant attention is paid to transference, countertransference, and unconscious communication as a clinical source for renewing ideas and for the integration of research results in clinical practice. This brings together the thinking and findings of research and clinical work as a path in the development of theory-building and a science of psychoanalytic treatment. The analysis of

Daniel's psychopathology is the most intensive empirical evidence, which gives a multi-dimensional picture of empirical ways to study psychoanalytic work and process, with a detailed study of the relationship between process and outcome, focusing on the ways of interaction between analyst and patient as they change during the various phases of treatment.

Maintaining the relationship between the problems presented by patients and the process of intervention is considered as the main evidence that is used as data, documented, classified, cross-referenced, and separated into layers over the course of the study. The raw data is used for interpretations to find linkages between the research objective and the therapeutic outcomes with reference to the original research questions. The case study method, with its use of multiple data collection and psychoanalytic techniques, provides strength to the research findings and conclusions. The analysis of the data necessitated a move beyond the initial research questions, but provided accurate and reliable findings. Throughout the evaluation and analysis, there is room for new insights and further research questions.

It is important to emphasize that evidence in this study is objectively based on collection of clinical data and is not based on the intuition of the therapist. The methodology involves looking at clinical material as empirical evidence—as data, rather than an illustration of a pre-decided theory. Therefore, this clinical research is considered an empirical study, involving the testing of hypotheses and supporting theories. The outcome is expected to be helpful in the treatment of people who have endured trauma, and specifically refugees, and useful for psychoanalysts and psychoanalytical psychotherapists, as well as critics of psychoanalysis. In this study, recognition is given to the fact that there can be no objective standards of enquiry and no real appropriation of criticism of conjectures.

The creation of several different and sometimes contradictory schools of psychoanalysis may be seen to undermine the basic theoretical language of psychoanalysis, which brings challenges for any type of research. However, many psychoanalysts, such as Bion (1959), Blum (1980, 1994, 2000), Cooper (1993), Ezriel (1950, 1956), Fonagy (2002), Heimann (1950), Hinshelwood (1994a, 1997, 1999), Isaacs (1952), Kernberg (1976, 1979, 1983, 1993), Laplanche and

Pontalis (1973), Mace (1995), Stekel (1939), Symington (1986), and many others have laboured to bring some order and systematic observation to research. Psychoanalysis is an object of knowledge, at both the level of practice and that of empirical research as a tool of knowledge and transformation that becomes the object of psychoanalytic research as an object of knowledge. Psychoanalytic thought in all its manifestations has a strong capacity to view the operation of both the internal and external, indeed, the emotional and social, world of the person. In the life of a traumatized person, emotions are at times overwhelming to the point of precipitating self-destructive behaviour that may seep through to the surface and influence social experience. In some situations, internal fear, intense ambivalence, and psychological collapse might result in external disintegration, or at least a pervading sense of immobility in the face of overt and intangible danger.

So, what is required in therapy with traumatized people is dynamic thinking and being as flexible, as one can with other types of patients, with the aim of considering the internal and external world, the good and the bad, the strengths and the weaknesses, the past, present, and the future, as well as the immediacy of the present that is evident in the real life of a patient that may reflect in here and now transference situations. Therefore, the focus should be on the three areas of object relations, as well as reconstruction of history, for the personality development of the patient to be revealed, primarily on developing awareness of vulnerability and resilience, both building on inner psychic space as strength and the capacity for holding what is thought to be uncontainable, leading to a better sense of self by having the therapist as the listening other. Within the context of the therapeutic intervention, consider the innate and developing (but often covert) resilience of the person's internal world as well as attending to the external presentation, considering what the person feels inside. In psychoanalytical practice, both aspects of conscious–unconscious and the internal–external world are necessary components of the therapeutic task. The capacity to focus on the emotional world of the others allows for a psychic space of thinking so that resilience can be searched for, and be achieved.

With this method, the findings from the clinical work provide one kind of validation for psychoanalytic reconstructions, making it possible to provide a "satisfactory degree of certainty" in the attempt to integrate the patient's "psychic truth" with actual or historical truth that Freud (1937c) refers to. The use of reconstruction is an important dimension of the psychoanalytic technique that helps us to gain understanding of how an adult or part of an adult has remained a disturbed child with that particular psychopathology. The significance of reconstruction is important for restoring personality, continuity, and cohesion, and for explaining neurotic repetition as it has developed in life and in the analytic transference.

Freud (1905e, 1917e, 1937c) himself sought validity of his discoveries by emphasizing the importance of establishing an agreement between analytic reconstructions and the results of naturalistic child observation. Ahumada (1994) explains his view on the inductive workings of clinical psychoanalysis, in which mainly pragmatic facts evolve within a pragmatic relational field in ways that allow cognitions to emerge. He emphasized that his use of the term "induction" is meant in the wider sense in which Whewell (1858), Quine (1961), Russell (1948), and Von Wright (1957) conceive it, and not in the restrictive sense that Mill (1852), Braithwaite (1953) or Grünbaum (1984) have used it. He (Ahumada, 1994) says that the distinction between facts and theories is only relative, and uses Von Wright's (1957, p. 169) arguments, who, contrary to inductive generalization, operates on the saying, "the future will differ from the past". If evolution is considered as *facts*, the opening up of more psychic space in psychoanalysis brings unconscious processes to the preconscious and conscious domain, which becomes the central fact of the psychoanalytic method. Ahumada concludes that what the therapist will describe interpretatively as psychic facts are mainly the ways the patient puts into play the unconscious patterns or theories; for his/her part, the patient attains an ostensible insight into clinical facts when, helped along by the descriptive mappings conveyed by the interpretations, he/she attains an important and powerful position by double or multiple observations in individual concrete instances of the empirical falsification of the unconscious.

The same objectives later led Lichtenberg (1983) and Stern (1985) to produce evaluations of infant research findings on analytic developmental propositions. This utilization of reconstruction will be helpful to identify the linkage between historical events and the patient's intrapsychic structure through the process of transference interpretation and response to the here and now in transference, as well as the linkage between past and present childhood and adult psychopathology. Reconstruction may not always follow from the transference; it is rather an inferential and integrative act from resistance and amnesia, which may also be the result of the chemical processes of memories and biological syntheses interpretations for missing memories and gaps in history—in particular trauma related history—and the act of unhealthy dissociation. The reconstructive integration can identify patterns of patients' personalities and the interrelationship aspects of these, together with the consequences of intrapsychic configuration, rather than isolated conflicts and experiences. Therefore, developmental influences are more important than historical facts, and contribute to the formation, testing, and validation of psychoanalytic treatments and theory. Findings on the therapeutic efficacy of the interpretation and reconstruction of dissociated (both healthy and unhealthy) past conscious and unconscious conflicts and trauma can be observed by therapists in the process of being an ongoing, analytical listening other. It is important to pay attention to what Greenacre (1956) calls the "conflictual process" that helps to contain all the components of conflicts in both patient and therapist in every moment. The mutual responsiveness that develops in therapist–patient dyad stems from a complex conflictual object relationship that is similar to any other object relationship, in which transference and countertransference at all times simultaneously facilitate and interfere with the analytic work. The clinical process illustrates these related phenomena, including the use of signal conflict, the benign, and vulnerable or, at times, negative, transference and the function of countertransference structures, and the use of repetition compulsion and projection. By doing so, one's affects, thoughts, and actions trace the shifting nature of the transference resistance and help the level of the object relationship continuously being created between therapist and patient, thus helping to prevent what Steiner (1993) calls "psychic retreats". Steiner (1993) says:

> Patients who withdraw excessively to psychic retreats present major problems of technique. The frustration of having a stuck patient, who is at the same time out of reach, challenges the analyst, who has to avoid being driven either to give up in despair or to

over-react and try to overcome opposition and resistance in too forceful a way (p. 131). . . . The relief provided by the retreat is achieved at the cost of isolation, stagnation and withdrawal, and some patients find such a state distressing and complain about it. Others, however, accept the situation with resignation, relief and at times defiance or triumph, so that it is the analyst who has to carry the despair associated with the failure to make contact. Sometimes the retreat is experienced as a cruel place and the deadly nature of the situation is recognised by the patient, but more often the retreat is idealised and represented as a pleasant and even ideal haven. Whether idealised or persecutory, it is clung to as preferable to even worse states which the patient is convinced are the only alternatives. [p. 2]

Steiner (1993) discusses the idea that neurotic, perverse, borderline, and psychotic patients all have narcissistic structures in their personality, which he termed a psychic retreat that he found with stuck patients, using the retreat in a transient and discretionary way. Steiner also talked about technical problems relating to the nature of interpretations and how they are likely to be received by the intensely frightened and hostile patient who fears the abrupt and permanent loss of the psychic retreat. He offers some ideas to therapists in their attempts to stay with the patient, and to understand more clearly "what the stakes are" at critically difficult points in the work. His discussion is helpful in recognizing and understanding what is going on, and in being more open to those moments in which we sometimes become drawn into supporting the patient's pathological organization. He further discusses how and when to interpret the transference relationship to patients and to recognize when they are ready to receive them, and how we need to judge this from careful observation of the patient's presentations. He explores the idea of the patient's capacity to understand what it is they are doing, and whether or not the projection first has to be taken up in the analyst rather than in the patient. Once the perceived nature of the object is explored, the conditions for deeper understanding can become possible. These differences in emphasis deeply influence how we intervene, and whether or not our patient sees us as someone who can provide understanding. Steiner (1993) also outlines the delicate use of the countertransference, which he calls "analyst-centred interpretations", with patients as a method of understanding, explaining, and clarifying the patient's use of projective identification. This, he suggests, enables the patient to explore his disturbed perceptions of reality outside himself, located in the therapist, and avoids the problem of the patient's withdrawal and retreat when confronted by patient-centred interpretations that forcibly return to patients projections that may be threatening and be perceived as attacking through too much awareness too quickly. He indicated that the patient often has a profound feeling of not having an understanding object, and that is one reason for them to organize a psychic retreat in response to a world lacking in objects.

Tuckett (1994) argues that validation in the clinical process depends on being clear about the hypotheses, suggesting that, in sessions, interpretation is mainly based on intuitive and "quite spontaneous links arising from background orientations". He emphasized the importance of the patient's and therapist's external realities. He said that outside the session, a wider and more developed set of grounded hypotheses can be developed, intended to illuminate what seem to be the core issues that arise over time, and the core problems suffered by the patient. Often, such hypotheses will only be in the form of working orientations. If they can be conceptualized more precisely into specific hypotheses-explaining sets of observed events and predicting consequences, they can be better evaluated, either by the analyst working alone, or in group discussion through the achievement of genuine consensus (Tuckett, 1994, p. 1159). He further indicated:

> The validation in the clinical process, to a large extent, depends on being as clear and specific as possible about the hypotheses being put forward for validation. I am suggesting that while we make interpretations based on intuitive hypotheses arising from background orientations and clusters of observed clinical facts in the sessions, it is also appropriate to create, in an ongoing way outside the session, a wider and more developed set of grounded hypotheses intended to illuminate the core issues that arise and the core problems suffered by the patient. For much of the time such hypotheses may be more in the form of working orientations, as I have labelled them, but if they can be formulated into hypotheses explaining sets of events and predicting consequences, I think they can be more precisely thought through and then validated—that is,

partially or wholly refined so that they 'fit' better and/or are rejected as not fitting, whether by the analyst working alone or in group discussion through the achievement of genuine consensus. [*ibid.*, p.1174]

Hinshelwood (1994) in a critical discussion about research in psychiatry and the Random Control Trials (RCT) suggests that "objectification in psychiatry is problematic". He indicates that the key requirement is an objective indicator of change, and these changes usually relate to pathological signs, such as blood tests to investigate the levels of specific substances and their effects within physiological functioning. He also suggests that the main reason for this is to allow physicians to assess the possible treatments objectively. Thus, the aim is to "compare like with like.

Crucial to this is the objective quantification of the independent and dependent variables with regard to patients' presentations. Patients produced their memories of the past in two ways: (1) by recollecting in words; (2) by repeating, in some form, actual past events or phantasies, where re-creating or repeating in the relationship (the transference) an expressive act reveals contents of the patient's unconscious, which become a cornerstone of the psychoanalytic technique. It could be argued that this is perhaps the most important development in the clinical practice of psychoanalysis; it is more important than any of the multitude of developments in psychoanalytic theory because the transference is the tool through which all the evidence is gathered and testing of the theory takes place (Hinshelwood, 2002). Hinshelwood (*ibid.*) further argues that

> The psychiatric drive to objectify symptoms and diagnoses takes place inevitably in a framework made up of social attitudes held by doctors, patients and society at large. It could be said that analysing transference is a treatment focused on the nature and extent of compliance itself. If symptoms, syndromes and diagnoses are in part (maybe a large part) socially constructed by the common attitudes amongst patients and doctors, then 'cures' are just as likely to be socially constructed from the same ingredients—social expectations and the care relationship. A cure based on such 'subjective' ingredients is no less a cure, and indeed objectifying such changes may be possible. [p. 288]

The role of reconstruction in psychoanalytic technique, in investigating its technical value and in improving its therapeutic and conceptual basis, has been to some level ignored since Freud's death in 1939, although the use of it continued to exist in clinical practice. Figlio (1982) discusses that the relational context of psychotherapy has wider implications when trying to assess the effectiveness and evidence for it. He argues that the symptoms and their derivatives syndromes are, in many cases, socially constructed.

Blum (1980) discusses the relevance of reconstruction as a concept and as a specific technical intervention. He gives a comprehensive reassessment of reconstruction, and argues for the importance of applying and integrating it with other clinical and theoretical perspectives. His (1994) view is that almost every aspect of the problem of reconstruction is taken up, considered, and elucidated from different angles in which the patient affectively re-experiences the childhood trauma, and reworks the adaptation to it in the immediacy and safety of the analytic process and in the context provided by reconstruction. He later explained that if we accept the adult neurosis includes later development, but is built on childhood psychopathology and vulnerabilities, a patient's conscious remembrance as reminiscence should not simply be discarded as though it were entirely inaccurate and irrelevant. The patient's conscious account of their experiences and history, with its inevitable gaps, inconsistencies, distortions, and personal myths, provides the context in which the analyst begins to understand the patient. Reconstruction, therefore, proceeds in an analytic and historical context from surface to depth, from present to past, and back again. It will integrate reality and phantasy, past and present, cause and effect (Blum, 2000).

Some of the factors that influence an analytical reconstruction are the therapist's insights and development, preferences, training, and personality, as well as the patient's influence on the therapist. Reconstruction is of therapeutic value through the analysis of the repetition compulsion and projection in the transference. It is a risk when working with a traumatized patient to overemphasize the part played by the patient's innate propensities or the environment. This includes consideration of the repetition of an early life that manifests in the transference. The nature of the patient's internal objects in exploration and distortion of truths is an important factor. In times of crisis, patients may revert to past systems; recognition of this factor implies that the work of reconstruction will be as much an ongoing process as work with the transference, which, one hopes, forms part of one's equipment for future self examination and self analysis. It has to be acknowledged that the task of constructing self-descriptions in psychoanalytic therapy may encounter the problem of memory and its plasticity, the ease with which it can be distorted, and creates difficulties in reaching hypothetical real memory, much of which we consider infantile.

It is, therefore, the patient's and the therapist's sense of self that is the important factor in the assessment and treatment of traumatized patients, and in establishing the level of resilience and vulnerability and the types of dissociation (healthy or unhealthy). In his book, *The Restoration of the Self*, Kohut (1977) expressed that in all he had written on the psychology of the self, he had purposely not defined the self, knowing that some would be critical of him for that omission. He explained that it had become impossible to base his work on his predecessors because he would have been entangled in a *thicket* of similar, overlapping, or identical terms and concepts, which did not carry the same meaning and were not employed as a part of the same conceptual context. He refers to a patient whose personality disturbance was marked by a vertical split in his personality. One fragment in this patient was characterized by a sense of superiority and messianic identification that resulted from a merger with his mother, who had idealized him and encouraged the grandiosity. Kohut also refers to cognitive impenetrability and says "introspectively or empathically perceived psychological manifestations are open to us" (*ibid.*, p. 311). The self for Kohut, he said, is "the way a person experiences himself as himself" (p. xv), a permanent mental structure consisting of feelings, memories, and behaviours that are subjectively experienced as being continuous in time and as being "me". The self is also a "felt centre of independent initiative" and an "independent recipient of impression" (*ibid.*, p. xv), as the centre of the individual's psychological universe and not simply a representation. Kohut also says, 'our transient individuality also possesses a significance that extends beyond the borders of our life' (*ibid.*, p. 180), and describes "cosmic narcissism", which transcends the boundaries of the individual.

However, the question in some cases is that if there is no important connection between childhood events and adult psychopathology, and if memory cannot be trusted to construct a self-
description, then what does one do to understand one's psychological difficulties? In therapy we listen, and we focus on the here
and now, on problem-solving, and on helping patients to find new
strategies and ways of interacting with the important people in
their lives, but we also have to give attention to the patient's presentation of their past and its effect on the present, without putting too
much emphasis on this, at least at the beginning. By doing this,
through memories and associations, the patient will come to
explore the mysterious otherness of one's self, which is the job of
reconstruction.

I argue that in the interactive matrix of psychoanalytic treatment, vulnerability and dissociative behaviours have multiple
meanings that demand further exploration. I present a vignette of a
woman that I call Eden, who came to therapy with great confusion
and a strong sense of vulnerability. In exploring the main themes of
treatments, her feelings of abandonment, her insecurity because of
an asylum application, lack of welfare support, destitution, and
homelessness, her attachment to a seemingly lifeless object was a
key issue in the treatment of Eden. I give examples of how this
patient's phantasies were enacted as a form of sexual surrender that
allowed access to historical experiences of trauma, atrocity, oppres-
sion, and hope.

This is a small fraction of the treatment of trauma as it was
explored over the course of four years in psychoanalytic psychotherapy, three times a week. I concentrate on highlighting how
this patient and I engaged in a series of interactions that brought
her history of abuse and abandonment, her repeated outrage, as
well as her sadomasochistic fantasy life, which she was dissociating unhealthily, into treatment. In exploring the main themes of her
treatment, her childhood abandonment, which was projected to
her insecurity owing to her asylum situation, was the main issue
addressed in her analysis. Eden's phantasy life was enacted by
unhealthy dissociations as a form of sexual surrender that allowed
her access to her own historical traumatic experience of atrocity. As
therapy progressed and she could associate and engage with reality,
she started developing some sense of self and hope for her future.

Eden

A thirty-two-year-old single woman from the Middle-East living with a friend at the time, Eden referred herself for therapy due to the high level of anxiety, suicidal thoughts, and fear of death she was experiencing. She had been in therapy previously, two years in individual therapy and eighteen months in group. In our initial sessions, she said that her biological mother had given her to her grandmother one day after her birth because she was a girl and was not welcomed by her father and paternal extended family, as there were already four girls and only one boy in the family. Although she explained that this is normal in her cultural environment, this set up the major themes of her treatment and her reflection on her life, her feeling of abandonment, and a strong and confusing sense of loss that was an ongoing theme in our work. She presented a traumatic history of both personal and political atrocities. She had been sexually, emotionally, and physically abused by her grandfather, who was a survivor of war, her uncle, who was a survivor of torture in prison, and her only biological brother, who stayed with them occasionally from the age of six. Eden presented strong feelings of guilt, anger, frustration, and loneliness, with constant masochistic suicidal fantasies that she has acted upon few times. She could easily be diagnosed with borderline personality disorder.

She said her reason for coming to therapy was the hope that someone could save her from the pain that she had borne ever since she could remember, and which she was not able to tolerate any more. She found it difficult to make eye contact, and from our very first meeting Eden held a key in her hand, fidgeting with it or looking at it when she was talking to me. I found this quite symbolic, and, although it was the end of the assessment session, I asked her whether that was the key to happiness. She did not respond verbally, just gazed at me and smiled.

It is important to note that Eden showed up an hour early for her first session and sat in the waiting area. I went to fetch her and she followed me to the room, holding the key which was to become her (our) constant companion in the process. She spent most of our time together pleading with me not to abandon her as her birth mother and her last two therapists had. She revealed a long history of severe physical and sexual abuse. It seemed that personal trauma had become Eden's ordinary life experience and had affected her chronically, colouring her personality and resulting in her being prescribed heavy psychiatric medication. I became concerned as to whether, with such traumas, it would be possible for her to achieve some level of resilience, or whether I would be another therapist who would ultimately reject and abandon her.

Eden described her upbringing under the totalitarian rule of her grandfather, with no freedom. Even as a grown-up woman, she was not allowed to work or have relationships, especially romantic ones, with people outside the family. Eden described in detail her grandfather's violence, and how she understood it to be a reaction to her displays of emotion during her childhood. She related that to her grandfather's history as a war survivor, which had left him unable to tolerate emotional expression. She recalled that whenever she complained, her grandfather would tell her, "The authorities attacked us and my mother and my brother were killed in front of me—why are you such a silly girl?" Over time, as Eden was able to relate to me as her listening other, she revealed many incidents of abuse at her grandfather's hands, and became able to associate, with horrifying awareness, that both her mother and her grand-mother were aware of what was happening and were unwilling to stop him.

Over the first year of our work, Eden described a series of molestations and rapes that had been perpetrated upon her. She had vague memories of having been molested as a very young child by a man who may have been her father. Her grandfather's brother also molested her on a number of occasions. Eden told her grand-parents about this, but they never confronted this great-uncle, although at some point they stopped leaving Eden alone with him. Starting in early adolescence, she began to get herself into situations that she knew to be dangerous; this included "colluding" in being raped by her teacher, who was forty-eight years senior to her, when she was only thirteen. After this event, she became promiscuous and also started using drugs. She had to sleep with people to earn money to fund her habit, and without using drugs she could not do that, thus creating a vicious circle. She soon developed a relation-ship with highly abusive man over forty years older than her who was supporting her drug habit. Despite this situation, Eden completed her secondary school education with very high marks and passed her entry examination to go to university. Although there continued to be problematic patterns of behaviour in her life in general and in her abusive relationships, indeed, her alcohol and drug misuse, she performed well academically and graduated at twenty-one with a high academic achievement.

She started working with young people, as well as having an academic position at university. She was involved with political activity and, as a result, she had to leave her country. She came to the UK, seeking asylum. When she received her refugee status here and was allowed to work, she found a job in a children's home. She enjoyed taking care of abused and troubled children. She said: "I became emotionally attached to the children I worked with very quickly. Because of that I encouraged my boyfriend (an Englishman close to her own age), who was recovering from a psychotic break-down and was out of job, to become a volunteer in working with the children. I was sure that this was good for both sides: for him, as he himself was severely abused in his childhood, and for these children, who needed support from someone who could relate to them. I encouraged the children to trust my boyfriend as they trusted me." She was tearful and stressed at this point. After a period of silence, she continued, "I noticed that he became more preoccupied with childhood sexual abuse, but I convinced myself that this was now a work-related issue . . . until one day one of the boys punched my boyfriend quite violently, and told me, 'You are evil' and ran away crying." I did not say anything, as I felt she needed space to talk about her experience and she needed me to be her listening other. After a brief silence, Eden said,

"I was horrified; I came to realize that I had made a big mistake. I asked my boyfriend and he confessed to his paedophilic feelings and told me that his psychiatrist is aware of the problem and knows that he has been controlling it, but his psychiatric team told him they are not sure if he is ready to work with young people . . . but, because he did not want to lose me he decided not to tell me and didn't tell his psychiatric service people, whom he met every day, that he had volunteered to work with vulnerable children because he liked his situation. I felt mortified that I had persuaded the children I loved so much into such a dangerous situation. . . . I struggled for a while to come to terms with what he had done, but I was troubled and beside myself . . . I remember a few weeks later, while we were out and he was driving I jumped out of the car while it was moving at some speed. He pulled over, hit me in the face, and left me on the side of the road . . . I walked home, I didn't know why, I knew I couldn't continue and I didn't want to live any more. I was tired of this . . . I went to the bathroom and took all my medication; I was heartbroken: not so much over the horrible ending of my life, but because I had colluded in doing harm to children who trusted me and I loved them so much and wanted to protect them."

I said, "I can see how your past experience, with all the men in your family and others in wider society abusing you, would lead you to desperately want to trust your boyfriend, who was an Englishman who was not from your background, and therefore you unintentionally exposed children in your care to his inappropriate behaviour. You said before that he was violent to you and he was quite ill and under psychiatric treatment. That left me wondering what led you to encourage him to work with vulnerable children. I am wondering whether in your new environment you needed to become more isolated socially and confined yourself in your house, which didn't feel like your home, with this exploitative man. You led yourself to believe, as your grandfather led you to believe, that you couldn't go out into the world because it is not safe, but the reality is that even in your childhood you knew your home didn't feel safe either. You were deprived of any meaning and value, but that was what you knew, so, I am wondering whether unconsciously you needed to reconstruct that here in London to feel at home, which, in fact, you did. I am also wondering whether you needed to live through those vulnerable children and, by seeing them going through a similar experience to those you have had, unconsciously believed that might break the ring of your isolation and loneliness, and whether you needed to go through this experience to be able to relate to the state of mind of your mother, who left you in an abusive situation."

While I was talking, Eden was crying. She particularly referred to the pain of being abandoned and rejected by her biological mother. She said, "I have no one, I have never been loved for who I am . . . perhaps there is some truth in all you said, although I have not been conscious of it at all . . . but, hearing what you said, it all makes sense to me now . . . please don't reject me, tell me anything you want me to do, but please don't you leave me as well . . ."

This became a thematic thread for her in our relationship and in the general context of her life. I was angry with her, so I was conscious that I should not use any more confrontational interpretations against unhealthy dissociations, but, in response to her pleading, I briefly said, "I have no intention of rejecting you or leaving my work, and working with you is part of it." On reflection, I realized that even this brief response was quite dismissive.

At the end of another session, once again I became curious about the key that Eden always brought into her sessions. As things had not been so stressful for her in that particular session, I decided to explore the significance of her key, especially because she was playing with and looking at it throughout the session, as had been common in all other sessions. I asked her in an inoffensive manner, at which Eden became agitated and walked out.

At this stage (her second year in therapy), Eden began, with her sadomasochistic behaviour, to set herself up for rejection and abandonment in her fantasy, something that she has feared from the beginning of our relationship. I viewed this as an improvement. Our relationship at this point had reached the stage where Eden perceived me as her listening other, who was helping her to develop some psychic space to deal with her fear and create a better sense of self in reality, rather than through enactment. I also realized that I had to monitor my countertransference feelings and be careful not to submit to her sadomasochistic enactments. I realized that, by drawing attention to her key, I had touched on her sadistic phantasies. In the next session, while she was sincerely apologizing she said, "Please you can punish me in any way you think I should be punished; it doesn't upset me, I still love you, but, please don't stop me from coming to therapy and please don't ask to take my key away from me."

Her behaviour seemed rather bizarre in this session. I decided not to respond to this, partly because I was not clear about what was going on and I needed more time to reflect on it. Although Eden and I continued to struggle to work with our analytic relationship, I found that the process was becoming more challenging for me. For a long time Eden's need and her fear were in constant conflict, without any direction. At times she would come to sessions full of rage with me; she would leave the session if I tried to make any interpretations, and then would return with confusion and with terrifying thoughts that I would exact revenge and give her tit for tat by rejecting her. But between these two extreme modes of her re-enactment we did manage some analytic work.

The memory of trauma and atrocity that Eden had endured was underpinning her daily life. Through the traumatic enactments, Eden was unconsciously sharing her life with the perpetrators of her abuse. Winnicott (1974) viewed the fear of breakdown as the fear of a previous event, rather than a future one. I argue that in cases such as Eden's, this relates to past as well as current, and ongoing, conditions of internalized atrocity, rather than to an actual or certain future of hope and recovery. Along similar lines, Sullivan (1953) described the interpersonal security operations that may be called into effect to dissociate the internal conditions inherent in unbearable states of preparation. When a traumatic event occurs, the traumatized person may not be able to recall the specific details of the event as the emotional impact of it has not been registered, or has been unhealthily dissociated from. He (Sullivan, 1962) viewed these types of reactions as human processes. He considered that such a psychotic state of mind exists at the extreme end of a continuum between mental health and mental illness. Sullivan's (1964) ideas form a foundation of contemporary interpersonal and relational psychoanalytic theory, and posited that schizophrenia and other psychotic illness are cultural phenomena related to early and/or ongoing failures in a patient's environment, representing a form of acculturation to chaotic and traumatic environments that can be transmitted through empathic linkages between care-takers and a child. Winnicott (1965) echoed such thinking in his assertion that there is no such thing as a baby, only the infant–mother (or mothering one), the *self* as inseparable from the inter-relationship of *self and other* in which, when atrocity occurs, there is no escape.

Underlying Eden's capitulation was her deep desire that she needed to know people around her. She had to be the knower, in the penetrative and often painful process of gaining access to her other inner experiences, carrying the implication and association of defeat, a quality of liberation and expansion of her sense of self as a result of the letting down of defensive barriers. Her longing masochistic desire was to give up her defensive barriers and be accepted for who she was. Due to the traumas Eden had endured, she had the desire to be in the presence of a potentially dangerous other, without consciously acknowledging it. This provided her with the opportunity to confirm her needed submission in the inter-action and repetition of the earlier trauma, or to refute her surren-der by breaking the cycle of repetition and her experience of the environment as being wholly malevolent.

Taking all these factors into account, Eden unhealthily dissoci-ated her deep desire to seek violent behaviour, and her masochistic submission held out the promise of that, seducing, exciting, enslav-ing, and, in the end, cheating the seeker-turned-victim out of her plan of wanting to get well, offering in its place only her intense masochism as her living testimony. The far-reaching means that she found to protect her sense of self and to develop a stable psychic space for her self-continuity and her integrity find the middle ground for her later ability to grow and become able to relate to me as her listening other, rather than functioning on her masochism, which was her way of taking care of herself to survive. Masochistic surrounding was her core, real and safe, until, as a result of many reflections in the process, she gained insight that it was wrong. Eden's masochistic character was a powerful expression of her hope, until she could relate to me more freely as her listening other. As a result, she found a clearer sense of self. I, as her listening other, became her safe container.

In one session, Eden talked about her dream and recounted that:

> There was very strong physical struggle between you and me . . . I was not sure if we were seriously fighting or we were playing . . . it also seemed physical . . . sensual . . . I felt both happy and scared when I woke up . . . the dream was like a soft porn show . . . because when I woke up I had a feeling of extreme sexual desire, my mood was grow-ing and my feeling for you shifted so strongly . . . it was crazy . . . but, nice . . .

She reported this at the end of the session, so we could not explore it further at that time. She came back to the next session and started by asking if I was angry with her.

I said, "It might be some comfort in seeing me as someone who was angry with you for associating with me freely."

She was silent for few minutes then said, "I am feeling lost and I think that you know what it is all about . . ."

I said, "Tell me what all is about . . ."

She said, "No, I would feel ashamed, humiliated, and embarrassed . . ."

Here, although she was presenting a different part of herself, I could see improvement in her. She developed enough psychic space that she could own her feelings, even the undesirable ones, and, thus, she has an internal space in which to become aware of, and to think about, them and to be able to talk about them.

I said, "Are you talking about *your* thoughts about the dream you had about us?"

Eden said: "You know, not just about dreams . . . here I sometimes feel something like an orgasm . . . like we are having sex in my mind, although it is only in my mind—we are together—I don't know how to say it . . . but, we are together, I am not alone . . . I am with you. I feel embarrassed and ashamed to talk about it. I am also scared [she was close to tears and at this point starts weeping]. I would like to have good sex . . . with someone I can love and trust . . . I never ever had any feelings for women . . . but, recently here with you, there is another me who can think nicely about sex and enjoy even the thought of it . . . you know sex has always been very painful for me . . .

Here Eden becomes in touch with her internal space, but in a very concrete, bodily way. I said, "This experience must be very confusing. Here, you are in a relationship in which you feel reasonably safe and the only way you can think about it is through concrete body contact to feel that it is real. It must be quite difficult and painful for you."

Eden replied, "Not until now."

I said, "Not until now?"

She said, "Even now it is very difficult to talk to you . . . it is mad . . . I wanted to walk out of here and never come back again to face this embarrassment. I cannot believe I am talking to you about it. But I worry that you will think that I am avoiding thinking about myself in this way. I wish I hadn't told you about it."

I replied, "And now you have told me we have to hold it together and work it through; something which might be unfamiliar to you."

She started weeping and said, "I never felt that I had a place . . . my life has been a torturous event, not the torture I experienced at the hands of my enemies . . . a torture in which I never felt I belonged because no one had ever made room for me as the person I am . . . I think that is why I decided to work with children and had my life back again . . . because with children I had to make room for them without expecting anything back . . . but, they are kind to me . . ."

This was ambiguous. On the one hand she was saying that there is no space (no room) for her, and on the other hand she was saying that she feels she does have enough space to think about having no space. Also, the issue of working with children puzzled me, as I thought that she already gained insight that the child parts of her wanted to be with deprived children. However, I decided not to raise this at this particular time and to focus instead on her erotic dream and transference.

I asked her, "What would you expect if you could build an equal relationship with another adult in your life?"

She replied, "I am not really sure, as I never imagined I could have such a relationship, but coming to see you, especially today, felt so good. I was looking forward to coming, which is unfamiliar feeling for me. I always dread seeing people. On the way here, I was imagining sharing my good experience with you. It was the first time I realized that I always shared my bad experiences with you and I always wanted you to know that I was feeling really bad. I always wanted you to help me not to feel that way without feeling safe enough to let you in."

I said, "Are you saying thinking and talking about our relationship is difficult and unfamiliar for you and it is easier if you think of it as physical contact rather than psychological and emotional connection?"

Eden said, "For all my life I have been trusting people, and they have hurt me every single time. Of course, having this experience here is unfamiliar and weird for me . . ."

I said, "I can imagine that this experience might be quite painful for you."

Eden said, "Yes, it is very painful. Do you know why? Because it is so difficult to let you know what I am deeply feeling when I am with you in this room. I never wanted to let you know. They are my thoughts and feelings, but I was sure when you found out you would accuse me of avoiding it."

It was the end of the session, so I merely said, "And now you can share your thoughts and feelings with me, you don't feel alone and we have to hold it together."

She came back to the next session and said, "It is so weird to think that I do have a place without any torture, where there is peace, where there is room for me as I am . . . but the thought of the fact that I was going to see you today stopped me feeling bad. I now know that you are here to help me and that is so good. I can be myself and feel safe to let you into my world and let you to bring me out of it. I am sure you know it is not a very nice internal world to be in."

Before this session, I was planning to bring up the issues of the previous session and to interpret our conversation as an expression of Eden's archaic id impulse, but, with this presentation, I decided to reserve my judgement and interpretations. I accepted it as an interpersonal risk, and an admission of her defeat that she needed to submit in order to feel accepted by me, which led to more psychic space for her thinking and relating, indeed, a further development of her sense of self.

In her relationship with me, as in all of her other relationships and experiences, Eden had recreated the internal atrocity with maximum vulnerability, the place in which others had abused, raped, humiliated, and abandoned her, leaving her in a state of not having any sense of self and no psychic space in which to find her real self. She took a courageous and heroic risk by sharing this lonely place, initially through sexual phantasy, representing her stealthy sexualized phantasy of our relationship as well as her hope for emotional contact with me as her listening other in order to let me into her malevolently populated world and to bring her out of it . She shared her feelings in the way she knew how, by enacting a primitive, somatic sexuality that had only existed in isolation, and that needed to be experienced with the one person she felt could either annihilate her or help her to save herself.

Our analytical relationship lasted for five years. In the process, Eden's personality transformed into that of a resilient woman with clear boundaries in all her social interactions.

In the next chapter, I present another vignette to demonstrate the qualitative process analysis of the psychotherapy of a severely traumatized patient whom I shall call Ahmed, who did change in the process by becoming able to express his feelings. I give a case history as an example of data for analysis, and discuss the methods used in this case. I also give an account of the way in which I worked with patients such as Eden, presented here, and others.

One of my first tasks always is to listen, receiving and organizing my knowledge of the patient's experience and, together with patient, to make meanings. This process provides a containing environment and space for the patient to become able to relate to me as the listening other, which is the beginning of an object relation they may have been deprived of in their early life.

In clinical practice, my object of the study is a therapeutic dialogue, with each patient beginning a journey from the reality of the speaking: that is, the patient presents and I listen as therapist with the hope of understanding and providing interpretation. The process, the reflection of the process, and analysis of the outcome is shown through my notes, transcripts of analysis and working through, as well as verbal reports in supervision and consultation. The point of this process is not just to ground the text or the result as part of the validation process, but to also to impart facts and knowledge. Consequently, the emphasis can be on pragmatic validation, that is, the outcome, and the usefulness of the results. This is due to the fact that psychoanalytic process is an open feedback system, where both patient and therapist are constantly making more or less explicit adjustments, which requires a specific research methodology adjusted to allow for this characteristic. Therefore, the emphasis on the tentativeness of the conclusion can only be in qualitative methods.

The intention of an analytic intervention in the process is to broaden and deepen the patients' knowledge about themselves and their patterns of relating to others. It is in the broadening of these aspects that interpretations are made. The use of language, text, and narratives are understood in context, and, indeed, the first interpretation of a context may not be the final one, but, rather, the beginning of a journey towards an insight.

As a result, qualitative research here is presented as text, narratives, dialogues, and descriptions, and, although it is possible to do so, analytic process cannot be reduced to quantitative measurement of fixed categories. The reduction of an often unmanageable quantity is determined not only by statistical principles, but, among other things, by the point of view that is consciously chosen on the material; thus, in quantitative methods, there is no space for analysis of the unconscious and transference interpretations, although they may include observation, the attribution of meaning or significance to historical facts, and the researcher's choice of material to be analysed for presentation. In qualitative methods, the criteria for election and the way of evaluating outcome are based on phenomena significant from the therapeutic point of view, not on their statistical mean. So, the process aims at, and focuses on, the new and specific material at both the conscious and unconscious level of the patient–therapist dyad. In other words, in qualitative research the phenomena are analysed and generalized in their context; the text creates the structure of meanings, which is then, through written case presentation, conveyed to the reader. This makes a distinction between the use of the word and the significant meaning attached to it and its effect on the text, based on individual patient presentation and aiming to relate to a person's internal structure and the way it is constructed: that is, the internal coherence as a creation for validity and resilience, or the lack of it, which corresponds to the traditional meaning or shared understanding, constructing a way for knowledge and theories of psychoanalytic interpretation or hermeneutics. So, the significance of a text must be understood as referring to, or trying to say something about, the world and as having a message about a phenomenon that may not be shared by different patients, or, indeed, by patient and therapist, at least at the beginning. This is in contrast with the aim of quantitative methods, which are designed with the intention of determining whether or not a hypothetical property is presented as the mean, and generalized standardized testing methods.

It is important to note that as part of training, psychoanalysts and psychoanalytic psychotherapists have to learn to observe in session presentations on a scale of seconds and minutes; to have ongoing careful monitoring and evaluation; and to evaluate the outcome changes in people's lives once every six months. This is done by considering aspects of what are identified as the person's problematic experiences and how they are negotiated and by studying each one separately and over time. The therapists, therefore, need to consider the following:

- how the patient's experiences are understood as derivatives of painful experiences;
- how they may be understood in an object-relational perspective;
- how to observe and analyse dialogical patterns as they appear in relational scenarios;
- how to take into consideration complex mental schemata in transference;
- how to note the expressed emotion in explicit and implicit patterns of behaviour and the pattern of communications.

All this will be a learning process, enabling the therapist to look at the patient's unwanted thoughts and ambiguous or formless presentation. With feedback, clarification, and interpretation, the therapist's job is to elucidate and recognize the problem, to help the patient in further explorations in order to increase the ability to verbalize thoughts, and to gain insight. This is done in an atmosphere that is safe enough, enabling the patient to open up some psychic space and make use of the therapist as the listening other for working through in order to have a better sense of self. This process enhances the patient's ability for healthy dissociations and problem-solving, thus gradually creating ego strength, autonomy, and resilience.

For instance, a patient may enter therapy with problems at any level of assimilation. Subsequently, in the process, movement of any distance along the continuum can be considered progress on an individual basis. If, in the initial meetings, the therapist assesses and becomes aware of some aspects of resilience in a patient, that will provide a foundation to use and build on that part of the personality and also provide possibilities for the patient to exercise their ability to deal with their vulnerabilities in the process. So, this is a dialogical view on therapy, coherent with object relations view, which, by means of transference–countertransference, focuses on encounters between the patient and the therapist's inner world, at both the conscious and unconscious levels. Thus, all speech, including the inner speech of the patient, is addressing the patient's listening other, that is, the therapist in the consulting room, which consciously or unconsciously becomes part of this process as a second party through transference. This, of course, can be perceived by the patient as a third party at a conscious level, that is to say, there is always something beyond the immediate transference object. The dual nature of responsive understanding allows the message to stay with the therapist without being given a final meaning, but instead allowing a new meaning to appear. This is the integral essence of analytical process, providing holding and containing that brings a more psychic space for the patient.

Another important aspect of this method that therapists should take into consideration is that when a patient talks about an experience, they make a transition from a non-symbolized position, where experience is represented mostly as bodily signs and behaviour, to an embryonic and basic ability to formulate traces of the experience and verbalizing it, thus gaining a better sense of self. So, when speaking about the experience, the patient establishes the ability to place it in a time perspective and also situate it in relation to different social and psychological contexts, a development of psychic space, resilience, and good sense of self. The therapist, as the listening other, observes words, sounds, and expressions, and distinguishes between what the patient is saying about their experience (that is, speaking about a particular experience or reflecting on the experience) and what the therapist is feeling in the transference. When reflecting on the experience, if the patient develops a better sense of self and of the therapist as the listening other, they will be able to explore the emotional meaning of the experience together, which, if successfully communicated, will result in more psychic space. This will provide the patient with the opportunity to look at the reorganization of the self and, therefore, to open up a readiness for sublimation, integration, and further resilience. At each level, the therapist as a listening other is placed in specific transference positions by the patient, who, consciously or unconsciously, demands a specific form of responsive understanding and containing. Therefore, the therapist's ability to learn to make these distinctions is necessary to gain knowledge of the way the words are organized, articulated, and communicated by the patient, together with the expressions presented by the patient. Patterns and sequences of transference–countertransference communications can frequently be derived from the patient's self-narratives, and how they relate to various aspects of themselves.

Prototypical communication mediated by non-verbal signs and the metaphorical aspect of meanings in the patient–therapist discourse also need to be identified and relayed to patient in transference interpretations. The therapist's countertransference feelings and fantasies can be used for identifying non-verbal communication patterns.

To summarize, in order to observe and analyse each situation a number of steps need to be taken in the process.

1. Define the patient's position in terms of both explicit and implicit object relation positions.
2. Observe, identify, and clarify the meaning of the patient's presentations.
3. Establish the self-aspect presentation of *I* or *Me*, as well as the use of *You* in communications to see which *I*, *Me*, or *You* the patient is referring to when talking about self.
4. Learn from which position the patient is speaking, thus distinguishing which *I* or *Me*, the patient, is speaking to which *You*, the therapist in transference.
5. Identify which part of the self the patient is referring to and what is the quality of the sense of self.
6. Establish what are the patient's associations and dissociations, and if patient can dissociate healthily.
7. Find out which is the part that is difficult for the patient to make direct associations with.
8. Identify the ways in which a patient can or will relate to, and associate with, their dreams, their wishes, phantasies, and fears, and how these results are presented, along with what is being addressed by transference interpretations within object relations, and the outcome.
9. Learn how the development of these positions followed in order to identify sequences and clarifications.
10. Identify the pattern of transference changes in the process, and clarify whether and when more than one position is presented in transference. This is important when working with people who have been affected by multiple traumas, as they may have difficulties in expressing themselves and may have a fear of being themselves with an other.

Conclusion

This chapter discusses the methodology used in the study. As the author's practice is informed by psychoanalysis, a brief review of the literature on methodology from the psychoanalytic perspective is considered. Whether the reader agrees that psychoanalysis has the capacity to be scientific in this sense depends upon their reading of the work on the philosophy of science, which is briefly referred to in this chapter, and the chapter on literature. However, I consider this study to be empirical, involving the testing of hypotheses and supporting theories, using psychoanalytic treatments for research purposes. What may be helpful from the psychoanalytic viewpoint, and, indeed, from that of the critics of psychoanalysis, is the emphasis on the fact that all human knowledge is mixed with errors, prejudices, and assumptions, and there is no such idea as an ultimate source of knowledge. The centrality of the three areas of object relations, and specifically transference and countertransference, are emphasized as windows of opportunity and as important methods of psychoanalysis, as is the need for a creative and flexible intercultural approach to therapy and reconstruction. One of the main points drawn from this chapter is how to consider in what sense clinical material is evidence: it is data, rather than an illustration of a preconceived theory. Without this recognition there can be no objective standards of enquiry; no real appreciation of criticism of conjectures; no need for further investigation into current knowledge to search for the unknown; and no quest for new knowledge.

However, it is important to repeat that the main discussion in this study is based on three main concepts: trauma, resilience, and dissociation.

CHAPTER THREE

Psychological trauma

Introduction

The focus of this chapter is to look at the meaning of trauma and to expand a possible classification of traumatic events that have an impact on individual functioning. I start with a description of trauma to offer a general understanding of the term, before looking at possible causes, various kinds of trauma, its dynamics, its mechanisms, and the diverse areas of functioning that trauma potentially has an impact on. The chapter also looks at the consequences of trauma and the relevance of these in resilience, with a brief discussion about post traumatic stress disorder (PTSD). Emphasis throughout is given to the fact that people have subjective reactions to objective events and no two persons will experience or respond to a stressor of the same traumatic occurrence in the same way.

What is trauma?

In the *Oxford English Dictionary* trauma is defined as:

1.   A deeply distressing experience;

2.   Med. Physical injury;
3.   Emotional shock following a stressful event.

Traumatize: cause (someone) to experience lasting shock as a result of a disturbing experience or injury.

The key meaning of psychological trauma refers to an event that is extremely stressful and overwhelming for the person involved and may affect their ability to cope. However, it is my view that the accumulation of non-traumatic stressors, sufferings, or dilemmas can create a trauma-like experience and can produce effects similar to trauma, eventuating traumatic symptoms. They can also add to real traumas and amplify their effects. Any negative socio-cultural attitudes and non-supportive responses towards the traumatized individual can create a chain of post trauma stressors which may cause secondary traumatizations. This is clearly of particular relevance when considering the trauma endured in adult life.

There are events outside the range of the individual's usual experience that constitute exceptional mental and psychological stress. The ranges of events traumatic to individuals can be as diverse as trauma responses. Regular life stressors, in different areas of human experience, are ordinary and have high expectancy, probability of happening, and controllability. Emotional trauma can result from occurrences such as a car accident, the break-up of a significant relationship, a humiliating or deeply disappointing experience of a loved one, the discovery of a life-threatening illness or disabling condition, rape, persecutions, torture, and other violent events. This includes responses to chronic and repetitive experiences, such as child abuse, neglect, warfare, urban violence, concentration camps, racism and prejudice, domestic violence, and deprivation.

Traumatizing events can have an acute emotional effects on individuals, even if the event did not cause physical injury or immediate psychological problems. The definition of what is psychologically traumatic, therefore, is fairly broad and varies according to the personality structure of the individual's response as well as the severity of the event and its aftermaths. Consequently, it is difficult to determine and generalize what particular event is traumatic. One way to identify trauma and its adaptive symptoms is to ask the person to provide a narrative of the event, rather than what went wrong. The central theme in this study is the possible intrusion of the past experience into the present, and consequent regression and fixation confronting the patient.

Trauma from a psychoanalytic viewpoint

Laplanche and Pontalis, in *The Language of Psychoanalysis* (1973), define trauma as:

> An event in the subject's life defined by its intensity, by the subject's incapacity to respond adequately to it, and by the upheaval and long-lasting effects that it brings about in the psychical organization. In economic terms, the trauma is characterized by an influx of excitations that is excessive by the standard of the subject's tolerance and capacity to master such excitations and work them out psychically. [p. 465]

Trauma is a complex combination of biological, psychological, and social phenomena that can create lasting emotional difficulties and plays a significant role in the psychogenesis of violence (e.g., Johnson, Cohen, Brown, Smailes, & Bernstein, 1999). One way to determine whether an emotional or psychological trauma has occurred, perhaps even early in life before language or conscious awareness were in place, is to look at the kinds of recurring problems that patients might be experiencing. Observing these can serve as clues to an earlier situation that caused a deregulation in the structure or function of the personality. Forward-looking neurological research, which is not the subject of this study, is beginning to show to what degree trauma affects people on a biological and hormonal basis, as well as psychologically, cognitively, and behaviourally. In traumatic experiences and interruptions of normal development in childhood, hypervigilance of individual autonomic structures may be compounded and reinforced by significant changes in the brain.

Looking back in psychoanalytic literature, there are three main issues to consider. First is the fact that Freud, in his works, provides awareness of three powerful forces and their demands on people. Back when everyone believed people were rational, he showed how much of our behaviour was based on biology. When everyone conceived people as individually responsible for their actions, he demonstrated the impact of society. When everyone thought of male and female as roles determined by nature or God, he showed how much they depended on family and gender dynamics.

Second is the basic theory of certain neurotic symptoms as caused by psychological traumas and the psychoanalytic theory of neurosis (Fenichel, 1945; Freud, 1895a, 1905d, 1920g). Although most theorists no longer believe that all neuroses can be so explained, or that it is necessary to relive the trauma to get better, it has become a common understanding that a childhood full of neglect, abuse, and tragedy tends to lead to an unhappy adulthood.

Third is the idea of ego defences (Freud 1895f, 1899a, 1905d, 1920g). Even if one is uncomfortable with Freud's idea of the unconscious, it is clear that we engage in little manipulations of reality and our memories to suit our own needs and desire.

In summary, the whole psychoanalytic theory of development is based on trauma. The basic form of therapy has been largely set by Freud and followed by contemporary psychoanalysts. Except for some behaviourist therapies, most therapy is still considered as "the talking cure" and involves a physically and socially relaxed atmosphere. And, even if other theorists do not care for the idea of unconscious and transference, the highly personal nature of the therapeutic relationship is generally accepted as important to success.

Understanding the nature of trauma is essential if treatment of traumatic experiences is to be effective. Garland (1998) indicates that trauma has the capacity to touch and disrupt the core of one's identity, so, addressing that level of disturbance requires time and space to restore meaning and integration into the patient's life again. She suggests that with people who survived the holocaust, although they have a strong wish to put their horrific experiences behind them, in many instances their hidden or denied psychological devastation is passed from one generation to another, thus unconsciously transferring the the traumatic experience to the children and grandchildren of the survivors.

In line with Freud's later idea (1920g), Garland (1998) suggests that a person experiences trauma when there is a disruption of a protective barrier in the person's mind, which protects the person from harmful and painfully excessive stimulation. If, in the early years, there is development of the child's protective function, provided by the m/other's sensitivity in knowing what the child is able to manage at any one time, on the whole, when that child reaches adulthood, s/he can take over these filtering protective functions with varying degrees of success.

Internal and external trauma

A traumatic event, which is almost impossible to forget, can result in either psychological difficulty or psychological growth. Object relations theory is helpful in distinguishing fundamental differences between internal and external trauma, and their consequences. The external characteristics of the potential traumatic event can start indirectly and become the most severe and direct trauma. Trauma can be the factitious result of early experience and development of one's mind. Stimuli can be either internally induced or externally inflicted, such as with a natural disaster or man-made traumatic events such as torture, war, rape, domestic violence, and so on. Bion (in Hinshelwood, 1999) hypothesized that the first cognitive working of the mind entails a link between something innate (the organism itself) and something foreign (experience perceived in external reality).

Objective and subjective views of trauma

There are, in general, two components to a traumatic experience: the subjective and the objective. Usually, the subjective experience of the objective event constitutes the trauma. An important factor to consider in the assessment and treatment of a traumatized patient is the subjectiveness of the trauma experience. It is one's subjective experience and the level of resilience one has that determines whether an event is traumatic or not, and if it is, to what degree. This is because the more one feels and believes one is endangered, the more traumatized one becomes. Therefore, psychological trauma may be any type of event or encounter which causes an overwhelming emotion and a feeling of helplessness. Whether or not there is actual physical or psychological harm, this can result in psychological disturbances and create confusion between mind and body. This plays a most important role in the long-term effects and presentation of psychological trauma. Therefore, endurance of the same traumatic occurrence is distinct according to how one is experiencing it, and the specific aspects of an event that is traumatic can also vary from one individual to another.

Differentiating between stress and trauma

One area that seems to be overlooked in the literature is the difference between experiencing emotional trauma and experiencing stress. Stress can deregulate nervous systems for a relatively short period of time, and it may take a few days or weeks before the nervous system calms down and reverts to a normal state of equilibrium. This return to normality is often not the case when one has been affected by traumatic events. One way to determine the difference between ordinary stress and the emotional effect of trauma, in my view, is by looking at the degree to which an upsetting event remains affecting a person's relationships and overall functioning. When one is in the realm of stress, if the reason for distress is communicated and responded to adequately, then the person can be returned to a state of equilibrium. If a person turns out to be in a state of active emotional intensity, it is a sign of emotional trauma rather than stress, although sometimes this may not be in conscious awareness. The level of distress one is experiencing by using defence mechanisms as a means of coping with trauma is also different from ordinary life stress. There is a great deal of psychological and psychiatric literature on the subject of PTSD (e.g., Everly & Mitchell, 2000; Foa, Hearst-Ikeda, & Perry, 1995; Gelpin, Bonne, Peri, Brandes, & Shalev, 1996).

Why events cause different responses in different people

There are simple factors affecting people's responses, such as the severity of the event, the individual's resilience or vulnerability, and the ability for healthy dissociation or lack of it, which is due to developmental and past experiences. However, the profound meaning an event represents and the more traumatic effect it will have on one's psyche is not straightforward. People can go through the same, or very similar, harmful event and some might be traumatized while others remain relatively unharmed or even become more resilient and stronger. This depends on numerous factors which influence one's personality structure: values, way of thinking, level of resilience, coping mechanisms, environmental factors, and availability of support from family, friends, or professionals. The idea of resilience as a protective shield or layer is an important concept which allows only tolerable quantities of excitations, as is the ability to dissociate healthily from excessive or unbearable experiences. This is specifically important in relation to vulnerability factors for people who have endured trauma in adult life.

The trauma of being a refugee

As all cases presented in this study have refugee backgrounds, discussing some of the factors affecting the trauma of refugees is important. Experiences of war or political violence for refugees are enormous in scale. They are brutal, repeated, extended, and volatile. From the psychoanalytic viewpoint, if we consider object relations as a formation of social bonds and of symbolizations, for a refugee who lacks resilience, the external trauma and the cultural shock of the new environment may break this bond and leave the person in disarray, full of violent and anxious feelings. This may take away the person's capacity to think, which is different from the innate tendency to repression. One of the difficult tasks for people who are affected by trauma is the feeling of loss, including the loss of the self, or at least, a part of the self, and the lack of mourning of the self which is lost, or at least, partly lost: loss of social life, as well as ownership and sense of belonging, such as work, income, home, family, friends, social and professional status, language and other cultural aspects. This is quite different from childhood mourning in the process of development.

The stage and severity of people's traumatic experiences before becoming refugees and facing problems related to immigration matters are influential on asylum seekers' states of mind, and determine the impact of the person's ongoing stressors. This may have differing emotional impacts, particularly just after arrival in the new country, but these are existential stresses. It is my assertion that an important component sometimes is the avoidance of thinking about or remembering the trauma, which actually may for a time be *helpful* if people can dissociate these intrusive thoughts healthily and want to manage their process of resettlement and integration without psychological collapse. It is my proposition that those who successfully avoid having intrusive memories and emotions related to them have a reasonably stable sense of self, enough psychic space, and, therefore, the capacity for healthy dissociation.

Healthy dissociation, or lack of it, can, therefore, be an indicator for distinguishing whether patients presenting with intrusive thoughts and anxiety are suffering from PTSD, or whether it is existential anxiety or trauma related anxiety, in which somatic presentation involves inhibition of the sympathetic nervous system, a restriction in the range of system variability, resulting in physiological rigidity at rest and when confronted. The most common problems and symptoms of a typical, unresolved psychological trauma of refugees with increased sensitivity or arousal fits into three categories, as detailed below.

1. Physical: eating and sleep disturbances, sexual dysfunction, low energy, and chronic unexplained pain in the body, specifically in back and knee, hypervigilance, jumpiness.
2. Emotional: depression, spontaneous crying, despair and hopelessness, extreme anxiety and a sense of being on guard , panic attacks, fearfulness, compulsive and obsessional behaviours, feeling out of control, irritability, detachment, guilt feelings connected with survival and omission, grief reactions, sudden unprovoked anger and resentment, obsessional fears about death, emotional numbness, sleep disturbances such as nightmares, withdrawal from normal routine, and inability to form and or maintain healthy relationships.
3. Cognitive: memory lapses especially, difficulty making decisions, amnesia, decreased ability to concentrate, avoidance of situations that resemble the initial event, an altered sense of time, flashbacks or re-experiencing the trauma, and feeling distracted or disorientated.

Disturbances in multiple value processing sub-systems due to trauma

Some traumatic events can affect more than one value processing sub-system. For instance, incest can disturb a healthy relationship, resilience, and autonomy, while genocide can disturb collective identity, interdependence, and community subsystems, which may demobilize one's psychological resources, overruling all other subsystems. This type of experience can shatter the schema, beliefs, assumptions, representations, and judgements associated with one's sense of self and relating to others, the view of the world, and, indeed, the efficacy of the existing value processing mechanisms that one possesses. Refugees, like others, interrelate within a set of connections that provide emotional, social, and material support as well as a sense of being socially entrenched, and having a sense of belonging and meaning in life. There is also the development of a system of accustomed social contingencies that are rooted psychologically and emotionally as the basis of feelings of safety, security, and belonging. Events such as torture, for example, are traumatic and can threaten these allied networks and well-established connections. For instance, involuntary displacement means the loss of connectedness to the familiar environment.

The formation of a sense of self, agency, and self-efficacy is a developmental milestone en route to adulthood with positive consequences for individual well-being. From a psychoanalytic point of view, it is important to assess what is specifically traumatic for a patient: is it the fear of castration (or anything that could resemble and remind of castration) and a narcissistic wounding to the sense of self; is it disturbances of positive identity as the foundation of emotional independence which leads to feelings of being competent, adequate, and having enough psychic space to be in control over oneself and in relation to others? Trauma in general can disturb psychological connectedness and cause feelings of loss, leaving the person helpless, and disturbs the development of resilience, healthy object relations, autonomy, and identity formation. What distinguishes the trauma of refugees, and specifically political refugees, who have been persecuted and cannot go back to their home country, is the loss of home and psycho-social being, which can cause added stress.

Trauma in early life (which is the case with many refugee children, both those coming with family and unaccompanied children) have an impact on the shared affective exchange in relating. It creates a lack of feelings of warmth, connectedness, security, and trust. Early childhood trauma affects the formation of personality through the whole sequence of emotional development, and can result in avoidant or muddled and confused object relations. It can generate relationship and personality difficulties, trigger assumptions and beliefs about self and objects, and have an impact on emotional as well as cognitive functioning in the area of object relations.

Some of the common patterns of emotional trauma may result in compulsive behaviour patterns, self-destructive, uncontrollable reactive thoughts, inability to develop a positive sense of self, splitting off parts of the self, helplessness in making choices, unhealthy dissociative behaviour, and the incapability of maintaining close relationships. Moreover, these can be compounded by witnessing life-threatening events, and in some cases being violent to others and embracing the identity of an executioner. Other situations, such as kidnapping, imprisonment, torture, and domestic violence, are, on the whole, associated with a longer period of helplessness and fear of injury or death. People who have been tortured in prison and lacking any support and community engagement may be further traumatized as a consequence of possible disclosure. For some political prisoners, witnessing someone else being tortured (this is common in political prisons as one method of torture) can be extremely traumatic, and the greater the attachment to the person, the greater the stress will be. Coercive power used in prisons, detention centres, concentration and refugee camps, and sometimes in the community as a whole (Rwanda or the Balkans), can be overwhelming.

The impact of refugee trauma on perception of the self

The enduring effects of a past event, such as torture, sexual assault, and violation as a weapon of torture, can lead to a change in the perception of self, others, and of the world. In these types of circumstances, there are people who can build the capacity to alter beliefs about self and the world to the extreme, in order to feel in control.

As a result, a person who might be persecuted may believe all officials are potential perpetrators and the world is not a safe place. It is possible to fail to assimilate and alter external resources to match previous beliefs. The person may come to believe that a bad thing happened to "me" and "I" must be getting punished for something terrible "I" did; life is dangerous and "I" should always fear what could potentially happen. For a traumatized patient who has lost trust completely as the result of environmental factors, and believes the world is not always a just and fair place, the therapeutic goal is to accommodate the experience of the trauma into the past life experiences; this means altering beliefs to incorporate the new information with the aim of helping patient to recognize that there can be exceptions. With this change in perception, a person with negative beliefs can change and form the view that "I" am not a bad person for being persecuted or having to leave as a result of war; and sometimes bad things happen to good people, and although "I" had bad experiences, the world is not an unsafe and insecure place altogether. This change initially may be temporary, and it is reasonable for the person to have recurring symptoms in the form of fears, intrusive thoughts, and loss of trust, which may be projected to such issues as their asylum application being rejected, meaning a possible return to the dangerous situation they have fled. Although these fears and intrusions might be rational and justified, because sometimes this is a normal reaction to an abnormal situation and is the result of existential anxiety, the progression of adjustment to the unpredictable might be challenging, as there are unconscious elements of trauma and recovery.

The self of a traumatized person, grouping, and the creation of an enemy

The development of a sense of self—its integration, its separation, its protection, and the resilience or lack of it—begins in the early developmental process. Although group is not the subject of this study, when looking at refugee types of traumas, it is important to look at group and grouping: the concepts of enemy and ally, the sense of self and the sense of belonging. Being part of a group or nation is largely dependent on individuals' sense of self and individuals within the community, ethnic, or national group. People tend to have the potential to see their group as a privileged group—what Erikson (1950) calls "pseudo-species". Thus, an enemy group seen as sub-human is threatening and generates reactive defences. Questions arising here are:

1. What is the extent and degree of defensiveness that is characteristic of conflict behaviour that represents the personal and emotional needs of individuals to hate an enemy in order to keep the conflicted selves together?
2. To what extent does the group or state, as superego, play a role in the individual mind of a person who endured trauma within the social and political system?
3. To what extent does the traumatized person have the capacity for splitting and projecting, which can play a part in how one sees and feels about the others?
4. Through the process of projective identification, how can one make others feel?

Future-orientated intrusive thoughts

If the focus of threat to life is not based on a past event for patients, but is based on the future (as is the case with many asylum-seeker patients, who are anxious about being rejected and returned to their country by the immigration authorities), the intrusions and re-experiencing of symptoms that occur as part of post trauma stress is a different type than those experienced by individuals exposed to traumas in the past and who are anxious about present situations, but can distinguish the two. There is a lack of literature in relation to asylum seekers' trauma, as the past and current literature focuses on re-experiencing symptoms, which commonly acts as a pointer to PTSD, and is based on past trauma exposure, rather than future-orientated events.

    Some of the asylum seekers seeking help suffer intrusions that consist of the past event, but also present and future-orientated events, such as: will the Home Office accept my asylum application? Will my children progress with their education in this country? Will I see my home town again in my life? Will I ever learn the

English language? Will I ever be able to work again? What will happen to me if they send me back? Will my children be provided for if I die? The list can go on and on. So, there is as much uncertainty about the present and the future as about the past. Within this context, it is not post trauma alone that affects asylum seekers' situations; it is past as well as ongoing and, indeed, future orientated, and the latter aspect is neglected in the literature.

Specific studies of PTSD that are relevant to the psychoanalytic model and concepts are important. This study focuses on a new way of thinking, originating from psychoanalytic theory, for the provision of appropriate help for people who have experienced trauma if the intrusive thoughts are focused both on the discrete past event and possible future-orientated events. Such knowledge and understanding can bring to light tangible evidence that the rates and patterns of experience are not as different across stressors as initially thought. Conceptualizing post trauma syndromes that may be characteristic of, and specific to, a particular patient is important, and could yield useful information about past and future impact and the coping structure. Having a sense of self, psychic space, the capacity for healthy dissociation, the ability to adjust, and the management of a life in a new environment are signs that can be used to establish the effect of trauma on an individual.

History of diagnosis and treatments of war neuroses and PTSD

It is important to look at theory developed after the First World War when studying what are sometimes known as "traumatic war neuroses". Freud himself initially wrote little about war neuroses, yet the subject had a profound impact on psychoanalytical theory and resulted in his publication of "Introduction to psycho-analysis and the war neuroses" (1919d). In that paper, he attempts to reconcile the existence of what he calls "danger-neuroses" with the view that neuroses are caused by a conflict between repressed libidinal impulses and the "ego instincts" of self preservation. He suggests:

> In traumatic and war neuroses the human ego is defending itself from a danger which threatens it from without or which is embodied in a shape assumed by the ego itself. In the transference

neuroses of peace the enemy from which the ego is defending itself is actually the libido, whose demands seem to it to be menacing. In both cases the ego is afraid of being damaged – in the latter case by the libido and in the former by external violence. It might, indeed, be said that in the case of the war neuroses, in contrast to the pure traumatic neuroses and in approximation to the transference neuroses, what is feared is nevertheless an internal enemy. The theoretical difficulties standing in the way of a unifying hypothesis of this kind do not seem insuperable: after all, we have a perfect right to describe repression, which lies at the basis of every neurosis, as a reaction to a trauma as an elementary traumatic neurosis. [p. 210]

In *Beyond the Pleasure Principle*, Freud (1920g) introduced the concepts of repetition compulsion and death drive to account for the impact of trauma on the mind and suggests that the trauma is repeated and repeated in order to master the stimuli and bring it under the domination of the pleasure–pain principle. His analysis of children's games showed that the trauma is mastered through a process of symbolization, thus hinting at a theory about the origin of human language itself. The stories of Siegfried Sassoon, Wilfred Owen, and others who were treated for shell shock during the First World War by the psychiatrist and anthropologist William Rivers at Craiglockhart hospital in Scotland, written about in Pat Barker's (1991) novel *Regeneration*, is an invaluable example. Rivers was influenced by Freud, but did not agree with Freud's view that neuroses were caused by sexual factors. Rivers used dream analysis, which Freud had already moved away from (by the time of the First World War) towards analysis of the transference neurosis. He (Rivers, 1918) suggests that the disappearance or improvement of symptoms on the cessation of voluntary repression may be due to the action of one form of the principle of catharsis, which is operative when a suppressed or dissociated body of experience is brought to the surface so that it becomes reintegrated with the ordinary personality. Another form of catharsis, which often happens in cases of war neuroses, as in neurosis in general, is that the person does not repress their painful thoughts, but dwells on them until their experience starts to have exaggerated and often distorted importance. In such cases, Rivers believes communication can provide relief for these troubles.

There is a rising body of research and literature (e.g., Everly & Mitchell, 2000; Foa, Davidson, Frances, & Ross, 1999; Foa, Hearst-Ikeda, & Perry, 1995; Gelpin, Bonne, Peri, Brandes, & Shalev, 1996; Herman, 1992; Mayou, Ehlers, & Hobbs, 2000; Pynoos & Eth, 1986) on identifying, diagnosing, and treating psychological trauma and trauma-related mental health problems, and also on culturally determined means of communicating psychological distress and articulating symptoms. This is associated with the need to make available suitable services to a rapidly growing population of war veterans, displaced people, immigrants, and refugees deracinated in a global situation of armed conflict, which shows no signs of ending or lessening. This is a psychoanalytic study, but it is important to acknowledge non-psychoanalytic studies that have been developed since the 1980s as trauma treatment models, such as "trauma debriefing models" (Herbert & Sageman, 2004; Litz, Gray, Bryant, & Adler, 2002; Macy et al., 2004; Ortlepp & Friedman, 2002). One common factor of these models is to encourage the traumatized person to re-tell the trauma story in as much detail as possible. While this study does not allow for a detailed discussion of these methods, their variations, or a critique of their sufficiency, it is important to point out that there is no convincing evidence yet as to whether trauma debriefing aids or hampers the traumatized person's psychological recovery, or whether it just provides temporary symptom relief.

The World Mental Health Report (WHO, 1995) provides a table summarizing eleven studies of PTSD and its prevalence rates in different populations that have suffered natural or man-made disasters, war, torture, or repression. The occurrence rates vary from a low of 3.5% among flood victims in Puerto Rico and 4% among refugees at a health-screening clinic in the USA, to 88% in Laotian refugees attending an Indo-Chinese mental health programme in the USA. These wide-ranging differences can be attributed in part to diverse assessment methods, scales, and interview programmes and to differences between child and adult populations, as well as help-seeking cultures. It is suggested that refugees, and in particular individuals who have experienced torture, are at high risk for developing mental health problems. Another common finding noted in these studies is the high frequency of comorbid psychiatric conditions, especially major depression. This, however, differs from my approach, which considers the therapist as a listening other to what the patient presents and works with that, rather than using medical categorizing and generalizing.

Understanding trauma and creating psychic space

The most devastating effect of traumatic events on a person is the disruption of ordinary life. Refugees and displaced persons may have been forced to leave their home due to their circumstances, losing their familiar way of life, and indeed, often not able to say goodbye to their loved ones. Coping with this very much depends on the person's resilience or lack of it, which is related to events that occurred before this stage of life. Understanding both the inner and outer worlds of the individual, and the ways in which the past affects the present, is an important factor in understanding the effects of trauma on an individual's psyche. For example, the way in which the individual becomes a refugee and how the person recounts their life story in their present circumstances is vital when considering whether the person's psychological presentation is related to the trauma in adulthood or is related to their earlier developmental experiences and has been triggered by the current event in their adult life. The observation and conception that people have is a central factor in the way in which they handle their experiences, which is a process that could contribute to creating more psychic space or losing it. The manner in which a patient may relate their stories in the present provides evidence of the interplay of these components. The ways in which some patients experienced physical and psychic invasion is made all the more moving by the accompanying description of their capacity for creating a psychic space. In spite of the extreme and overwhelming external circumstances designed for punishment by the authorities, sometimes the life histories of many resilient people bear witness to processes of reparation and creativity. This is evidence for the existence of psychic space, in which people in some ways are enabled to regulate the traumatic experiences, either in phantasy or through action, which helps them to move on in life, rather than being stuck in the aftermath of trauma. The ability to create a psychic space for thinking is linked to the sense of self and quality of object representations and their relation to external events and opportunities. The mental capacity to have a psychic space has direct associations to the psychological formulation of a sense of self. I hypothesize that for resilient individuals, this psychic space did exist, but was temporarily lost due to an unbearable traumatic experience, which, through having a listening other in therapy, can be reclaimed and recreated. It is the creation of this psychic space that will allow healthy dissociation—a defence mechanism which I argue to be foundation of resilience. This is of central importance in this study, and will be discussed further, with clinical material, to develop my line of reasoning.

However, it is important to note that the effect of trauma, irrespective of previous personality structures, influences people and their capacity. Memory is an important factor in recounting the experience, and the way in which people's affects are regulated during recall are related to a narrative according to whether the traumatic association is direct or in relation to another factor, such as early development and object relation. This is extremely important, but it is not always an either/or question, as both forms of association can be present at different times in the same person. It is related to a dynamic balance, which can be influenced by ongoing events, rather than a single traumatic event. One could speculate that some of the mechanisms of defence have peculiar functions. It seems less likely, for example, that someone would be filled with a sense of adventure and excitement while peering out at wild animals from a torture chamber, or seeing his sister being raped in front of him as a torture weapon. Many other examples can be cited where a person has been at a severe disadvantage and yet has enough capacity to cope with the situation. The concept of resilience and survival strategies, therefore, is not intended to overlook the fact that people are deeply affected by trauma, regardless of how well they may have been able to compensate for it. The move from isolation and helplessness to connectedness and preserving a sense of self and others by use of healthy dissociation—indeed, having the ability to recognize that therapeutic help is needed and seeking it to deal with the psychological effects of trauma, being creative in supportive networks, and using a sense of humour as coping skills—are characteristic qualities in a resilient person.

Individual resilience and response to the unpredictable

An emotional trauma contains the common elements that: (1) it is unexpected; (2) shocking; (3) the person was unprepared; (4) helplessness—nothing the person could do to prevent it. Despite this, it is not easy to determine what is traumatic to someone and the level of it. But a person's resilience, and how one experiences the event in the subjectivity of trauma, determines how one will react to an unpredictable event. If one is used to being in control of emotions, it may be surprising and even embarrassing to discover that something can be so debilitating and out of control. Thus, an event or situation may create psychological trauma as it devastates one's perceived ability to cope, and leaves the person feeling emotionally, cognitively, and physically overwhelmed, fearing death, annihilation, and mutilation.

My argument is that the effects of chronic traumatic stress on physical, psychological, relational, and social functions are dependent on the degree of the person's resilience and ability to dissociate healthily. While relatively minor stressors may trigger a symptom in a vulnerable person, an event must be catastrophic to induce a similar reaction in a resilient person. However, multiple inflicted external traumas as the result of environmental situations can construct psychological difficulty even in the resilient person. For example, people with a history of childhood abuse, which affects their adequate development and creation of a good sense of self and enough psychic space for self-processing structures, react differently to traumatic events than those with reasonably secure childhoods who are exposed to traumatic events in adult life.

Although it is beyond the remit of this study, it is important to note that the interaction between genes and environment also adds to the complex dynamic of trauma. This is an important factor, as we are biosocial organisms with unique genes, unique personal values, and self-structures that mediate the psycho–socio–physiological reactions to environmental stressors and traumas. This is important, because trauma can cause physiological changes in the central and peripheral nervous systems that regulate physiological interactions and body functioning as well as psychological functioning. Ordinary human experience contributes to shaping the structures of individuals' value processing system in development

from infant to adult. Traumatic events can disturb, rebuild, or reinforce the existing, stable resilience, and damage self-processing
structures. This study conjectures that traumatic events can
contribute to either the disturbance of resilience, or to the creation
of it and the development of a sense of self and a self-system with
more psychic space that helps one to process and cope with traumatic experiences. This is based on the subjective experience, the
processing mode, the area of functioning, the objective characteristics of the events, and the ability to create psychic space and healthy
dissociation.

Trauma symptoms as adaptive

Two primary configurations of psychopathology derive from individuals' attempts to cope with severe disruptions of normal dialectical developmental processes and efforts made to handle
developmental disruptions. One may become excessively preoccupied with one aspect of developmental issues, such as relatedness
and self-definition, and defensively avoid another. This dynamic
formulation of psychopathology as deriving from distortions and
disruptions of normal psychological development provides a paradigm that organizes various forms of psychopathology in different
ways. It is important to observe adapting strategies that people
develop in order to survive after traumatic exposure when we
assess the presenting symptoms in a patient, thus making it easier
to solicit what rationale these strategies have in terms of helping a
patient to cope with traumatic memories of the past in the present.
With further exploration derived from the patient, we should look
at those patterns and determine whether those behaviours are a
new characteristic adaptation as the result of a traumatic experience, or are based on personality structure.

To summarize, this chapter provides explorations of what the
term trauma means in general and in psychoanalysis. Causes,
consequences, dynamics, and mechanisms of psychological trauma
were discussed, and some attention was given to refugees' experience of trauma, since the clinical data in this study are from refugee
patients. An appreciation of what is meant by trauma is a necessary
backdrop for this thesis, providing a springboard for the discussion

of post trauma stress as an example of vulnerability beyond the medical view and within psychoanalytic concepts. Freud's perspectives on trauma were offered to set the psychoanalytic context. Stress is placed on the individualized nature of the experience of traumatic events. This considered important to establish, as it is the origin and nature of individual differences in vulnerability and resilience, the sense of self, psychic space, and the type of dissociation (healthy and unhealthy). In order to present a blend of clinical and theoretical material, I give a vignette of a patient whom I call Ahmed.

Ahmed

Ahmed is from the Middle-east and had been imprisoned for two years, severely tortured, and forced to witness other people being tortured, including his wife, his child, and his sister. Ahmed left his country to escape from further persecution and lost contact with his family. He subsequently tried to trace his family members through the Red Cross in the UK, but with no success. In his referral letter, it was reported that he made frequent visits to his GP with psychosomatic presentations and was advised to think about whether his problems might be psychological. Initially, he was defensive and not keen on the idea, but, after consideration, he informed his GP that he would like to receive psychological help. Ahmed and I had three sessions for assessment to decide whether I could be helpful to him. He presented himself as somebody who could avoid and resist accepting problems and who tried hard to be positive and optimistic and wanted a quick fix. His response to my question about this position was "I needed other people's approval so I found myself constantly worried about disappointing others in their view of me."

Looking down at his knees, he recalled occasions where he had actually explained to others that he was vulnerable and in need of help, and said, "Instead of being helped, I only received a response of dislike and rejection, which was disappointing and caused me further pain and stress. Then I stopped asking."

It became apparent that his avoidance of, and dissociating from, dealing with his problem was perhaps a sign of an effort to cover up and cope with his helplessness. In this particular session, he talked of the importance of not disclosing problems for fear of making people worry and then experiencing rejection. This way, although he could be aware of his difficulties, he could keep them to himself so as not to cause himself further pain. I asked him to tell me more, and Ahmed insisted that I needed to understand his position and not see it in terms of him being a defensive patient without good reason. He said, "When a person from my country comes to see me, you do not start to disappoint the person with your problem or what happened to you . . . They do not like to be disappointed. So therefore you try to keep your problem to yourself, to not cause worry for them."

In this short statement, Ahmed starts referring to himself within the cultural context of his country. He began by referring to himself as "me" or "I", but as the issue became more difficult for him in relation to others, he refers to himself and his action by using "you", although he was aware that he was referring to his own thoughts and feelings with me, his listening other. Here, through his healthy dissociation, he protected himself from too much pain while still having a sense of self and enough psychic space to talk about his painful experience. This session provided evidence that Ahmed was concerned about showing his vulnerability. During the session, I provided him with gentle encouragement, and relayed to him that if he talked about his painful experience, I would survive and would not be disappointed with him, which worked. He immediately became tearful, and talked about some aspects of his experience. However, Ahmed's helplessness and powerlessness in the face of his problematic experience was repeatedly represented in transference as an implicit procedure of the situation where he needed help, he being subjected to rejection or abuse. Indirectly, he was telling me that he needed my approval and my confirmation that I could be his listening other before talking. When, in later sessions, we explored his pattern of defence at the heart of his quest for advice, his response was, "When a person comes to you and begs you for something or he and you both know about severe torture on you or your family or to someone else who was in prison . . . it is a very, very difficult situation . . . you are out and not in prison, but you know your friends and family are still suffering in prison . . . in your mind you want to kill one of your torturers if you can reach them."

Here, Ahmed's helplessness and the dreadful aspect of his murderous feelings was revealed. In his phantasy, he sees himself as capable of becoming a killer. I shall not go into detail here, but at this point I did address this with him, and he affirmed and voiced the violent feelings he harboured and reassured me that he was in control. With further exploration, Ahmed reacted to interpretations given with an appeal for help to deal with his helplessness. He reached insight into his aggressive feelings and made the link between his aggression and his vulnerability. As I mentioned before, at the beginning of treatment Ahmed demonstrated a culturally accepted way out of his conflict. But at this stage of therapy (after four months), he becomes able to break away from his cultural defences. This resulted in recognition and acceptance of his conflict, which was his helplessness when facing his own rage, hatred, and murderous feelings, and not of others. It became clear to him that his feeling was strong when he was thinking of his torturer, and later in the process it became apparent that his murderous feelings were not limited to his torturer but could be directed at anyone who made him feel inadequate, insecure, and worthless. However, at this stage, memory of his own experience and the atrocities he had witnessed being inflicted on others continued to haunt him, which manifested in his dreams and his remembering. The scene of witnessing members of his family being tortured was recurrent, one of which was when his wife and his sister were raped and assaulted in front of him. His inability to find words for his overwhelming feelings and to express what he had experienced was evident in his tension, as well as, at times, in his fragmented verbal communications. (Ahmed's verbal communications were varied; he could present himself in a clear and articulate manner, but on occasion he would become totally fragmented.) When he was not able to verbalize his thoughts and feelings clearly, our transference relationship would change and he would become angry and frustrated with me, as I had to seek clarification from him.

Ten months into therapy, revisiting Ahmed's experiences and his problematic pattern of relating to others brought about the dilemma of facing his aggressive part, reciprocal responses that stood in sharp contrast to his conscious ethical and social values; specifically, his view of himself as a forgiving and supportive person in relation to others. I decided that we needed to look at the tension that Ahmed described in his first account of being rejected and, in this context, elaborate meaning that could not be regarded as a symptomatic response to the intensified conflict caused by the two incompatible characteristic patterns he had adopted. In doing so, it became clear that these were in conflict with each other, and when he was confronted with his murderous self, and the blurring with his victim self as a helpless person, it became clear to him that he had no clear sense of self, due to not having enough psychic space to process his thought, his fear of breaking down, and his fear of not being able to contain his feelings. He then understood that it was for these reason that he developed psychosomatic and bodily reactions. By being able to accept me as his listening other, and expressing his true feelings, Ahmed achieved some psychic space that led to integration of his sense of self in order to deal with his problematic experience and his conflicting thoughts. This was associated with his increased emotional differentiation, and he became able to deal with his complex emotions of sadness, sorrow, guilt, grief, and shame, from which previously he was dissociating in an unhealthy manner.

Focusing on the theme presented by Ahmed as problematic experiences in the process, which I considered as a phenomenological account of how the theme developed and how Ahmed related to his problematic area, here I present another short passage of the process that highlights some of the sequences of his psychological development; indeed, his developing ability to create healthy dissociations. In one of our sessions, Ahmed was overwhelmed after talking about what he had encountered in prison and he experienced a breakdown in the session. He said,

"Sometimes when I am feeling this pain I don't feel any problem in my head, but now I am sitting here and feeling, I'm feeling this pain here in my head, everything connected in my body with my head. I don't feel it always, now I'm feeling it just in my head and feeling something like itching, something very strange, it is not an ordinary feeling. I can't say it's pain, I can't name it."

There was a long silence, and then he carried on. "It is really in the back and front of my head. And this time I feel some sort of tension. Some sort of mmm . . ."

Ahmed was pointing to his head. I felt rather confused, wondering whether his presentation was symbolic or whether he was actually talking of physical pain, so I reserved any interpretation and asked,

"You are telling me that you feel some sort of tension just now?"

Ahmed said, "Yes!"

I asked again, "Can you help me to understand better please?"

With very heavy breathing and in a loud voice, he said, "I don't know. It just came."

He breathed more heavily, and then was silent for a while, and then started again.

"Please, can I?" looking at the couch while he was breathing heavily.

I said, "Would you like to lie down on the couch?"

(I never encourage patients that I am seeing once a week to use the couch, so I was rather shocked and could not think how to respond to what I saw as his peculiar behaviour.)

Ahmed said, "Yes, please. Can I?"

He moved and lay on the couch without my permission/confirmation and did not say anything, until the end of the session (for twenty-three minutes precisely), but his anxiety seemed to be relieved and he was breathing normally when we finished the session. He did not talk about this episode on our next session or for some while afterwards, and I decided not to raise it either, as I thought his feeling associated with this may yet be too overwhelming for him at this stage, taking into consideration that I was seeing him once a week.

The next segment is part of a session from when Ahmed had been in therapy for a year. He had told me about an episode where he was questioned by some officials and, as a result, became ill. I shall not give any details of his story here, in order to protect his identity, but I recall what followed.

I said to him, "You like people in any circumstances to respect one other. You value that very much, and you have experienced that in prison people are not respected. Am I right to think that you are trying to convey to me that you are very sensitive about this type of interaction between people? It made you very angry to be disrespected and to see other people being disrespected in your presence."

Ahmed interrupted and said, "Yes, yes, of course I become very angry. I get so angry I can't even explain it, I actually don't think anger is the right word, I think I need a much stronger word. I don't remember what I said to them. I was very, very sick. I was tired. I was ill and exhausted. I was angry and tired, I was so tired, I never have been so tired and angry in my life. I am so pleased that you understand what I am talking about. I don't need to hide myself here and that feels good."

He became silent and started to cry, and was in tears until the end of the session.

In this session, Ahmed seemed to feel me as his listening other, helping him to move towards connecting his emotions and bodily reactions with his present situation and his past experiences. He started moving towards making statements and clarifications, connecting his feelings with his past and present state of mind, and to making connections with his psychosomatic problems. He gained insight to his own rage and ability to associate with what had happened to him rather than to others. He moved from social dilemma to his personal dilemma, and no longer needed to work with constant projections. This was a great improvement, as by this time he had not visited his GP's surgery for over four months, whereas before we started therapy he had visited it at least four times a week. This I considered a positive therapeutic outcome.

Using the above example himself, three months later Ahmed showed a further improvement in working with difficult experiences in depth. His murderous anger at this stage had dropped to a lower level, gradually making more psychic space for his sadness and his delayed mourning of the losses he had endured.

Here, I bring in a theme in which Ahmed met a young girl who had been shot. He said,

"And she was talking about her situation in the region where she was living. She was often saying she was very sorry for no reason. She told me that someone had shot her and the bullet was in her body and she didn't know why the person shot her. Can you believe this?"

He was silent. I knew he needed my encouragement as his listening other, so I said,

"I get a sense that you need me to confirm that I am listening carefully."

He started to cry, and after a few moments carried on in tears.

"She was crying so deeply and she was in pain, I was in pain . . . my pain."

Ahmed became quite stressed and he started weeping, expressing deep sadness. This was the first time he was able to relate to his pain as his own pain, and was not crying about projections—the pain of others that he was always tearful about before.

I said, "It is difficult to realize that all the sadness was yours . . . and you had to swallow your tears for yourself for such a long time."

Ahmed said, "Mmm. Mmm. It was. It is."

I felt it was now safe to encourage Ahmed to focus more directly on his own pain, rather than working with projections of shared pain. I said,

"Witnessing or hearing such injustice happening around you is quite painful. And of course it is not easy to live with a situation you have been in. It is incomprehensible. I am especially thinking about how you carry with you the memory of your own child being tortured, and you could not do anything about it, as that could put both of your lives in more danger."

Ahmed, in tears, confirmed this by saying, "Mmm. Mmm"

I allowed some silence for few moments, and then I said,

"It is very sad."

He said, "It is very sad. It was very very painful . . ."

Silence again and then he said tearfully, "It is very, very sad."

The session came to an end in silence.

In this session, Ahmed managed to express his sadness and allow himself to experience that his sadness can be contained by me as his listening other without needing to become overwhelmed (by anger and frustrations) or becoming physically ill (psychosomatic). This was a sign of increased mental capacity with more psychic space, which resulted in a further change of his dissociative patterns of behaviour from unhealthy to healthy.

At this stage, he developed a better sense of self and became able to show his more integrated self with pride. This improvement in Ahmed was shown both in his transference with me and in his accounts of his outside interaction with others. When he felt help-less and needy, although not comfortable, he did not expect rejection, abuse, or humiliation to the same extent as he did before. He developed insight into his situation and therefore became more engaged, reclaiming his resilience. He developed a state of mind whereby he could see that emotions could be contained and become more differentiated, approaching a level of understanding and insight. Consequently, I was able to use more direct interpretation in transference. More mature, though not less difficult, emotions began to dominate our work. We were at a stage where difficult emotions could be met by understanding and containment. Ahmed became able to free associate and he would not show defensive behaviour towards my interpretations and, as a result, became self-integrated with greater awareness of himself and of others. The pattern of our work changed and he would come back to session with his thoughts on issues that had been discussed in previous session/s, even when he found it difficult. For example, he came to one session and said,

"Yes, so always if a person or people I know come to me, they don't disappoint me in reaction to my problem or what happened to me. They . . . they . . . they themselves don't like to be disappointed, so they try to manage their fears in this way by projecting them to me. Perhaps cutting or changing the subject is their strategy for coping. After the last session, I was thinking I must actually have been so self-obscured to share my experiences with people who have no idea. You know, although it is part of my life, I now know it is quite alien to others. It is quite disturbing."

In this passage, it was clear that Ahmed initially found it hard to verbalize what he wanted to convey to me, but when he gathered his thoughts, then he was all right. He recognized his internalized aggression and was able to connect to his own inner psyche. He became silent here. I felt he may need some encouragement, but I only said, "I see."

He continued, "The reason for not talking about my problems is because I do not like to make other people feel sorry for me, and also do not want to upset them. Now, I don't think it is being defensive. I think it is knowing your place and the people around you. I don't think I am defensive. I talk about everything here. But, it was wrong for me to talk about all those painful issues to people who don't have any idea."

I said, "So, it may be that when you are talking about your problems you may also be thinking about not making me too worried. Bringing this out now, perhaps part of you needs my reassurance for you to continue to associate freely and have me listen to you."

Ahmed said, "Yeah yeah yeah. Something like that . . . Sometimes . . . Yeah, exactly."

He then focused on the time when he was talking about the prison and torture; he said, "It is not easy to forget your experience and with that experience always in your mind it is very difficult to be able to feel safe and trust other people—you know."

I felt that although Ahmed had been expressing his comfort in talking with me without fear of hurting me, there was some complaint that I may not appreciate his fear and vulnerability in the situations that he had been in.

I said, "It seems to me that by referring to other people's coping strategy, perhaps you are telling me that there are issues you still cannot trust me enough to share." I then asked him for his feeling related to his experience, the particular type of feeling he experiences, hoping to establish deeper aspects of his internal voice.

Ahmed said, "Uh . . . I was very bad sometimes in my . . . uh . . . feeling very bad from that, no good feeling . . . Yeah. No . . ."

Then he was silent for two minutes before starting again.

"There were very bad things and although I want to forget them, I can't. I remember those things and when I think about them . . . it makes . . . it makes me feel sick. I feel so mean talking to you like this, but this is how I feel. I feel something that I cannot tell you. It has really been very difficult for me to tell you what I'm feeling about one particular experience. That is what I have not told you yet. Umm . . . I'm feeling . . . um . . . something in my body happening just now. Um . . . It was very inhuman and I never thought that people could do that. . . . But they were doing something worse than that . . . they were torturing children and women. Mmm . . . they tortured my son in front of me. You know? Uhuhuhm . . ."

I said, "You are shifting from one thing to another and losing your focus again and causing yourself stress. Can we focus on you for now? Tell me what was going in your mind before I asked you the question about our relationship."

He was silent for a while, and then said, "They weren't . . . they . . . they were not feeling ashamed of that. They were doing everything bad and the problem is, if you can advise me, I know I should not ask you, but if only you can advise me what to do, if I see one of that group or some of that group or some of the people who were torturing me, how can I control my murderous feeling? I need you to tell me. How can I stop myself from hurting them, the way they were hurting my six-year-old child, my wife, my sister, my other family members and me . . . If you could only tell me . . ."

Ahmed was shaking and unable to make any eye contact. I decided not push this further, although I was aware that he needed to talk about something very difficult for him which at the time I felt he was not ready for, or perhaps I was not ready yet—I did not pursue it.

On reflection, it became apparent that his memories of the torture could still provoke strong feelings of helplessness, as well as anger, which Ahmed now was turning into an active position by asking for my advice. I thought he was trying to modify his rage and was willing to find a way of trying to resolve the fragmentation and confusion he feels. In asking me how he could relate to his feelings, he was asking himself what to do, and he was able to accept his helplessness. By confiding in me as his listening other, Ahmed now could trust that together we could work to help him stop his constant unhealthy dissociation when he recalled his traumatic experiences. This was enhancing his psychic space and his capacity to relate, enhancing his ability to finish his horrific thought without panic, bodily pain, and fragmentation, and to have a dialogue about his experiences outside himself with me and finish his thought. This was to restore his sense of self and regain his resilience.

I became aware that when Ahmed started to talk about his experience in prison, and as his memories of torture evoked strong feelings of helplessness that were too much for him, he turned it into an active decision by asking me for advice. I also bear in mind that this was a culturally codified way of trying to resolve a problem, which he learnt to do in order not to fully display his helplessness. I had to learn to respond to this aspect of his personality with careful respect for his culture, confirming to him that I appreciated his attempts to teach me about his culture, and help me to learn. On those occasions, I tried not to use direct interpretation so as not to be perceived by him as being judgemental. Instead, where I felt I needed to interpret what had been said, I encouraged him to undertake further exploration in order to help him identify the pattern of his defences. By identifying the most important themes, analysing the pattern and structure of Ahmed's presentation, and following his improvement through the therapeutic process, it became possible for Ahmed to examine and re-examine his position. In the process, after his initial culturally defined resistance to free association and his fragmentation, or what he called "being stuck" when recalling his traumatic memory, he was very perceptive and quick to learn to contain his high arousal. Although the detail of the whole process is not included here, I observed a massive improvement in Ahmed's psychological well-being; in session events, and in short- and long-term process, the outcomes of his changing behaviour in transference with me, indeed, with his outside relations and interaction that he reported.

Ahmed's presentation of his experiences could be formulated as: when faced with thoughts and memories of the atrocities and trauma he had endured, he would feel needy and helpless, expecting to be rejected by other/s, which in turn made him very angry and frustrated. These also activated another state of mind, where he experienced murderous feelings and hatred towards others he interacted and felt helpless with.

The goal of therapeutic intervention with Ahmed was to first gain a thorough history and become familiar with the material he was presenting, with great fragmentation at the beginning, and to become his listening other, facilitating his thinking and reflection. The parts of the sessions presented here had to be carefully selected, providing a catalogue of verbal and non-verbal aspects of his presentation and the changing process. Themes had to be carefully chosen and defined to evaluate Ahmed's behaviour and assess different areas of his object relations; this was also the case with events or situations which his cultural attitudes or actions expressed. Ahmed's action is expressed as narratives of experiences, phantasies, memories, feelings, bodily sensations, and dreams, organized and presented in dialogical sequence pattern. I very much focused on what Ahmed said and how he said it, and on his reactions to my clarifications or interpretations, and how I had to learn about his pattern and culturally defined defences. The progression of his presentations demonstrated that one dominant theme in our work was his relation to the atrocities he had experienced and witnessed, and the violent feelings he would have when confronted, either in reality or in his phantasy, by his perpetrators and with those by whom he had felt humiliated, and, indeed, in transference with me. Significant words such as "torture", "interrogation", "killing", "suffering", "rape", "tension", "pain", "soldiers", "guards", "culture", "good", "bad", "evil", "domain", "kind", "human" were used by Ahmed on a regular basis to express his thoughts and feelings. His non-verbal communication was a way of expressing his suffering that included signs such as crying, hyperventilation, and anger. These gradually changed as the therapy progressed.

However, in the process, I needed to do more than just make meanings with Ahmed. I used a narrative construction based on certain assumptions. Ahmed's self-narrative was concealed (or retreated from) another narrative, which he did not recognize as his own. I work on the basis that the aim of therapy is to introduce Ahmed to the non-self-narrative that exists in him, but is for the time out of his reach as he, through unhealthy dissociation, was retreating from it. In the process of ending, we discussed and considered the outcome as a success. This, of course, is not ordinary science. One could ask how I might know that that is Ahmed's subjectivity and not mine. And how do I know that the hidden narrative of Ahmed is there in him, and it is not my expectations of him that he feels obliged to respond to. The outcome of therapy is the evidence that it was his and not mine.

To strengthen my points, I refer to some literature that I revisited in the process. I have found the numerous works of Freud pertinent, in particular those predominantly concentrating on the elaboration of psychoanalytical technique and religious and cultural history, including *Totem and Taboo* (1912–1913), "The theme of the three caskets" (1913f), and "The claims of psycho-analysis to scientific interest" (1913j), his metapsychological works, "Instincts and their vicissitudes" (1915c), "Repression" (1915d), and "The unconscious" (1915e). In other work (i.e., in his essay "Thoughts for the times on war and death" (1915b)), Freud elaborates his ideas about the outbreak of the First World War and the consequences of the conflict between culture and instinctual life. This was helpful in assisting me to work with Ahmed in reconstructing his experiences and his memory of them. Working with transference as an important psychoanalytical tool, and assessing the outcome, I have also taken into account Ezriel's (1956) suggestion that the methodology of psychoanalysis had to be clarified before the discipline could be regarded as scientifically validated. He pointed out how the customary method of investigation is observation of events in the "here and now", as opposed to history or archaeology, which reconstructs particular events from the past in order to explain present conditions. Freud compared the analyst to the archaeologist in the way he "digs up" a patient's past in the form of memories, associations, and so on. Ezriel (1956) argues that this view missed the here and now aspect of material which was "unconsciously selected for [the analyst] by the subject of his investigation, the patient . . . presented to him . . . both spontaneously and in response to the analyst's interventions" (p. 31). In attempting to understand a patient's behaviour, Ezriel would ask himself what made the patient do and say particular things in front of him at specific moments in time. Then he passed interpretative comments back to the patient, who he said was "a kind of reality testing and arguably the essence of psychoanalytic therapy" (p. 39). He demonstrates how the use of recordings of sessions made it possible to test hypotheses of human behaviour through closely observing interactions between the patient and therapist. He noted the importance of transference in the therapeutic process, suggesting that it could have both positive and negative effects on the patient and result in either improvement or deterioration in its "aim at avoiding frightening impulses towards the analyst" (p. 47).

The other specific concept that I have taken into account as a relevant concept in working with Ahmed, and, indeed, other similar patients, is Steiner's (1993) "psychic retreats", which I understand to be states of mind into which patients can withdraw in order to evade anxiety and mental pain, in which patients become restricted in their lives and "stuck" in their treatment, or experience a total withdrawal from reality. The essence of Steiner's discussion is relational, in which if a therapist is able to successfully contain elements of projections from the patient, the patient may feel understood. This relational interaction was helpful process that led to Ahmed's improvement and his greater integration and development. Steiner's discussion is helpful, but limited for the healthy and unhealthy types of dissociation that I am discussing in this study.

Ahmed's life, very much affected by trauma and his experiences, has made him lonely, isolated, and sometimes out of touch with others, and in some instances out of touch with his own experience. This is external trauma experienced in adult life, and it is distinguished from the traumas of birth and childhood. Although patient childhood trauma is very important in the development of personality formation, a patient such as Ahmed may present extra and specific schemata as the result of external trauma in adult life.

CHAPTER FOUR

Literature and post traumatic stress disorder

Introduction

Trauma plays a significant role in the psychogenesis of violence (e.g., Johnson, Cohen, Brown, Smailes, & Bernstein, 1999). A normal awareness of the relationship between internal and external reality is not universal, but rather a developmental achievement (Fonagy & Target, 1996, 1997). If they are exposed to or suffer multiple traumas during their lives, people, in general, will have some psychological difficulties, and for those who have actually experienced trauma, these difficulties hinder the process of adaptation to, and integration in, a different environment. There is a need to think about this and search for appropriate help for efficient integration. Another issue that this study will consider is: what is it in the personality of traumatized people that makes some resilient to their traumatic experiences, but leaves others vulnerable to psychological collapse (i.e., development of PTSD)? As it is not something that lies in the objective external event, what is it about the personality that enables, or disables, resilience?

What is the cause of psychological trauma?

Experts in the field of mental health define psychological trauma in different ways. There are events that are outside the range of the individual's usual experience that constitute exceptional mental and physical stressors. However, the ranges of events that are traumatic to the individuals are as diverse as trauma responses. Traumatic events are the ultimate or most severe stressors. Regular life stressors, in different areas of human experience, are ordinary and have high expectancy and probability of happening, and, therefore, are more controllable. Traumas are the out of ordinary stressors that have low expectancy, probability, and controllability. Emotional trauma can result from such occurrences as a car accident, the break-up of a significant relationship, a humiliating or deeply disappointing experience of a loved one, the discovery of a life-threatening illness or disabling condition, or other similar situations. It can also result from experiencing natural disasters, rape, persecution, torture, and other violent events, including responses to chronic or repetitive instances of child abuse, neglect, warfare, urban violence, concentration camps, racism and prejudice, battering relationships, and enduring deprivation.

Traumatizing events can have an acute emotional effect on individuals involved, even if the event did not cause physical injury or immediate psychological problems. The definition of what is psychologically traumatic, consequently, is fairly broad, and includes responses to powerful occurrences. It is difficult to determine in general whether a particular event is traumatic. For the purpose of identifying trauma and its adaptive symptoms, it is useful to ask the person what has happened rather than what is wrong. Usually, the intrusion of the past into the present is one of the main problems confronting the person who has endured trauma.

Coping with trauma

The idea of a protective shield or layer that allows only tolerable quantities of excitation is very important in coping mechanisms—vulnerability and resilience for the clinical assessment of people who have endured trauma. The manifestation of dissociation, either healthy or unhealthy, can be considered a predictive factor. Stress can deregulate nervous systems for a relatively short period of time, for a few days or weeks, before the nervous system calms down and reverts to a normal state of equilibrium. This return to normalcy often is not the case when one has been affected by traumatic events. One way of telling the difference between ordinary stress and the emotional effect of trauma is by looking at how much remaining effect an upsetting event is having on a person's life, relationships, and overall functioning. If we can communicate distress to people and can respond adequately and return to a state of equilibrium, we are in the realm of stress. But if we turn out to be distant in a state of active emotional intensity, we are experiencing an emotional trauma, though sometimes we may not be consciously aware of the level of distress we are experiencing.

The accumulation of non-traumatic stressors, sufferings, or dilemmas can create a trauma-like experience, producing similar effects as, and eventuating, PTSD-like symptoms. They can also add to real traumas and amplify their effects. Negative socio-cultural attitudes and non-supportive responses towards the traumatized individual can create a chain of post trauma stressors which may cause secondary traumatization.

Throughout this study, I will look at psychoanalytical therapeutic intervention in order to examine patients' ability in relation to resilience and vulnerability; specifically, at how resilient people can manage their traumatic experience by employing mechanisms of healthy dissociation while vulnerable people have certain unconscious mechanisms that interrupt and disable their coping mechanism for such necessary healthy dissociation. I suggest that healthy dissociation links with the idea of an inner psychic space, which can be fostered by having a listening other, such as can be provided in therapy, if there has been a developmental deficit for the patient, which both contribute to a coherent and relatively robust sense of self.

A single traumatic event and repeated or ongoing trauma

There is a distinction between a single trauma and repeated traumas. Single shocking events, such as earthquakes, hurricanes, floods, volcanoes, plane crashes, chemical spills, nuclear failures, robbery, rape, and homicide can certainly produce trauma reactions, but the traumatic experiences that result in the most serious mental health problems are usually prolonged and repeated, at times continued over many years of a person's life.

The single, unexpected, direct trauma may cause typical symptoms of relentless flashbacks and persistent avoidance and increased arousal. It does not appear to cause the massive denials, psychic numbing, self-anaesthesia, or development of a personality disorder that characterizes the PTSD symptoms, though this type of trauma can impair some areas of psychological functioning.

In contrast, complex traumas are continuous and repetitive ordeals that gain prolonged and appalling anticipation in one area of human functioning produce the most severe effects on mental health, such as dissociation, somatization, and depersonalization. Such trauma creates enormous defence mechanisms of repression, denial, dissociation, somatization, self-anaesthesia, self-hypnosis, identification with the aggressor, and aggression against the self. The impairment in emotional processing includes the absence of feelings, a sense of constant anger and frustration, deep sadness, and fear. Protracted stressors inflicted with intent by other persons are much more difficult to tolerate than accidents or natural disasters. If harm was inflicted deliberately in the context of a relationship, the predicaments are greater than those of an incident. In situations where the injury is caused deliberately in a relationship with a person on whom the injured party is dependent, mainly by a parent or care-giver in relation to a child, the effect can be horrendous. Sadistic abuses of the subject of interpersonal violence by a care-giver as an eruption of passion in the severest forms are those inflicted deliberately. Premeditated cruelty usually can be more terrifying in the long term, and more injurious, than impulsive violence.

Experiences of war or political violence are usually enormous in scale: they are brutal, repeated, extended, and volatile. Moreover, they are often compounded by the traumatized person witnessing life-threatening events, and possibly by doing violence to others and embracing the identity of an executioner. Other situations, such as kidnapping, torture, rape, and domestic violence are disturbances usually associated with a longer period of helplessness, fear of injury or death, lack of support, and negative consequences from disclosure. Witnessing someone else being beaten is stressful, and the greater the attachment to the person, the greater is the stress. In some cases, watching violence directed towards a parent or caregiver is devastating for a child, due to the fear of losing his/her primary source of security. Coercive power, which has been used in prison, concentration camps, and in some families, has overwhelming and destructive effects on the receiver.

The difference between a single traumatic event and ongoing trauma

The enduring effects of a past event, such as torture or sexual assault in childhood and as an adult, can lead to a change in the person's perception of their sense of self, of others, and of the world. One may lack the capacity to cope, or form a capacity to alter beliefs about self and the world to the extreme, in order to feel in control. One may believe that all officials might be potential perpetrators or rapists, and the world is not a safe place. It is also possible to fail to assimilate the reality of a situation and alter external resources to match previous beliefs, and come to believe that the reason a bad thing happened to "me" is because "I" must be getting punished for something terrible "I" did, because bad things only happen to bad people. This leads to a belief that life is dangerous and that "I" should always fear what could potentially happen, thus preventing the development of a psychic self. However, during normal processing of a past trauma, the goal is to accommodate the trauma into our life, which means altering our beliefs to incorporate the new information. If we lack this capacity, then we develop negative beliefs which exacerbate the stressors. For example, a traumatized patient may start to believe that the world is not always a just and fair place, but there are exceptions, and "I" am a bad person for being persecuted or abused, and sometimes that bad things happen to good people, and the world is not altogether an unsafe and insecure place. However, if this person has a reappearance of the symptoms, or there is a fear of, and intrusive thoughts about, something such as being forced to return to the dangerous situation they have fled, fears and intrusions might be justified, and, therefore, the progression towards adjustment to the unpredictable might be challenging, but this is a normal reaction to an abnormal situation.

Why can an event cause different responses in different people?

There are simple factors relating to the reason why the same event can cause different reactions in people: the severity of the event, the individual's developmental process and past experiences, strengths, and weaknesses, all affect a person's response to trauma. The greater the meaning an event represents to us, the more traumatic is the effect it will have on our psyche. This also depends on numerous factors that influence our personality structure and our coping mechanisms and strategies, such as healthy and unhealthy dissociation, our values and the way we think, our psychic space and our sense of self, the availability of, and the reactions and support from, our family, friends, and/or professionals whose help we may seek, and our ability to make use of our listening other. Different people can go through the same harmful event and some might be traumatized while others remain relatively unharmed or even become stronger as a result of the experience. This difference in reaction correlates with the individual's ability to be resilient or tendency to be vulnerable.

Disturbances of attachment due to trauma

Attachment disturbances have an impact on the shared affective exchange with parents or care-givers for the infant and child and on companionship for the adult. It affects the feeling of warmth and connectedness for the adult and the feeling of security and trust for the child, who depends on the attachment figure. Early childhood trauma that affects attachment includes abandonment, death of parents, a parent's affairs, or divorce. Loss of very close significant others, such as a long-term child-minder or care-giver also can disturb the whole sequence of emotional development and can result in an avoidant or muddled and confused attachment style, which in turn can create relationship and personality difficulties, and can also give rise to assumptions and beliefs about self and objects and affect emotional as well as cognitive functioning in the area of object relations.

The formation of a sense of identity, agency, and self-efficacy is a developmental milestone on the road to adulthood with affirmative consequences for an individual's well being. Self-sufficiency or development of a positive identity builds emotional independence in the individual, which leads to feelings of being competent, adequate, self-aware, and of control over self and in relation with others. Trauma such as sexual and physical abuse, domestic violence, rape, slavery, being a prisoner of war, torture, and genocide can disturb attachments and cause feelings of loss of self and helplessness in an adult, and in childhood can disturb the development of healthy attachment, autonomy, and identity formation.

We interrelate within a set of connections that gives us emotional, social, and material support as well as a sense of social entrenchment, belonging, and meaning to life. We also develop a system of accustomed social contingencies that are rooted psychologically and emotionally as the bases of feelings of safety, security, and belonging. Events that threaten these networks and well-established connections can be traumatic. Displacement means the loss of attachment through suspension of normally available connections.

Disturbances of social behaviour due to trauma

Our social behaviour usually is motivated by the pursuit of goals that are central to our perception; the value of our behaviour is based on our evaluations of our prospective targets. So, our failure to achieve a target that is perceived as essential can also be traumatic.

Disturbances in multiple value processing sub-systems due to trauma

Some traumatic events can affect more than one value processing sub-system. For instance, incest can disturb both attachment and autonomy, and genocide can disturb collective identity, interdependence, and community sub-systems and demobilize our psychological resources to respond, which can overrule all our other sub-systems. This experience can cause doubt about an individual's sense of self as well as shattering the schema, beliefs, assumptions, representation, and judgement about one's view of the world, and about the efficacy of the existing value processing mechanisms that we possess.

Disturbances of automatic schema due to trauma

Traumatic events can also disturb the automatic functions that execute the activation of schema. They may be beyond the existing repertoire of schemata that direct the adaptive response to such an event. This may create a demand for new value processing structures. Furthermore, as a result of trauma, we commit behaviours that do not match our personality and value system prior to the trauma. For example, a person may, under ordinary circumstance, have a resilient personality and fully employ the four traits found in resilient behaviour: (a) the psychic space, (b) a listening other, (c) the sense of self, and (d) healthy dissociation. However, the experience of trauma can result in an inability to make use of these factors in a normal way, thus disturbing the automatic activation of resilience.

What are the possible effects and symptoms of emotional trauma?

Some of the common patterns of emotional trauma may result in compulsive behaviour patterns, self-destructive, uncontrollable reactive thoughts, an inability to make choices, dissociative symptoms through splitting off parts of the self, and an inability to maintain close relationships. However, as mentioned above, the reaction to emotional trauma can vary, based on individual levels of resilience or vulnerability.

Emotional trauma can create lasting difficulties. One way to determine whether an emotional or psychological trauma has occurred, perhaps even early in life before language or conscious awareness were in place, is to look at the kinds of recurring problems one might be experiencing. These can serve as clues to an earlier situation that caused a deregulation in the structure or function of the brain. In traumatic experiences and interruptions to normal development in childhood, hyper-vigilance of an individual's autonomic structure is compounded and reinforced by significant blocks in psychological functioning and the function of the brain. So, we can say that trauma is a complex combination of biological, psychological, and social phenomena.

Common reactions to trauma

Most people who directly experience a major trauma have problems in the immediate aftermath. Many feel better within a few months of the event, are able to healthily dissociate from the event, and are able to maintain their sense of self. Others recover more slowly and some do not recover without the help of a listening other. Some of the most common problems after a traumatic experience are amnesia, flashbacks or re-experiencing the trauma, avoidance of situations that resemble the initial event, nightmares, numbness, detachment, depression, guilt feelings, grief reactions, an altered sense of time, increased sensitivity or arousal, such as hyper-vigilance, jumpiness, extreme anxiety and a sense of being on guard, increased sensitivity and overreactions, including sudden unprovoked anger, insomnia, obsessions with death, sleep disturbances or nightmares, emotional numbing, fear, relationship problems, and substance misuse. Some of these are described in more detail below.

Avoidance and numbness

Avoidance is an ordinary way of managing trauma-related pain. The most common is avoiding situations that are reminders of the trauma, such as the place where it happened, or going out in the evening if the trauma occurred at night. This is a defence mechanism used to separate and dissociate the self from the event that was traumatic. Another way to reduce discomfort is to try to push away painful thoughts and feelings. This can lead to feelings of numbness, where people find it difficult to have either frightening or enjoyable and affectionate feelings. Sometimes painful thoughts or feelings may be so intense that the mind blocks them out altogether, and in some cases people may not remember parts of the traumatic event.

Fear and anxiety

Anxiety is a common and natural response to a dangerous situation. For many, it lasts long after the trauma ended. This occurs when views of the world and a sense of safety have changed. People may become anxious when they remember the event. Other things that may trigger or signal anxiety include a place, time, smell, noise, or situation that is associated with the trauma.

Re-experiencing the trauma, or flashbacks

Intrusive thoughts, flashbacks, sudden floods of emotions or images related to the traumatic event are common for people who have endured traumatic experiences. People may re-experience unwanted thoughts of the trauma and vivid images, as if the trauma were occurring again here and now.

Nightmares

Nightmares are common. These symptoms occur because a traumatic experience is so shocking and so different from everyday experiences that it cannot fit into the customary world. Thus, in order to understand what happened, the mind keeps bringing the memory back, not only to better digest it, but also to make it fit with the sense of self.

Increased sensitivity

Increased arousal is also a common response to trauma. This includes feeling jumpy, stressed out, agitated and shaky, being easily startled, apprehensive, and having difficulty with concentrating and sleeping. If unattended, continuous arousal can lead to impatience, irritability, and, in severe cases, personality change.

People who have been traumatized often see the world as filled with danger, so their bodies are on constant alert, always ready to respond immediately to any attack. This increased arousal is useful in truly dangerous situations, but it can become very uncomfortable when it continues for a long time or occurs in safe situations when it is not needed. An additional reaction to threat that can occur after a traumatic event is to freeze up, thus not only dissociating from the traumatic event, but also from reality.

Anger

Many people who have been traumatized feel angry and irritable. If they are not used to feeling angry this may seem scary. Some people may feel angry in view of the fact that they are feeling irritable so often without knowing the reason. Anger can also arise from a feeling that the world is not an adequate and fair place any more, or as a result of loss or multiple losses.

Guilt

Trauma often leads to feelings of guilt and shame. Many people blame themselves for things they did or did not do to survive, or feel ashamed because during the trauma they acted in ways that they would not have in ordinary circumstances. Feeling guilty in relation to the trauma means assuming liability for what has happened. While this may help a person feel more in control initially, if sustained for a long time it can also lead to feelings of helplessness and depression, which can be the case in traumatized people who have vulnerable tendencies. In resilient cases, the person is more likely to recognize/accept the real source and root of the guilt and shame, and maintain a sense of self that is healthily dissociated from the trauma.

Grief and depression

Grief and depression are also frequent reactions to trauma. These can embrace feeling "down", miserable, hopeless, or despondent, losing interest in people and activities, feeling that life is not worth living, and having sleep disturbances. These feelings can lead to thoughts of wishing to be dead or having suicidal ideation. Because the trauma has changed so much of how a person sees the world and their self, it makes sense for them to feel sad and to grieve for what has been lost as the result of the trauma. Grief and depression triggered by trauma can be seen in both vulnerable and resilient personalities.

Low self-esteem

Self-esteem, confidence, self-image, and also one's view of the world often become negative after a traumatic event. Many people view themselves as a disapproving personality after the trauma. It is also common to view others more unenthusiastically and to develop an idea that the world is unsafe and no one can be trusted. These negative thoughts are processed over and over again, leading people to feel that they have been changed entirely as a result of the trauma. In cases of resilient personalities, low self-esteem is less likely to occur and if it does it may not have a long-term effect, as a result of healthy dissociation from the traumatic event.

Relationships

Having or building relationships can become difficult after traumatic events. Some people may find it difficult to feel sexual, or to maintain intimate relationships. This is particularly the case for individuals who have been sexually assaulted, where, in addition to their difficulties with trusting people, sex itself can be a reminder of the trauma. However, seeking help from, and building a relationship with, a therapist as a listening other is an important step in dealing with the effects of trauma, as this can help to restore the sense of self that may have been lost. Making use of a listening other is an important factor in regaining some resilience.

Substance misuse

After traumatic experiences, some people may become more intense users of alcohol or other substances to self-medicate, which can slow down recovery and cause additional problems. The more potentially detrimental the effects of trauma are, the greater the stressor and the greater the need of substance use may be. Substance misuse can be seen as a more active way of unhealthily dissociating from, and coping with, emotional trauma and its effects.

Trauma in childhood

Childhood trauma, starting when the individual's personality is forming, shapes one's perceptions and beliefs about everything. Traumatic stress in childhood that influences the brain is usually caused by poor or inadequate relationships with a primary care-giver. Sources of this relational trauma include forced separation in early life from a primary care-giver and chronic lack of attunement of a care-giver to child's attachment signals, possibly for reasons such as physical or mental illness, depression, or grief. Early life trauma may create weak defences and vulnerability to experiencing future traumatic responses. Childhood trauma can also cause the disruption of basic developmental tasks and can cause deficits in abilities such as self love and respect, seeing the world as a safe place, trusting others, and organized thinking for decision making as well as avoiding exploitation. Disruption of these tasks in child-hood can result in adaptive behaviour: for example, self love and respect will be replaced by low self-esteem and agitation, paranoia, a lack of organized thinking for decision making, or psychosis, self-harm, self-destructiveness, and self-sabotage.

Trauma experienced at early points in psychological develop-ment may severely compromise the survivor's core sense of self and the capacity for secure object relations, as well as having suffi-cient psychic space and, therefore, relational representation. As a result, the strong sense and fear of harm, of death, and of terror take away the patient's sense of self and the psychic space for thinking and replace them with irreparable psychic damage. The unhealthy dissociations, therefore, become the patient's frame of reference, so treatment such as trauma exposure, or, with fear-based PTSD, re-experiencing the trauma memories and associated emotions in a narrative-building and control-enhancing manner may not be useful interventions and may not work at all, as the patient does not have enough psychic space and ability to associate with the self and with the memory of the trauma endured. So, therapeutic interven-tion needs to support the patient's capacities to diachronically (experiences relating to or involving the developmental process of early life, especially the learning of language and reflection through time) or synchronically (relating to ego development or lack of it, especially the use of language, as it exists at a point of assessment) manage unhealthy dissociation and primitive affect and impulses.

However, there seems to be too much emphasis on, and attention to, the diagnosis of PTSD in traumatized patients who are suffering from acute stress symptoms. Qualitative and quantitative analyses are needed to determine the types of intrusive thoughts that traumatized patients experience, and to re-examine categorizations of these experiences as being future or past event orientated. Existing research examining PTSD across the diagnosis and treatment range for traumatized patients has shown that the diagnosis is not straightforward in this group of patients, as there has not been any clinical research to evaluate whether some intrusions are future orientated and do not belong to the past. The best way to examine this empirically is to ask patients about the content of their intrusive thoughts, rather than making assumptions.

Results reported from controlled trials indicate that a majority of adults with chronic PTSD do not engage with, or benefit from, psychoanalytic psychotherapy. I will explore two complementary strategies to address this dilemma: first, identifying treatment responders so as to proactively match similar individuals with the target intervention in the future, and second, identifying characteristics of non-responders in order to guide the development of alternative interventions. From the perspective of object relationship, therapeutic intervention in this study explains how the response and non-response depends upon the identification of measurable features of treatment recipients that interact variably with the treatment outcome from the psychoanalytic point of view. Two characteristics that may show promise for optimizing treatment of chronic psychological problems are related to a history of early childhood trauma and the associated symptoms, or what Herman (1992) calls complex PTSD. People with unhealthy dissociations who endured trauma in childhood during their developmental process exhibit greater sympathetic reactivity than people who have encountered trauma in adult life but who had a reasonably healthy childhood without trauma or neglect. This suggests direct connections beween traumatic object relations in the developmental process and inefficient psychological regulatory functions and maladaptive infant and adult mental health.

The stressors identified in the group of patients presented in this study as vignettes and case studies are commonly related to abuse of power, betrayal of trust, humiliation, entrapment, helplessness, pain, confused and disorganized object relations, and/or loss. There are similarities and patterns of response across the range of stressors and hurt, and there is a need to think broadly about trauma.

I conceptualize dissociations (both healthy and unhealthy) and resilience as a constellation of chronic problems very much related to the regulation of the sense of self, consciousness, and relationships that are not formally recognized as a diagnostic entity (American Psychiatric Association, 1994). I hypothesize that unhealthy dissociations occur when extreme traumatization compromises the fundamental sense of self and object relational trust at critical developmental periods (e.g., child abuse; Herman, 1992; Roth, Newman, Pelcovitz, van der Kolk, & Mandel, 1997), and therefore has been posited to be a set of associated features of trauma and memory of trauma linked to interpersonal childhood trauma (*ibid.*). The effects of trauma in this study were identified as:

- alterations in affect or impulse regulation, such as severe anger, suicidality, risk of violent behaviour, and aggression;
- alterations in consciousness or attention to the trauma and reality, such as unhealthy or pathological dissociation—the lack of psychic space;
- alterations in the sense of self and self-perception, in which the self is viewed by the patient as humiliated, damaged, shamed, unloved, and misunderstood, and alterations in systems of meaning, such as hopelessness and helplessness;
- alterations in perception of the perpetrator, such as a distorted view of the perpetrator, or identification with an aggressor;
- alterations in relations with others, such as not trusting people, which means not having a listening other, colluding with the victim role, victimizing others as a result of introjection and projection;
- somatization, such as unexplained or exacerbated physical complaints.

Ford, Fisher, and Larson (1997), in their study, used patients' object relations and PTSD as predictors of treatment outcome measures and treatment programmes. Moderate *vs.* low object relations were predictive of reliable change independent of demographics, personality disorder diagnosis, baseline symptom severity, or trauma exposure. They indicated that those with PTSD and moderate object relations levels showed substantial positive gains, while those with lower object relations levels and PTSD tended to be unchanged and to deteriorate. They identified substantial variance in treatment outcome, which they accounted for the symptomatic severity priors to treatment that remained unexplained, but resulted in the outcome unexplained variance. Given the possibility that childhood trauma might have been a factor in the severity of post traumatic symptoms, further analyses with the same patients needed to be conducted to examine the role of early childhood trauma as a predictor of treatment outcome. However, these types of rigid structure are avoided in psychoanalytically orientated intervention. In psychoanalytic therapy, the therapist's focus is not on pre-formulated aspects of the patient's psyche, or on structured interventions. The job of the therapist in psychoanalytically informed treatment is to work on the unconscious, including working with free association, transference and countertransference, and dream interepretation. This method, if pursued with a focus on object relations, both historically and in the here and now in transference, helps to prevent undesirable variables in treatment outcome.

However, in cases of trauma, it can be beneficial for the therapist to keep in mind the four factors of resilience—the psychic space, a listening other, the sense of self, and healthy dissociation—in order to help build healthy defences and resilient behaviour as a means of coping with the trauma.

Assessment or initial interview

Psychoanalytic assessment and treatment is a consistent and robust predictor of treatment outcome with patients who have endured trauma, both in adult life and those with a history of early childhood trauma. Through the process of assessment, the patient may display traits of resilience or vulnerability, insight into which can be developed when exploring the four factors of resilience in the patient.

Whereas a diagnosis of PTSD predicts an increased likelihood of clinically meaningful change, the psychoanalytic approach predicts a substantially decreased likelihood of clinically meaningful and personality change in the patient. The clinical data in this study showed clear evidence that a psychoanalytic approach is appropriate treatment for a range of diagnostic conditions. The strength of the evidence varies across clinical cases presented I carried out a systematic investigation; the outcome, therefore, is comparable to other scientific therapeutic methods. There are psychological problems resulting from traumatic experiences (e.g., trauma-related problems such as unhealthy dissociation, obsessive–compulsive disorder, depression, and anxiety) where the outcome of psychoanalytic psychotherapy is better for long-term recovery than that of alternative treatments. The multivariable changes in my data gathering on patients' functioning, or lack of it, at different stages (i.e., pre-therapy, presentation in the process of assessment, and the progress observed during the two-year interventions) are evidence. All patients initially presented with severe vulnerability in the assessment process, but as therapy progressed, the severe vulnerability subsided and there was a variable but clear movement from unhealthy dissociations to healthy ones. These were associated with improvement on measuring the quality of patients' lives, their way of relating to others, and their anxiety: indeed, the pattern of dissociation and unhealthy dissociative conditions that, technically, had been a significant barrier to the patients' psychological recovery. In the reliable change analyses, the types of dissociation initially were predicted and presented with transference being dramatically decreased and improvements in patients' quality of life, and object relationships in transference and, indeed, outside therapy, provided evidence of this. Thus, assessment and treatment for chronic trauma symptoms need to focus not only on PTSD symptoms, such as fear, avoidance, and hyperarousal, but also on complex alterations in affect regulation, consciousness, interpersonal relationships, and meaning. Most patients with predominant dissociation as the result of exposure to trauma initially report experiences in adulthood rather than in childhood, which results in several precedents and implications in both assessment and treatment.

The ability to create a safe environment and to get an idea of the patient's frame of reference requires major clinical skills. When working with traumatized people, for example refugees, in the initial assessment the therapist needs to cover the full social, political, and psychological disturbance, which may take more than one meeting. Sullivan (1953) writes about the psychiatric interview and its purpose as elucidating characteristic patterns of the life of the subject. He believes that, if consideration is given to the non-verbal but, none the less, primarily vocal aspects of the exchange, it is actually feasible to make a crude formulation of many people within an hour and a half. In such assessments, the therapist needs to take care not to imply rigidity, but to retain flexibility towards the varying concerns and communication patterns of different individuals. The paramount objective is to establish rapport with the patient in a working alliance and ensure that the listening other is available so that the patient can make use of him/her. Indeed, from the first encounter with a patient, the assessor begins to form a working image of the person. This working image will not necessarily be divulged to the patient, but is a set of hypotheses concerning the patient's strengths, coping strategies, and limitations, establishing their level of vulnerability or resilience. Thus, working with traumatized people, such as refugees, in the therapeutic setting, the poverty of their ability to convey what is going on in their mind and their life in the past as well as in the present must be experienced and appreciated before making a diagnosis or undertaking further treatment. We need to be very sensitive to a refugee patient's identity and personality, because, at times, a patient may be incapable of verbalizing her or his experiences. It is challenging to hypothesize and to form an opinion as to whether a patient's mental disturbance arises out of traumatic experience or is a specific clinical characteristic. In other words, is it the result of external or internal reality or both, and to what level?

It might be helpful if, in the first place, efforts are made to classify cases into clinically established diagnostic categories, even though some phenomena are incomprehensible, at least in the light of psychoanalysis (for instance, PTSD).

We need also to determine whether disturbances arise from development, or from a cultural or social belief system. Coltart (1988) says that the assessment interview may be the most momentous occasion in the patient's life. The experience of being listened to intently and exclusively may be quite unique, and a profoundly positive and idealizing relationship may develop on this basis, without making an interpretation. She said the effect of interpretation is to draw attention to those aspects of the patient of which the patient is unaware and may wish to remain unaware. The importance of a listening other plays an important role throughout the therapeutic process. The lack of it is also potentially there prior to the start of therapeutic intervention. For example, if a patient refers themselves for therapeutic help, the seeking out of a listening other can been seen as indicative of resilient behaviour.

Hinshelwood (1991, 1995) indicated that clinical material is best approached as pictures in three areas of object relationships: first, the current life situation; second, infantile object relations, as described in the patient's history, or hypothesized from what is known; and third, the relationship with the assessor which, for all intents and purposes, is the beginning of a transference (p. 157). Working interculturally, I would summarize the central themes of the patient's current and past life situation, and their perception of internal psychic space and sense of self, in the initial interview, as well as the patient's resilience or vulnerability, and assign a developmental level to the patient's personality organization. By the end of the interview, I like to have covered the main features of the patient's current circumstances, family background, detailed developmental history, especially psychosexual history, history of major losses and trauma, dreams, main areas of interest and aptitude, and to have some idea about sources of both stress and support. Where relevant, I would also gather some knowledge of past psychiatric history, including history of hospital admission, psychotropic drugs, suicide attempts, and substance abuse, as well as mental states, such as depressive, obsessional, and psychotic phenomena, which, as mentioned above, would be indicative of the patient's experience of trauma, its effect on the patient, and the patient's reaction to any potential emotional trauma.

I would try to recognize the distinction between Oedipal—three person—neurotic difficulties, and object-related or pre-Oedipal—two person—borderline and narcissistic problems as fundamental in early development, as well as looking for strengths of ego, self, or drive. It is also basic for my practice to assess gender, power and its implication in the initial encounter, and maternal and paternal relationships within the specific cultural context for the patient as an individual, and within a group. It is my view that in order to analyse the mechanisms that control all aspects of gender differences, we need to outline the concept of femininity and masculinity. Generally speaking, some characteristics are gender-specific in all cultures: women and men have different experiences, attitudes to relationship, and concerns. The therapist must understand and work with these differences, in order to provide the patient with a comprehensive listening other. Consider the interaction between the intrapsychic and the social reality of one's life: the ability to differentiate the internal world from external reality in a traumatized person in therapy.

These issues may play a major role in revealing what gender means, how it operates, and how it is negotiated in personal relationships. The key question for the therapist is how gender beliefs are organized and function in that specific culture and community, what effects this has on patients' conscious and unconscious, as well as the level of integration and its effect on the process of resettlement in the new environment. For example, in all cultures, sexual and physical abuse is associated with great humiliation and fear of permanent damage. The psychological consequences of sexual violence depend on the culture or sub-culture, their social role, and relationships. In some cultures, deflowering may result in a woman no longer being acceptable as a marriage partner. In other cultures, rape may result in a woman becoming stigmatized as a "whore", ostracized even by her husband and her own family, as well as by the wider community. What would be the result of sexual abuse and rape in one's daily life, therefore, cannot be generalized. What distinction is drawn between rape by prison officials as part of torture, and rape in other circumstances also can be different between cultures. There is psychological evidence that abused woman often have disorders such as nervousness, insomnia, depression, reduced self-esteem, and guilt feelings. Moreover, where sexual abuse was part of torture, further mental problems were found to interfere with cognitive function, such as lack of concentration, memory disorder, flashbacks, nightmares, intrusive thoughts, suspicion, and delusions. Such people also have more sexual dysfunction. There is a distinction between the consequences of sexual violence in

Western and non-Western culture and society, especially for women.

Looking at gender differences in all societies, both nature and culture influence the definition of any individual. Culture determines how the individual, as a man or a woman, thinks, acts, perceives, and feels. For example, in some cultures, having a boy is honourable, but having a girl is shameful, and the man's role is to protect family honour. Generally, looking at a fundamentalist religious community, women are considered to be strong, and to need to be kept under control to prevent them from tempting the men to forsake their social and religious duties. From this perspective, rape is blamed on the woman herself, and may result in social rejection; as a result, such women may keep silent about rape. In particular, in some Middle Eastern, Asian, and some other Muslim families, women are expected to be dependent on men (fathers and brothers before marriage, and husbands after marriage) and men are expected to control women and children. In these cultures, the only way to enter adulthood for women is marriage. Also in such cultures, behaviour such as homosexuality, or freedom to choose a partner, is out of the question. Women having sex before marriage is abnormal, and cannot be tolerated. Women must exert self-control even in their private life, for the sake of family honour and their own future in the community. Family honour, especially men's honour, may be damaged and replaced by shame if a female member of the family is raped. In such cultures, a raped woman is not a victim, but simply a "dirty woman", a "whore"; and thus learns never to tell their father, brother, or husband, as their "protector", what has happened to them. It is a secret shared only with the rapist, in the hope that she may be able to forget it, believing that knowledge of her rape may result in her being killed, or may destroy her family. Therefore, she carries the burden alone, in order to survive and protect the family. Such an isolated woman builds an internal relationship with her abuser, which has more destructive potential.

In this study, I have focused upon a group of traumatized patients who have endured external trauma in adult life as a result of their socio-political environment as well as whose biological needs for nurture and comfort were adequately met, but whose mothers or primary carers never related to them beyond simple care-taking. They never smiled at their children and had no pleasure from playing with them or in the children's emerging sense of aliveness. It appears that the mothers used their children as transitional objects, and did not function as a listening other for the children, thus preventing their psychic space and sense of self from developing. In turn, the children's emotional development became fixated in the in-between transitional space. This fixation led to specific types of character structure and ego defects. Early development levels did not form a smooth continuum to higher, later acquired, adaptive ego states. There seem to be extensive holes in the layers of the psychic apparatus, which manifested themselves as defective modulating elements. Some patients who are suffering from structural defects respond to psychoanalytic treatment and standard psychoanalytic techniques. The patient who shows extreme behaviour, who is able to present him/herself as a functioning, sensible, and rational individual, can also present as extremely sensitive and demonstrate difficulty in relating to others. These issues can best be understood in terms of ego pathology character traits, as well as a traumatic developmental past, and can be addressed in clinical situations. Understanding the patient's specific developmental constellation, therefore, is the most important part of the assessment and treatment. It is a way of establishing the foundations of individual psychopathology that will enable the clinician to make connections and distinctions between different defences the patient presents in the process of treatment and the types of dissociation (healthy and unhealthy).

There are many such patients among those who seek treatment with initial presentations of adult external trauma. However, they present special problems in therapy, which can be explained in terms of the psychoanalytic paradox, which refers to a treatment impasse caused by an imbrication of psychopathology and various attributes of the psychoanalytic method. The mother's attitude toward her infant child has some similarity to the low-key, objective, analytic neutrality. These patients require different modes of relating which indicate that the therapist—here acting as the listening other—is, unlike the mother, very much concerned with the patient's developing autonomy and entering and exploring the external world. These variations in treatment are not modifications or deviations from psychoanalysis; they are, rather, elements of the analytic process necessary for the treatment of specific types of psychopathology. Just as each patient is unique and the transference manifests itself in a particular fashion which then causes the therapist to make certain interpretations, the variations of technique address the construction of a containing and holding environment appropriate in working with such a patient.

Independent psychoanalytic assessment and diagnoses of (1) early childhood trauma, and (2) trauma exposure in adult life and level of resilience or vulnerability that is perceived in self-control and quality of life, and severity of traumatic events, depressive and anxiety symptoms focuses on the individual's presentation without pre-assumption, indeed, without the need of fitting with particular structured assessment tools. Psychoanalytically orientated psychotherapy provides an intensive model of therapeutic care for exploratory, expressive, reflective, and psycho-educational modalities for individual patients. It is considered that individual psychoanalytical psychotherapy provided on a more than twice-weekly basis for the treatment of a chronically traumatized patient is the most appropriate approach for symptom relief and personal growth, helping to develop an ability to dissociate healthily and build a sense of self. The approach focuses on developing and overseeing an individualized evaluation, treatment, and rehabilitation plan for: (a) here-and-now coping skills (healthy dissociation), (b) community reintegration (developing a sense of self and building relationships with others), and (c) therapeutic exposure and narrative reconstruction of unresolved trauma from early developmental process (through the use of the listening other). A four- or five-times-weekly therapeutic process helps patients to experiment with, elaborate, integrate, and reinforce, skills for fear reduction, affect regulation, and self-schema unifications and rehabilitation from affects of trauma on an individual's body, health, relationships, dreams, and emotions, leading to trauma symptom control and trauma related stress management for things such as guilt and anger, and, indeed, relapse prevention.

Analysing the data and the outcomes of the patients that I worked with, particularly those presented here, indicated that the prevalence of early childhood trauma in vulnerable patients was quite high. Early trauma history and vulnerability were shown to be 100% interrelated. Variables in vignettes and case presentation are used in this study to describe a distribution that involves a number of random, but related, variables in analyses of variance for repeated symptom presentation of dissociative types, which provides evidence for measuring each individual classification and history of early childhood trauma between patients' independent variables and time of presentations (i.e., in assessment process or early intervention *vs.* post one-year intervention) as within the patients' independent unpredictability or adaptability.

Winnicott (1965) propounded the idea that at the preliminary stages of the development of mother–infant interaction, anxiety and the dread of annihilation are also closely connected to the notion of holding. It is holding that enables the baby to become a self; Winnicott refers to this as the "continuity of being", "the alternative to being is reacting, and reacting interrupts being and annihilates" (*ibid.*, p. 90).

Winnicott viewed the root of the tiny baby's terror in terms of being able just "to be". This idea differs from Kleinian theory, as he considered that aggression and destructiveness were not a function or projection of the death instinct, as the newborn baby could not hate until it was able to comprehend the notion of wholeness. For Winnicott, the capacity of hate occurred after the holding stage. Winnicott suggests that in this phase the ego changes from an unintegrated state to a structured integration, and so the infant becomes able to experience anxiety associated with disintegration. He believes that in a healthy development, at this stage the infant retains the capacity for re-experiencing this unintegrated state depending on the continuation of reliable maternal care or on the build-up in the infant of memories of maternal care beginning gradually to be perceived as such. The main function of Winnicott's holding environment, therefore, is the reduction of impingements to which the infant must react, with resultant annihilation of personal being.

Cross-generational transmission

Although the cross-generational transmission of trauma is not a major factor in this study, it is important to make note of it, as it could be applicable to some traumatized patients. Transmitted trauma is different between persons or generations, with different mechanisms, such as symbiosis, empathy, attachment, enmeshment, personal or collective identification, projective identification, introjections, dependency, co-dependency, interdependency, parenting, compensation, and acculturation. An individual coexists in a system or a network of intertwined relationships that transmit the effects of different significant events. An example is shared psychotic disorder: the development of a delusion in a person in the context of a close relationship with another person(s) who has an already established delusion (*DSM-IV*, 297.3). Traumas can have similar effects on persons in relationships, or with a strong collective identity, even they did not suffer the trauma themselves. In this context, trauma can happen not only to one person, but also to a social unit, to a community, or sometimes to a whole society, for example, genocide, civil war, and ethnic cleansing. However, the transmission of trauma does not automatically always occur, for the same reason as an extreme traumatic event may not necessarily result in post trauma symptoms in a resilient person. The transmission can happen from one person to another, or to a connected group that has been affected by trauma and collectively lost its healthy defences and coping mechanisms. There are also indirect traumas and their effects, which may transmit within a family system across generations, such as domestic or other types of violence, physical abuse, and incest. The intergenerational continuity of those family patterns is often expressed by young children becoming violent and being perpetrators of abuse themselves, or colluding with the victim's role, thus repeating the intergenerational cycle of victim and perpetrator of violence.

Projective identification is a possible mechanism that can facilitate the transmission of unresolved traumatic experiences. Projective identification in the context of parent–child relationships involves the parent's recruitment of the child to perform a particular role for the parent's externalized unconscious fantasies, and is thought to harm a child by weakening the child's capacity to experience his or her own subjective awareness, insight, and feelings as an acceptable reality. A child enacting the parent's projective fantasies leads to a collapse of the potential space within the parent–child relationship, thus not allowing the development of the child's autonomy, though this transmission is not automatic.

Collective cross-generational trauma transmission across generations can be divided into collective traumas, which is better -

described as a collective complex trauma, as it is inflicted on a group of people which has a specific group identity or affiliation to a collective culture, such as ethnicity, colour, national origin, religion, and political beliefs. Historical information prior to traumatization and the intensity of traumatic exposure, including the effects, is important. Historical trauma can predispose the individual to respond poorly to later traumas. Prior traumatization is generally associated with more symptoms and a longer recovery period. There is also the multi-generational transmission of political or structural violence that constitutes extreme social disparities created by generating deprived social structures.

Chronic and ongoing threats to a secure life that many asylum seekers experience can either stimulate or overwhelm their sense of survival. This can disturb their values and processing from one to all areas of psychological functioning. Further, the effects of deprivation through poverty, rights, citizenship, and immigration status may cause further trauma and lead to demoralization, socioeconomic disadvantage, lower levels of achievement, and an increased level of socio-psychological problems. Poverty may also effect the halting of intellectual development and lead to educational deprivation for many refugee and asylum seekers, especially children and young people, even for those who have no apparent biological restrictions in learning. The direct and indirect cross-generational consequences of such structural violations of basic human rights can be devastating and long-lasting for any human being. This type of ongoing traumatic condition is the type which can, and in many cases will, transmit across generations.

History of diagnosis and treatments of war neurosis and PTSD

The diagnosis of PTSD started after the First and Second World Wars. Later, in the 1980s, numerous trauma treatment models were developed which were collectively referred to as "trauma debriefing models". One common aim in these models was to encourage the traumatized person to re-tell the trauma story in as much detail as possible. While this chapter does not allow for a detailed discussion of these methods and their variations, or a critique of whether or not these are sufficient in themselves, it is important to say that there is no convincing evidence yet as to whether trauma debriefing aids or hampers the traumatized person's psychological recovery, or whether it just relieves the symptoms temporarily. Sometimes this approach, used out of context by a caring person who wants to help but has no counselling or other mental health training and qualifications or skills, is potentially dangerous. There is an increasing body of research and literature on identifying, diagnosing, and treating psychological trauma and trauma-related illnesses, and also on culturally determined means of communicating psychological distress and articulating symptoms. This augmented focus is associated with the need to make available suitable services to a rapidly growing population of displaced people, immigrants, and refugees deracinated in armed conflicts in various parts of the world, which, unfortunately, shows no signs of ending or of lessening. As indicated earlier (p. 71),The World Mental Health Report (WHO, 1995) provides interesting data resulting from eleven studies of post traumatic stress disorder (PTSD) among those who have experienced various disastrous events.

A useful approach in assessing PTSD is to make no assumptions regarding patients' explanations, illness, expectations for treatment, but verify their explanations explicitly with them. The underlying rationale is that all clinical encounters are in fact cross-cultural encounters and this is worth considering even when the patient and therapist are from the same cultural background. For example, the question, "What was the worst part of the traumatic experience for you?" can often yield very different and unexpected answers, even among people who have experienced the same event, and clarifies that they have not experienced the same trauma. Culture also shapes the experience of trauma, and may give the illusion of a common destiny that would obviate varying individual providence, while different destinies are contingently related, and, indeed, shape the effects of trauma and its intensity. Therefore, it is important to be aware of how the individual's psyche may find hidden paths within the constraints imposed by culture. In some non-Western cultures, trauma recovery also involves witnessing, testimony, and reparation. The experience of trauma and recovery is distinct from the narrative frames of Western societies, which are often linked to accepted Christian wisdom (conscience or unconscious) of catharsis, confession, reparation, and redemption. In some cultures, it is safe to speak out, as one may have a belief system that social testimonies are needed before healing can occur.

It is important to recognize that there is also controversy about diagnosing social and political problems related to violence, war, or poverty as psychological disorders. By making a diagnosis of PTSD, social protest or suffering becomes medicalized and people who are persecuted under a repressive regime, or as a result of ethnic cleansing, or particular beliefs or principles, are pathologized. In some cultures, distress is commonly understood and expressed in terms of disruptions to the social and moral order and no particular attention is paid to internal emotional matters in their own right. There is a great overlap between refugees' mental health and trauma, and we need more studies of people who have lived through war and other traumatic experiences in order to have more realistic expectations regarding trauma effects over time. In some cases, people who have experienced and/or witnessed massive trauma have been able to achieve productive levels of functioning. Psychosocial interventions, therefore, should focus more on increasing the capacity of patients, rather than reacting to predictable symptoms.

Diagnostic criteria of PTSD

In the tenth edition of the *International Classification of Mental and Behavioural Disorders* (*ICD-10*, F43.1) (World Health Organization, 1992), PTSD is defined as a disorder that people may develop in response to one or more traumatic event(s), such as deliberate acts of interpersonal violence, serious accidents, disaster, or military action. The disorder can occur at any age, including during childhood. The validated diagnostic instruments and most randomized controlled treatment trials of PTSD use the diagnostic criteria for PTSD defined in the fourth edition of the *Diagnostic and Statistical Manual of Mental Disorders* (*DSM-IV*) (American Psychiatric Association, 1994).

The diagnosis of PTSD is based on aetiology, and is restricted to people who have experienced exceptionally threatening and distressing events. The *ICD-10* definition states that PTSD may develop after "a stressful event or situation . . . of an exceptionally threatening or catastrophic nature, which is likely to cause pervasive distress in almost anyone" (p. 147). Thus, PTSD would not be diagnosed after other upsetting situations that are described as "traumatic" in everyday language, for example, divorce, loss of a job, or failing an exam. In these cases, a diagnosis of adjustment disorder may be considered. *DSM-IV* highlights that a traumatic stressor usually involves a perceived threat to life (either one's own life or that of another person) or physical integrity, and intense fear, helplessness, or horror. Other emotional responses of trauma survivors with PTSD include guilt, shame, intense anger, or emotional numbing.

Who is at risk of PTSD?

People at risk of PTSD include:

- victims of violent crime (e.g., physical and sexual assaults, sexual abuse, bombings, riots);
- military, police, journalists, prison service, fire service, ambulance and emergency personnel, including those no longer in service;
- victims of war, torture, state sanctioned violence, terrorism, and refugees;
- survivors of accidents and disasters;
- women following traumatic childbirth, and individuals diagnosed with a life-threatening illness;
- children in abusive environments.

Symptoms of PTSD

The most characteristic symptoms of PTSD are re-experiencing symptoms. PTSD sufferers involuntarily re-experience aspects of the traumatic event in a very vivid and distressing way. This includes flashbacks, in which the person acts or feels as if the event were recurring, nightmares, and repetitive and distressing intrusive images or other sensory impressions from the event. Reminders of the traumatic event arouse intense distress and/or physiological reactions. Symptoms of hyper-arousal include hyper-vigilance to threat, exaggerated startle responses, irritability, and difficulty in concentrating, as well as sleep problems and symptoms of emotional numbing. These include the inability to have any feelings, feeling detached from other people, giving up previously significant activities, and amnesia of significant parts of the events. Other associated symptoms include depression, generalized anxiety, shame, guilt, and reduced libido, which contribute to their distress and have an impact on their functioning.

Whether or not people develop PTSD depends on their subjective perception of the traumatic event, as well as the objective facts. For example, people who are threatened with a replica gun and believe that they are about to be shot, or people who sustain only minor injuries during a road traffic accident but believe at the time that they are about to die, may develop PTSD. Furthermore, those at risk of PTSD do not only include those that are directly affected by a horrific event, but also witnesses, perpetrators, and those who help PTSD sufferers (vicarious traumatization). So, what can have a traumatic affect on one person may not be perceived as traumatic for another person. Another factor in developing PSTD, similar to the discussion about the effect of trauma, is a person's predisposition to being resilient or vulnerable in dealing with the effects of the traumatic experience.

Effects of PTSD

PTSD symptoms cause considerable distress and can significantly interfere with social, educational, and occupational functioning. It is not uncommon for PTSD sufferers to lose their jobs, either because of re-experiencing symptoms, sleep disturbances, and concentration problems, or because one is unable to cope with reminders of the traumatic event at work. The resulting financial problems are a common source of additional stress, and may be a contributory factor to extreme hardship, such as homelessness. PTSD has adverse effects on the sufferer's social relationships, and social withdrawal, problems in the family, and break-up of significant relationships are by no means unusual. PTSD sufferers may also develop further, secondary psychological disorders as a complication of PTSD. The most common complications are: substance use disorders, depression, including the risk of suicide, anxiety disorders, such as panic disorder, which may lead to additional restrictions (for example, inability to use public transport), somatization, chronic pain, and poor health in general.

The main findings from the epidemiological research on PTSD are as listed below.

• The majority of people will experience at least one traumatic event in their lifetime (Kessler, Sonnega, & Bromet, 1995).

• Intentional acts of interpersonal violence, in particular sexual assault and combat, are more likely to lead to PTSD than accidents or disasters (Creamer et al., 2002; Kessler, Sonnega, & Bromet, 1995).

• Men tend to experience more traumatic events than women, but women experience higher impact events (i.e., those that are more likely to lead to PTSD; Kessler, Sonnega, & Bromet, 1995). In a large representative USA sample, Kessler, Sonnega, and Bromet (1995) estimated a lifetime prevalence of PTSD of 7.8% (women: 10.4%; men: 5.0%). using *DSM-IIIR* criteria. Estimates for the twelve-month prevalence range between 1.3% (Australia) and 3.6 % (USA). Estimates for one-month prevalence range between 1.5% and 1.8 %, using *DSM-IV* criteria (Andrews, 2000; Andrews, Sanderson, Corry, & Lapsley, 2000), and 3.4 % using the less strict *ICD-10* criteria (Andrews et al., 1999). PTSD remains common in later life but with the suggestion of a greater proportion of sub-syndromes PTSD in the older age group (van Zelst, de Beurs, Beekman, Deeg, & van Dyck, 2003).

Different types of traumatic events are associated with different PTSD rates. Rape was associated with the highest PTSD rates in several studies. For example, 65% of the men and 46% of the women who had been raped met PTSD criteria in Kessler, Sonnega, and Bromet's (1995) study. Other traumatic events associated with high PTSD rates included combat exposure, childhood neglect and physical abuse, sexual molestation, and for women only, physical attack and being threatened with a weapon, kidnapped, or held hostage. Accidents, witnessing death or injury, and fire or natural disasters were associated with lower lifetime PTSD (Kessler, Sonnega, & Bromet, 1995).

ICD10 and DSM-IV comparison of diagnostic criteria of PTSD

The *ICD-10* diagnosis of PTSD requires that the patient

(A) must have been exposed to a stressful event or situation of exceptionally threatening or catastrophic nature, which would be likely to cause pervasive distress in almost anyone;
(B) must persistently remember or "relive" the stressor in intrusive flashbacks, vivid memories, or recurring dreams, or in experiencing distress when exposed to circumstances resembling or associated with the stressor;
(C) must exhibit an actual or preferred avoidance of circumstances resembling or associated with the stressor, which was not present before exposure to the stressor;
(D) must demonstrate either of the following:

1. Inability to recall, either partially or completely, some important aspects of the period of exposure to the stressor.
2. Persistent symptoms of increased psychological sensitivity and arousal (not present before exposure to the stressor), shown by any two of the following:
    (a) difficulty in falling or staying asleep;
    (b) irritability or outbursts of anger;
    (c) difficulty in concentrating;
    (d) hyper-vigilance;
    (e) exaggerated startle response.

Criterias (b), (c), and (d) must all be met within six months of the stressful event or the end of a period of stress (delayed onset by more than six months is possible, but should be specified).

The *DSM-IV* diagnosis of PTSD is stricter in that it puts more emphasis on avoidance and emotional numbing symptoms. It requires a particular combination of symptoms (at least one re-experiencing symptom, three symptoms of avoidance and emotional numbing, and two hyper-arousal symptoms). In addition, *DSM-IV* requires that the symptoms cause significant distress or interference with social or occupational functioning.

In contrast to *ICD-10*, a *DSM-IV* diagnosis of PTSD further requires that the symptoms have persisted for at least one month.

In the first month after trauma, trauma survivors may be diagnosed as having acute stress disorder (ASD) according to *DSM-IV*, which is characterized by symptoms of PTSD and dissociative symptoms such as depersonalization, derealization, and emotional numbing. The *ICD-10* diagnosis does not require a minimum duration.

Standardized assessment instruments

The validated structured clinical interviews used to facilitate the diagnosis of PTSD include the

- Structured Clinical Interview (SCID) for *DSM-IV* (First et al., 1995);
- Clinician Administered PTSD Scale (CAPS);
- Post Traumatic Stress Interview (PTSI) (Foa, Riggs, Dancu, & Rothbaum, 1993).

All these instruments are based on the *DSM-IV* definition of PTSD.
There is a range of useful self-report instruments of PTSD symptoms, including the

- Impact of Event Scale (IES) (Sundin & Horowitz, 2002) and Impact of Event Scale—Revised (IES-R) (Marmar, Weiss, & Metzler, 1997);
- Post Traumatic Stress Diagnostic Scale (PDS) (Foa & Tolin, 2000; Foa, Riggs, Dancu, & Rothbaum, 1993);
- Davidson Trauma Scale (Davidson & Colket, 1997);
- PTSD Checklist (Weathers, Litz, Herman, Huska, & Keane, 1993).

Clinical aspects of the diagnostic interview

When establishing the diagnosis of PTSD, it is important to bear in mind that PTSD sufferers find talking about the traumatic experience very upsetting. They may find it hard to disclose the exact nature of the event and their associated re-experiencing of symptoms and feelings, and initially may not be able to talk about the most distressing aspects of their experience. This particularly may be the case for people who experienced the trauma many years ago or have delayed onset of their symptoms.

The main presenting complaint of sufferers does not necessarily include intrusive memories of the traumatic event; this may be as a result of dissociation, whether healthy or unhealthy, or as a result of a distorted sense of self. Patients may present with depression and general anxiety, fear of leaving their home, somatic complaints, irritability, inability to work, or sleep problems. They may not relate their symptoms to the traumatic event, especially if a significant amount of time has elapsed since the event.

Epidemiological research has shown that the diagnosis of PTSD is greatly underestimated if the interviewer does not directly ask about the occurrence of specific traumatic events (Davidson & Colket, 1997). It is suggested that checklists of common traumatic experiences and symptoms may be helpful for some patients who find it hard to name them. Both the CAPS and the PDS (Foa & Tolin, 2000; Foa, Riggs, Dancu, & Rothbaum, 1993).

The *DSM-IV* diagnostic category for PTSD is a widespread tool for measurement and comparison of symptoms, aiming towards accurate diagnosis and, thus, treatment of this condition. Perhaps more than other psychiatric diagnoses, though, the concept of trauma necessitates a broader view to enable a methodical perception of the experience, even when it is observed in a bio–psycho–social formulation. This may be due in part to the exceptional cause–effect nature of PTSD, where an event that threatens life or limb is essential to the diagnosis. This aetiology creates an opening for interpretation and a need to search for the meaning that a traumatic event has on an individual. Additionally, developmental process, psychological resilience, and other social factors that protect people from developing PTSD must be explored to understand why large numbers of people who have experienced trauma do not develop the illness as defined by the *DSM-IV* diagnostic category for PTSD classification. The *DSM-IV* has changed criterion A of PTSD by omitting the description of the stressor as "outside the range of normal human experience". Instead, criterion A now requires that the individual's experience in response to the stressor must include intense fear, helplessness, or horror. This definition expands the type of traumatic events that qualify for PTSD to include violence, personal assault, motor vehicle accidents, natural or manmade disasters, learning about the sudden, unexpected death of a family member or a close friend, learning that one's child has a life-threatening disease, or being diagnosed with a life-threatening disease oneself.

The defining characteristic of a traumatic stressor or of psychological trauma is the presence of an implicit or explicit threat to life and reactions that are extreme and generally negative. The development of PTSD may be only one of many related consequences of exposure to trauma. There are many other stressor effects that can be considered, most of which reflect the effects of life-threat on biological, emotional, or cognitive functioning. Traumatic stress may thus be associated with unusual or unique endocrine changes, immune system changes, upset and distress, cognitive distortions, and existential anxiety. These changes may occur as a function of direct threat, as when one is diagnosed with, and treated for, a serious illness, or more indirectly, as a function of witnessing. In either instance, the effects the experience can have on the psychic space and in one's sense of self can lead to the development of PTSD. For the most part, they occur because of the threat to life involved, and this threat or its direct implications form the core of an emotional complex that appears to need restructuring or changing one's perception of the world.

If the focus of threat to life is not based on a past event for patients, but is based on the future, which is the case in many groups, such as asylum seekers, the intrusions and re-experiencing symptoms that occur as part of post traumatic stress syndromes may be of a different type than those experienced by individuals exposed to traditional traumas. The re-experiencing symptoms that act as a pointer to PTSD is exclusively related to past trauma exposure, rather than future-orientated events. Some patients seeking psychological help who do have intrusions that consist of the past event may also have future-orientated intrusions (e.g., will the Home Office accept my asylum application? Will my children progress with their education in this country? Will I ever see my home town again?). The only way to examine this empirically is to ask patients about the content of their intrusive thoughts, rather than making assumptions.

There seems to be too much emphasis and attention to the diagnosis of PTSD in traumatized patients who are suffering from acute stress symptoms. Qualitative analyses are needed to determine the types of intrusive thoughts that the patients experience, and to re-examine categorizations of these experiences as being future or past event orientated. Existing research examining PTSD across the diagnosis and treatment range for traumatized patients who have been displaced has shown that the diagnosis is not straightforward in this group of patients, as there is no clinical research to evaluate whether some intrusions are future orientated and do not belong to the past. In contrast to a medicalized view, the literature on social suffering (Kleinman & Good, 1985) elaborates traumatic experiences and human problems in a much more meaningful manner and allows for a more humanistic understanding of the challenges that we all face in our lives. Suffering is described by Kleinman, Das, and Lock (1997) as a social experience that connects the moral, the political, and the medical, including health and social policy. The social constructionist emphasis is that there is not one correct or true way of viewing the world, rather, there are many different realities, all constructed within different contexts.

Principles of psychoanalysis and trauma

If we follow the fundamental rule of psychoanalysis and exclude as far as possible the purposive ideas of the ego, these derivatives, observed in the impulses of human beings, become clearer. Interpretation of a resistance and id impulse demonstrates the nature of a derivative part of the ego facilitating the finding. So, there is no interpretation merely of the unconscious components before they are represented by a preconscious derivative, which the patient can recognize as such by turning attention to it. Pointing out defences to a patient and explaining the nature of defences and the reason for using the therapist as the listening other can help the patient's ego to tolerate instinctual derivatives because they are being rendered less distorted. In the treatment of a traumatized patient, transference resistance interpretations show the *healthy dissociation* of the ego into a part which judges reasonably and a part which experiences the pain, the former comprehending that the latter is not necessary in the current situation, but is the result of unresolved matters from the past. This type of intervention reduces anxiety and results in less *unhealthy dissociation* and distorted derivatives. These types of dissociation, therefore, are different from pathological dissociation, and are used as a form of self-observation with the aim of keeping certain unbearable mental contents in isolation. Working with patients with these types of defences, it is important to make use of the positive transference and transient identifications.

Knowledge of the deeper psychic space comes to patients through ego toleration of the unconscious, and the ego participates in all analytic operations, having three functions:

1. The execution of the id and the source of object cathexis in transference.
2. The organization of the superego.
3. The institution that allows or prevents the discharge of the energy poured forth by the id.

In therapy, the personality of a patient passes under the ascendancy of the transference and countertransference, where instinct and repression are both represented—anti-cathexis due to anxiety used as a defence against the therapist as the potential listening other. Here, I present a brief case history without the process record of a young man I shall call Jonathan.

Jonathan

Jonathan, aged twenty, was referred by a special needs teacher at his college, who was concerned that this unusually small and intellectually bright young man seemed to have no capacity to socialize with the others in his group either inside college or outside. She was puzzled that though he seemed sweet and compliant in individual conversations with teachers, in the group situation of the classroom he quickly became very irritated. He seemed to have no capacity to understand or to learn the college rules, specifically with relation to the personal space and privacy of others. From our initial meeting, Jonathan demonstrated anti-cathexis that clearly originated from his past, when he was around four years old. Jonathan was numb emotionally. He told me that he was left with his grand-parents, who looked after him and took care of his physical needs, but did not help him to feel secure or reassure him that he was loved. He remembers that he was always in fear. He reported that these patterns were repeated over and over in all his relationships in his life, and, indeed, was evident in the transference with me in the process of therapy. Although I judged him to be borderline, I did not necessarily consider Jonathan's type of unhealthy dissocia-tion as a mark of a very serious personality disorder. I perceived it rather as a selective lack of psychic space in which to concentrate and as a distraction for the mental activities associated with unde-sirable thinking and the remembering of his trauma. The unhealthy dissociation presented by Jonathan and other similar patients is an intrinsic factor in the organism directed towards maintaining psychological health, hence the impossibility of healthy dissocia-tion. I assumed that these kinds of psychic activity were corre-sponding to the selectively unattended traumatic experiences that are dissociated unhealthily from self-conscious rational thinking. This aetiology evidently corresponded with Jonathan's personality, in the main as a creative activity. The basic direction of his psychic organism and his initial resistance to change was a characteristic of his unhealthy dissociation.

Jonathan's resistance and defensive response to transference interpretations in the beginning of our relationship took the form of inflexible and persistent silence. The only associations he could make were wrenched out with a great deal of ill humour. Working on Jonathan's unhealthy dissociation bit by bit provided him with an insight into the defensive nature of his attitude to therapy and to me as his potential listening other. As our relationship continued and he developed a positive attachment to me, he started getting in touch with the root of his anxiety. He became more reflective and responsive in transference and gained insight into his situation. One day, without any encouragement from me, he broke his silence by saying that he had become able to identify the fearful child in him, and said, "I would never want to be that scared little boy again."

This provided evidence that by having me as his listening other, Jonathan was able to create a better sense of self, enable more psy-chic space, and increase his level of resilience and ability to deal with his extreme anxiety, as well as his intense transferential feeling that was taking him back to his childhood situation. His response to gentle and careful interpretation of the transference increased his psychic space, enabling him to associate with his real experiences instead of employing unhealthy dissociation. By talking to me about his experience, he developed a better sense of self and managed to focus on his reality. Thus, his consciousness shifted from the centre of affective experience to intellectual contemplation, which helped him to gain insight into his current situation. As his therapist, I made an effort to draw that part of his ego to my side, and effectively put it in combat with the cathected segment of his unconscious and his unhealthy dissociation. The representation of his unhealthy dissociation process was linked to his superego formation in conflict with his id, taking place in his mature being, and he could foster a balancing contemplation to keep free from affect. The development of dissimilarity was followed by his amalgamation and integration. As he developed more psychic space, the function of his ego consisted in the striving, prompted by his instincts for self-preservation and pleasure, to connect, amalgamate, and unify, thus resulting in less conflict within his internal world.

His alienation from others and his sexual activity were understood by him in a different light and, with further reflection, when the powers of his mind were channelled, he could direct his attention to his conscious and separate out his distinct perception of others and his own characteristics. In the process, he became able to acknowledge a distinguishing aspect and quality of his personality. His acknowledgement heralded a clear notion of change, enabling him to see how the characteristic that was due to his conscious reflection presented itself. He then became interested in, and more in touch with, his internal world and his unconscious. He gained insight about his sleep patterns and his dreams, which were composed of two fundamental elements of his psyche with profound inhibition of his consciousness, and his somatic self that was composed of physical changes which effected his adaptation to the restoration of level-headedness. The duality of his sleep represented the isolated occurrence of the somatic element of his sleep, as well as his tendency towards "unhealthy dissociation", and differentiated it fundamentally from sleep, which is by nature immediately reversible and could be delayed or avoided as he wished. His unhealthy dissociation I considered to be the same mechanism of his defence and his general inhibition, but the effects of this same inhibitory force was limited to the configurations and his somatic function in the form of fear and a sudden inability to move in his sleep. These started to diffuse as therapy was progressing, in response to transference and dream interpretations, both simultaneously and concurrently. These types of attacks I considered to be Jonathan's expression of his affective dissolution of his vulnerability and his lack of capacity, which constitute the essential phenomenon and the necessary consequence of the formation of his inhibition in the first place.

As therapy progressed, and by getting much better, Jonathan became enabled to understand the significance of his past and the role it played in his present behaviours and his relationship with others, and in transference with me. The possibility of having satisfactory interpersonal relations and a new way of living gradually became interesting to Jonathan. This enabled him to talk more openly and helped him to gain insight of the fact that his troubles belonged to different stages of his personality development prior to his adolescence. Then it became apparent that one of his problems was closely related to his excessive masturbation. The role of experiencing was important in determining his sexual or genital behaviours, and the emotion of hunger for relating. Jonathan's vulnerability was embedded in, indeed, was the result of, the emotional deprivation and trauma he had endured. His lack of ability to understand the relevance of his past to his present situation was related to not having a clear and robust sense of self and, therefore, not understanding himself. Therapy facilitated his seeking an understanding of his past and the current social order in which he lived; this was in complete contrast to the beginning of therapy, where Jonathan was numb emotionally and out of touch with his surroundings.

Roth, Newman, Pelcovitz, van der Kolk, and Mandel (1997) reported that avoidant and emotional numbing symptomatology appears to be complicated by pathological dissociation and fragmentation of normal memory. In my view, conscious avoidance and unhealthy dissociation are used by the patient in order to deal with the unbearable memory of trauma and a sense of helplessness. Trauma-focused treatment (mainly practised through cognitive–behavioural therapy (CBT)), therefore, may inadvertently expose a patient such as Jonathan to overwhelming emotions and further increase his unhealthy dissociative avoidance and denial, which can result in an auxiliary personification of retraumatization, rather than working through his traumatic experience. Therefore, assessment of, and treatment for, post trauma problems should focus on fear, avoidance, and dissociations (healthy and unhealthy), as well as on complex alterations in affect, consciousness, and interpersonal relationship. This is because trauma experienced at an early developmental stage may severely compromise the person's core sense of self, leaving no psychic space for reflection and the capacity for thinking or relating to others, and having a therapist as the listening other can repair those developmental defects. Therapeutic intervention can provide space for the patient to reflect on fear of harm or a constant fear of being killed, which is infused with insecurity and lack of trust in others, indeed, with a sense of dread and constant anxiety in social settings. For patients such as Jonathan, there is always a fear of betrayal, which produces further fears of disappointment, anger, and frustration. Psychoanalytic therapeutic approaches recognize these types of fear, anger, and frustration, and pay attention to identifying the patient's strengths, which will result in the patient's gaining some level of resilience and autonomous control. This is especially important for a patient like Jonathan, who may be subject to sudden and overwhelming states of primitive rage without being able to reflect on why this is so. This can be achieved by encouraging the development of the four factors of resilience: the sense of self, psychic space, a listening other, and healthy dissociation.

The assessment of early childhood narratives and trauma history, therefore, is the key to personality formation and patterns of defence and is vital for identifying patients' engagement in, and response to, transference interpretations in treatment. Thus, a focus on understanding how childhood trauma can exacerbate intrusive re-experiencing of adult-related trauma memories is important. This is of great consequence, because it will have an effect on the psychic space, or lack of it, as well as pragmatic cognitive behaviour and functioning, and may decrease the patient's ability to have and to use the listening other who gives support and can be used to promote a good sense of self in the face of past overwhelming traumatic experiences.

CHAPTER FIVE

Resilience

Introduction

Resilience is central to this study and touched upon in the previous chapters as a means of illustrating why any two people can have different responses to potentially the same traumatic occurrences. The *Oxford English Dictionary*'s (2001) definition of resilient is: "adj. 1. able to recoil or spring back into shape after bending, stretching or being compressed. 2. able to recover quickly after difficult conditions".

The word resilience comes from the Latin *resalire* (to jump up again), and has passed into psychological idiom systematically since the 1960s. I define resilient as the ability to experience severe trauma or neglect without a collapse of psychological functioning or evidence of post traumatic stress disorder. This does not imply psychological well-being or positive mental health, which assumes an acceptable environment, but it is a reasonably effective psychological functioning with a protected inner space.

In this chapter, after a generalized definition, I look at the work of Werner and Garmezy, mentioned in Chapter One. From this, my understanding of the term resilience is offered with a list of the factors typically found in resilient people, expanding on some of the psychoanalytic concepts that can be viewed as the equivalent to resilience. These are then applied to two vignettes, illustrating one individual who demonstrates resilience and another who lacks resilience.

The psychic space, sense of self, and listening other are also touched upon in this chapter as major concepts in this study and as elements of the overall hypothesis for the foundation of resilience in relation to different types of dissociation.

What actually is resilience?

Resilience is a multi-faceted phenomenon that encompasses personal and environmental factors that interact in a synergistic fashion to produce competence despite adversity. It is complex, and assimilates personal characteristics as well as environmental, socio-economic, familial, academic, and community factors. Resilient people are not perfect and may experience emotional difficulties and stress-related health problems; they may need support even though they have a high level of competence. However, being aware of, and using, environmental supports, opportunities, and resources in a healthy manner are aspects of resilient characteristics. The development of resilience among individuals who have experienced trauma with a specific psychopathology is important. I assert that the development of such pathology in response to traumatic experiences in adult life has a clear connection to childhood and adolescence experiences. My clinical data provides evidence of patients' developmental milestones, including the ability to deal adaptively with stressful circumstances, developing an integrated sense of self and psychic space, and, from a relational perspective, the existence of good enough parents as the listening others, which lays the foundations for resilience.

Resilience and psychoanalysis

Although psychoanalysis is a form of treatment that enhances resilience, surprisingly, psychoanalytic literature has not directly referred to resilience, even though psychoanalytic intervention is intended to help maintain a focus on the healthy parts of the patient's life while working on the disturbed parts in order to achieve integration. So, the focus of psychoanalytic intervention is to enhance resilience by way of exploring vulnerability. The psychoanalytic view tends to focus on concepts such as ego strength, which is appealing to a factor of intrinsic resilience existing inside the isolated mind of the individual. As there is no direct focus on the concept of resilience in psychoanalytic literature, there is no empirical evidence as to whether resilience can be fostered and encouraged in the early years or not. So, this question perhaps could be answered in future research aimed at clearly determining the extent to which resilient features are innate or learnt.

Freud's preference (1900a), in line with the influential philosophy of Spencer and Darwin, was to think of resilience in terms of individual and cultural developmental shifts in time, as linear, back and forth, or up and down. He considered regression as overlapping linear events, but it is still hard to know to what degree we are caught in a vicious circle, under the destructive power of a repetition compulsion or, more optimistically, a progressive distortion. Some of the aspects that determine the difference between vulnerability and resilience in psychoanalytical literature are the "facilitating environment" (Winnicott, 1971) and "transitional space" (*ibid.*), a space which has profound psychological importance for the recovery from trauma, Bion's notions of "containment" and "the concept of container–contained" (1962c), and Bowlby's (1969, 1973, 1980) concepts of "a secure base" and "attachment".

Psychoanalytic concept equivalences to resilience

There are a number of processes and phrases in psychoanalysis that have aspects of resilience, such as:

- ego strength or ego function (Eissler, 1950; Kernberg, 1976; Saul, 1940);
- psychic strength (Kernberg, 1975; Klein, 1940, 1952b);
- self sufficiency (Kohut, 1971, 1972; Sandler, 1983; Sandler & Rosenblatt, 1962; Sandler & Sandler, 1992; Schafer, 1968)
- emotional strength (Colby, 1960; Parson, 1986; Greenberg, 1986; Grünbaum, 1986; Holt 1986);

- self regulation (Fonagy, 2002; Lewin, 1954; Reich, 1960; Schore, 1994);
- representativeness of pleasure giving (Brenner & Vinacke, 1979);
- reflective internal working model (Blatt & Blass, 1996; Bowlby, 1975; Bretherton, 1987; Eagle, 1995, 2003; Hinshelwood, 1994b; Holmes, 1993, 1997; Lichtenberg, 1989);
- Safe intrapsychic space (Bergmann, 1993; Davies, 1998; Frances & Dunn, 1975; Mahler, Pine, & Bergman, 1975).

The list can go on to

- insightfulness;
- integrated self;
- self cohesion;
- capacity to think;
- sublimation;
- self righting;
- ultimate self strength;
- sense of agency;
- cohesive state of mind.

Among other characteristics of resilience, I also add the following:

- an ability for healthy dissociation;
- being able to elicit positive attention from others;
- responding in a socially acceptable manner and being sensitive to the needs of others;
- displaying social competencies and the ability to communicate with empathy and care;
- having a good sense of humour that enables one to gain perspective and provides some helpful lightheartedness and the ability to laugh at oneself;
- the capacity for empathy, which enables tolerance for difficult situations, making connections with others, identifying an issue and resolving it in a positive manner, thereby helping to avoid hostility.

These resilient characteristics create a cushioning effect against overwhelming aggressive feelings and wishes, and allow a person to function without falling apart. Self-discipline, self-esteem, the ability to say no, the ability to act independently, to take charge of things when needed, and to have internal and external control are also important skills associated with resilience. Furthermore, it is also important to have intelligence and good reasoning and problem-solving skills, as well as the capability to accomplish tasks. However, it is my assertion that it is the development of autonomy and a sense of the self that is a major social milestone, a trait that enhances resilience.

Having a sense of future and purpose and the ability to set achievable goals, persistence, optimism, high expectations, educational aspirations, and a sense of meaning and coherence in life are typical characteristics of resilient individuals. The ability to work well, play well, love well, and expect well, are characteristics of resilient individuals who make good use of environmental supports and work to improve their life. Resilient people are more often able to assess what needs to be dealt with. They tend to possess a good cognitive capacity and adequate emotional stability. For resilient persons, things are seen as they are and are not easily dismissed; they can clearly distinguish between phantasy and reality. This enables such a person to respond more effectively in difficult situations, and not be paralysed by anxiety. Other characteristics of resilience are the capacity for self-reflection, and an awareness of others, characteristics that create self-respect and self-protection. Having a strong ego and clear ego boundaries is another feature of resilience, which protects one from becoming perplexed by other people's pathology, and enables one to maintain a good ear for listening and a respectful attitude.

Resilient people can, to some extent, control the impact of their environment by using strategic withdrawal—healthily dissociating activity or passivity, internally as well as externally. A resilient child in a dysfunctional family, for example, will be less likely to be an object of abuse than their more vulnerable siblings. Another example, often seen in work with children and adolescents and their role in the family, is what I call a "reversal of roles and responsibilities", that is, a situation where the child takes on the responsible role in relation to the parent/s, which is not uncommon in vulnerable families. A child has to become the carer for a vulnerable parent, cook for the family, take care of younger siblings, and in some refugee and immigrant families where parents do not speak English, interpret and translate for their parents (children learn the language much quicker than their parents and adopt the host culture more rapidly).

Resilient people are more aware and more tolerant of their feelings. This reflects in the treatment of patients who find their guilt feelings more manageable, and usually very little neurotic or unconscious guilt distorts their interpersonal relationships. A resilient person may experience less of the survivor's guilt, which is common among people who have witnessed the killing of close family members or friends. For resilient people, this guilt may more often be channelled into helping others, by working in a caring profession or getting involved in charitable, political, or other good causes. They may have a sense of confidence about the outcome of doing good and living peacefully, and have the ability to find safety among people they trust. This enables the person to take care of themselves more adequately and realistically and not get swallowed up in someone else's narcissistic or sadistic needs. Related to this is the ability to bring into their lives people who can help them with their needs or tasks without pitying them; people who have a strong sense of morality and a social and political consciousness and have genuine human concern. Another characteristic common in resilient people is positive and creative thinking with a sense of fulfilment—growing plants, for example, or getting involved in organizations, and making positive changes. It is certainly the case that some resilient people get satisfaction from being involved with good causes and making positive changes, even very small ones. Resilient individuals often have a need to prove that adversity can be overcome; they do not want to be identified as victims. However, whether any of these characteristics are inherited or can be influenced by the environment is an important issue for debate, which is beyond the remit of this study.

Resilience and dissociation

My focus here is on resilience and the pattern of dissociation, both healthy and unhealthy. It is possible that a psyche breaks its reliance on the consistency and resilience of its core at the time of an atrocity and defensively retreats into dissociation, as if the core self support systems, agency, continuity, cohesiveness, and affects, are disconnected by an act of dissociation during the actual trauma. Those can, of course, reconnect through recounting the memory of the traumatic event, but may not reconnect seamlessly. A conscious decision to dissociate (although there is always unconscious element in it) in these instances is healthy dissociation. This is a situation where the sense of self can lose the familiar ground on which it usually stands. It is an awareness that is never far from consciousness, and that can come into sharp relief in response to external or internal cues, but often is a complaint or drone in the background of experience, a knowledge of otherness, of the failure of the self and the self's ties, indeed, of the certainty of death.

Healthy dissociation as a resilient factor is an important reflective self-function that does not risk creating space for thinking too much about negative experiences. It is an ability to create psychic space and a mental state of intent (wish, belief, or want) unwilling to be confronted by a malevolent set of encoded traumatic experiences in the mind. Thus, the resilient individual possesses reflective self-function and has the potential to prevent negative experiences from the past influencing their current life and relationships. This is the resilience process that I claim exists in the patient and underlies the mechanism of defence that reflects in the transference (clinical observation of this dynamic will be presented in the second part of this book by examining two case studies). The concept of resilience, therefore, is helpful in considering aspects of patient personality formations and character beyond the trauma in adult life. In comparison to a vulnerable person, a resilient person who endured trauma has the capacity to suspend the demands of immediate connection with a very difficult and, at times, unbearable reality and contemplate alternative perceptions through the act of healthy dissociation, hence being able to distinguish between phantasy and reality, which is an advantage in dealing with trauma and life's hardship. To demonstrate this, I present a brief vignette of a resilient patient.

Iris

The patient I call Iris was in her thirties, and had been detained as a result of her political activity in a country where severe torture was inflicted on prisoners. She talked about her experiences in prison and the defences that she and few other female political prisoners adopted to cope with the extremely violent situation in the prison regime. She said, "Everything was geared by the authorities towards making the inmates lose their identity, their hope, their reason for living, and their sense of agency."

Iris explained how, with some other prisoners, she adopted a strategy of teaming up with one another in a small group, to look out for each other and for other vulnerable young prisoners. She said, "We supported each other physically and emotionally in the almost symbiotic ways that were necessary in such extreme circumstances, and we were getting stronger emotionally."

This is evidence of resilience, in that through their relationships, Iris and the other resilient prisoners, with a strong sense of self, created an island of sanity. They confirmed each other's identities as human beings. By having a sense of self and enough psychic space and capacity to relate, they became the listening other for each other and for other vulnerable prisoners, while owning their own sense of self. Iris adopted a positive attitude in order to survive her situation of torture and constant fear of execution.

Here, it is possible to recognize the processes of projection, introjection, and projective identification, and, importantly, a kind of dissociation used as a defence to deal with an ongoing trauma—this is a healthy dissociation. This example demonstrates an important characteristic in resilient people who can take responsibility for what has to be done and can take charge in difficult situations and do not collude with the victim role. Iris, in prison as a resilient person with a good sense of self and with sufficient inner psychic space, was able to be a listening other to other, more vulnerable prisoners in order to cope with her own captivity and torture.

In response to a question from me, Iris said, "I see no point in attaching a negative thought to this; it would only make me feel miserable and prevent me from being productive and enjoying the result of our activity in surviving such an atrocity, at least psychologically . . . because the physical scars are for life and there is nothing we could do about that . . . but I know they did not break me psychologically."

This supports my hypothesis that a resilient person has the ability to make use of facilitating aspects of the environment. It confirms that resilient individuals with a strong sense of self are able to build a safe enough environment and, with their good psychic space, they can talk to themselves to regulate pain and protect themselves from too many vulnerable feelings; they can dissociate healthily and use dissociation as a protective shell, not cutting off, splitting, or repressing, and thus are able to regulate their experience of trauma. This almost unbreakable part of the self protects the person from collapsing emotionally when the external world is unpredictable, overpowering, and life-threatening. It is a means of self-protection to maintain a safe inner psychic space, which is hypothesized in this study to be involved in dissociation.

It is important to repeat here that the characterization of vulnerability or resilience is related to childhood development and/or the outcome of therapeutic intervention. Development is ongoing throughout the lifespan, and psychoanalytic treatment is an opportunity to pick up what has been missed out, and start again to facilitate later development. Therefore, it is the therapist's job to take into consideration not just vulnerability, but also resilience, as an important factor in the process. The capacity to regulate experiential states and to maintain an integrated sense of self to deal with disruption is a resilient characteristic. Having some level of resilience can be considered vitally important in therapy in terms of the patient's capacity, or lack of capacity, to join the therapist in establishing the therapeutic alliance, and to accept the therapist as the listening other.

In contrast to the case above, I now bring an example of a vulnerable patient I shall call Abdul, who, by having a listening other (therapist) became able to gain some resilience in the process and replaced unhealthy dissociation with healthy dissociation.

Abdul

Abdul, a twelve-year-old from Central Africa, was referred for assessment and possible therapy due to his lack of concentration, not engaging with his peers, and his extreme withdrawal from his foster carers and his social worker. Abdul was silent throughout assessment sessions and only responded with "yes" and "no". The only information provided in the referral letter was that, at eight years old, Abdul saw his father and brothers shot by officials. His mother took him and his younger sister into the bushes and joined the rebels, hoping for her own survival and that of her children. Nothing prior to this was known. Four months into therapy, in one session he said,

> "My mother had impressed upon me two rules, one I must always smile and not complain, and two I must never tell anyone that my father and brothers were killed or what happened to my family in general."

> I told him, "You don't need to smile here, unless you want to, and if you feel sad, it is OK to cry."

He immediately stopped pressuring himself to smile, and was in silent tears for most of the session. With my encouragement, he said that his mother was repeatedly raped, tortured, and later killed by the rebels. After this process, Abdul changed and gradually developed a capacity to talk, and for about two months he talked about his past and his memories. He talked about school and social services with gratitude, and would report that everything and everybody around him was good. He was unhappy because he could not get up in the morning, could not pay attention to his teacher, and felt that he was letting everyone down. He started by repeatedly saying he was "bad". In listening to him, I often felt that his presentation still did not correspond with his level of depression.

Six months into therapy, Abdul broke down and had a period in hospital, resuming therapy after his discharge. Seven months later, he opened up for the first time and talked about the losses that he had experienced, his feelings of loneliness, of being strange and different, and of missing his mother. His memories were haunting him. He was not able to describe the contents of his vivid nightmares and flashbacks. He felt no one understood him, and he started to wonder what the point of talking about all this was.

In countertransference, my response to Abdul's emotional state was my controlled empathic attunement, which was both my greatest asset and liability. I needed to constantly work to protect myself and Abdul by imparting an understanding of the impact of the trauma he had endured and by addressing the effects upon us both. In the seclusion of the consulting room, I constantly found myself between numerous boundaries—between body and mind, past and present, conscious awareness and unconscious processes, self and other, material and intrapsychic, phantasy and reality, fact and fiction, desire for and fear of fulfilment, conflict and deficit, separateness and oneness. The list can be expanded to include all types of psychological and philosophical boundaries, in particular, ethical ones, which cropped up despite my intention to maintain neutrality as a therapist. More often than I wished, I found myself agonizing over dilemmas of good and bad, right and wrong, what is acceptable or unacceptable, and on so many occasions I found myself enraged about what had been done to this child. So many times I wanted to hug and hold him, protect him from further suffering, and tell him everything was going to be all right. I controlled myself, as I was aware that to be useful to Abdul I had to be ready to give space to his phantasies of destruction, sometimes through allowing him to project them to me, or attack and destroy what I had to offer. I am not referring only to open attacks, but to much deeper, largely unconscious, and symbolic destructiveness.

In one of the sessions, Abdul was quite frustrated, and I made some interpretation; he started weeping and howling with despair. Not to lose this moment, I encouraged him to talk. He said that even if he wanted to tell me more, he did not know what to say. We established that it was hard for him to find words to describe his memories and feelings. I thought we could use art and play to assist Abdul to express his feelings. We agreed that we could think about his experience together and he could draw pictures of the scenes in his mind, and then we would talk and together we could try to find the right words for them. He smiled—this was his first real smile since I met him almost two years before. As his experience was so overwhelming, we agreed to focus on his past experience and memories for the first thirty minutes of each session and for the last twenty minutes focus on his daily life here, and we could skip the first part of the session whenever he wished. Abdul agreed with a big smile again. Thus, systematic work on his experiences started.

His anger started to flare up as therapy progressed. He gained the ability to put his experience into words. He then started complaining about everyone he had encountered here in London.

He felt that people did not care about him. He viewed his social worker as sadistic, irresponsible, and careless; his teacher as a racist person who was picking on him for the mistakes of others; his fellow students bullied him and no one wanted to be his friend; his "selfish and racist" foster carers only kept him for the money and did not care if he died tomorrow. He was expressing strong feelings of not being loved or wanted. In transference, sometimes he was telling me that I did not care about him and I was only doing my job, and at other times was clinging, idealizing me, wanting me to be his mother, and finding it difficult to leave the sessions.

As we progressed further, Abdul was able to tell me that due to his size, he was not able to fight with a gun with a few other boys, and he had to dig holes to bury dead people, taking their clothes and valuables beforehand. Among the people he had to bury, he recognized his sister and later his mother, as well as a few other family members. Those images were always there, but he never could finish them, so, we had to finish them together. Finishing those unbearable memories helped him to recall other memory from his earlier childhood. His father was a "strong man" in the army and was quite restricting at home; he also had children with another woman. His mother was "strong and strict", especially with her sons. The memory he could recall from back home was of sitting outside every night until dark, waiting and hoping his father might come home, "because mum was happy and calmer and talked quietly, not shouting constantly, when father was there." This provided the opportunity to explore his current living environment, helping him to realize that people (foster carer, social worker, teacher, etc.) were not shouting at him and were interested to hear his opinion. He became more able to recognize that the foundation of his anger was in the past, and to stop projecting to people around him here and now. Gradually, he became interested in his education and involved with school activities, developed an attachment with his foster carer, and was proud to come to a session with his best friend waiting for him to go to play football after his appointment. The fact that he felt so proud of having a friend is evidence of how psychoanalytic intervention brought about great changes in this young person, who developed enough psychic space and an ability to relate.

Here, I present another vignette of a patient I shall call Jasmine, who had a strong sense of the self and enough psychic space and resilience to dissociate healthily.

Jasmine

A patient in her late thirties, Jasmine came from a wealthy as well as educated family but had to flee her country against her will as a result of persecution. Jasmine was detained and tortured severely; her brother was executed, and many members of her family have been persecuted. In a session at the time that I had been seeing her for four years, she informed me that she would be missing our sessions for the following two weeks, as they were moving to permanent accommodation. Through further exploration about their new accommodation, I discovered that they (a family of four with two school-age children) had been living in one small room during their six-year stay in London. I was shocked, not just to hear this, but by the fact that I never heard her complain about it.

I said, "It must have been very difficult . . ."

Jasmine said, "Well, we all are alive, healthy and reasonably happy . . . we wanted to stay in London to see people from our own community and also we want our children learn our language as well. We made this decision, knowing there is a shortage of housing in London and we may have to wait a long time. No one forced us; it was our decision. We could go outside London and have a nice large house . . . we are grateful that we had shelter and now we have been given a house that hopefully we will enjoy for years . . ."

In a session, when we were talking about the loss of her brother, I asked her whether she feels guilty being alive and in Britain, a safe environment.

She said, "No, I feel sad . . . not guilty—guilt is the feeling of people who do wrong . . . although I know they don't—those who killed him should feel guilty, not me . . . I feel sad, I miss him dearly and sometimes I feel angry, but I never feel guilty."

In my experience of working with traumatized people for three decades, this was the first time, and to date the last time, that I have seen such a resilient, healthy, and sensible approach to life. An important resilience characteristic in Jasmine was that she did not experience the survivor's guilt commonly identified with survivors of trauma. When she was psychologically not able to cope with the memory of the trauma she has endured, she was able to dissociate (healthily) herself from her unbearable memories and channel her feelings into helping others, which gave her great satisfaction.

Conclusion

In this chapter, the discussion of resilience opened with a definition of the term, before examining psychological aspects of it. A list of psychoanalytic concepts broadly equivalent to resilience was suggested. From this came an outline of what I understand about resilience and the factors commonly found in resilient people. It concludes that psychological theories of resilience are numerous, but psychoanalytic theories are fewer. I presented three vignettes.

First, Iris, who served to illustrate psychoanalytic concepts related to resilience, in particular, that of sense of self and a safe psychic space.

Second, Abdul, who presented extreme vulnerability. This case illustrates the psychopathology related to vulnerability and how by having me, his therapist, as a listening other, Abdul could create a psychic space and, therefore, a sense of self, which changed Abdul from being just someone existing with severe depression to a young adolescent who became alive again.

Third, Jasmine presented clear resilience characteristics. Jasmine's tremendous capacity to deal with adversity, and her ability to dissociate healthily when she was not able to deal with the situation, were evidence in therapy and in every aspect of her life that she was bringing to therapy.

The three vignettes serve to corroborate the theory of having a listening other as being important in contributing to resilience in the individual, and link with the research question stemming from the literature review. Having a listening other proved to be an important factor for psychological functioning and for both developing and reclaiming resilience in all three vignettes. The prisoners in the first vignette had each other as the listening others for support; in the second vignette, Abdul had me as a therapist; in the third vignette, Jasmine had her early good object relations, combined with having me, her therapist, as her new listening other to help her deal with traumas that she had endured in adult life.

As this study is primarily focused on psychoanalytical intervention, the second vignette provides useful data on vulnerability and the development of resilience in therapy through the therapist being the listening other. Abdul came to therapy with severe vulnerability and without any sign of resilience, but developed into a capable and resilient young man through what I call "secondary developmental processes". From a psychoanalytic perspective, this is important, as it can be taken to mean that resilience could be part of specific character traits, which is relational, and that those traits are developed from interpersonal relations, or are interpersonally supported. I conclude that existing psychological and psychoanalytic perspectives on resilience are not satisfactory in relation to external trauma and its relation to the person's resilient or vulnerable characteristics. This will be discussed in more detail, with further vignettes, in the next chapter, which focuses on dissociation. However, questions arising from this chapter are: what is it in the personality that makes some people resilient to their traumatic experiences, but leaves others vulnerable to psychological collapse (i.e., development of PTSD)? And, as it is not something that lies in the objective external event, what is it about the personality that enables, or disables resilience? This opens the door for a new theory central to dissociation.

CHAPTER SIX

Dissociation

Introduction

T he explanations of trauma and resilience in previous chapters should be helpful in making plain that when we are faced with life-threatening and traumatic situations, a common response is to dissociate. When we are overwhelmed with a sense of danger and we do not have a way to protect ourselves, our nervous systems can automatically go into dissociation as a response to situations that threaten our survival and we may lose our ability to accurately perceive what is happening in our environment. This helplessness I consider to be a normal reaction to an abnormal situation.

Despite its clinical importance, dissociation is an open term, leading to conceptual confusion which restrict its value. The term dissociation (healthy and unhealthy) used and discussed in this study has qualitatively distinct types: it is pathological *vs.* nonpathological, in which detachment from unbearable memories of trauma is considered as a healthy and appropriate defence against fragmentation or compartmentalization. Distinctive of dissociations in this study is the level of awareness and consciousness that is perceptive and offers penetrating relief in response to external cues to protect the internal world. Although the effects may still vibrate in the unconscious, dissociation makes it possible to cut off the thoughts, feelings, and memories of particular trauma. This can be effected through knowledge of otherness, or of the failure of the self and the self's connections, or of the principle and certainty of death, which is a way of successful mourning that allows one to overcome the severity of trauma and its memory. Even an unhealthy dissociation (which will be illustrated in detail in Daniel's case in the second part of the book) is not a simple negation of the self, but a negation of the part of the self affected by the trauma and its memory. It is this obstruction that reduces the ability to sublimate, therefore reducing creativity. This is because memories are not some sort of bland mental background patterns that simply provide surroundings for the self. They are alive, free, from time to time unknown, and, on occasion, dangerous mental representations, which can be overwhelming and force capitulation. They are an intrinsic part of the mental function and holders of the content of the self.

The diagnosis and treatment of people who have experienced trauma is complex. The complexity of traumatization and treatment are mainly derived from the theory of post traumatic stress disorder and personality disorder, trauma-related conversion disorder (*DSM-IV*), dissociative disorders of movement and sensation (*ICD-10*), and dissociative identity disorder. This complexity can overwhelm and confuse clinicians, and can lead to treatment impasses and problematic countertransferential reactions in the therapeutic encounter. Dissociation, both healthy and unhealthy, I consider to be the most important concept in working with traumatized people. These types of dissociation consist in an essential dividedness between one or more parts of the person, for example, one that engages in the functions of daily life and one that is fixated on traumatic memories, engaging in defence reactions when exposed to real or perceived threats.

These functions are realized through action systems derived from evolution, such as object relation, exploration, play, and defence, and will be manifested in particular mental and behavioural action tendencies. I assert that the two types of dissociation, a healthy dissociation, which is linked to resilience, and an unhealthy dissociation, which is indicative of vulnerability, are equally important in provision of therapy to people who have endured trauma.

The vignettes of vulnerable and resilient patients in the previous chapter demonstrate the characteristics that enable or inhibit healthy dissociation in both conscious and unconscious mechanisms in the mind of a traumatized person, which can be either relatively less or, in some cases, absent in patients. The types of dissociation presented by people span the whole range of healthy and unhealthy dissociative reactions. However, I argue that healthy dissociation is a healthy defence and not dysfunction. If we assume that dissociation is the disruption of the usually integrated functions of consciousness, memory, identity, or sensitivity to the environment, there is an important question: how is it that through the act of dissociation some people survive massive trauma and human rights violations?

A quick look at PEP and other psychoanalytic literature does indicate that psychoanalysts are occasionally using the notion of dissociation again now, but the term is used in an inconsistent way, especially in relation to trauma, for example Sinason (1993, 1996, 2002, 2003, 2006), and the term sometimes is used indistinguishably from *splitting* and *repression*. Freyd (1996) described how dissociation can be indistinguishable from "memory repression" or "traumatic amnesia". Sometimes, it has a more conscious connotation, like that intended by Fonagy, Gergely, Jurist, and Target (2002) who calls it going into "pretend mode of mentalising". However, this is not quite how the term is considered in this work. I argue that healthy dissociation is a defence mechanism and coping strategy consciously adopted (although there are always unconscious connotations). The combination of traumatic experiences may result in extreme vulnerability and helplessness, so, for a person with healthy developmental processes who possesses some level of resilience, the traumatic events may cause temporary depression and anxiety, but not psychotic breakdown. In my view, the occurrence of dissociative phenomena in clinical treatment of a traumatized person may manifest in hysteria, memory loss, depersonalization, identity diffusion, fear of death, disruption of ego functioning, or disruption of the self. I have given examples of these in the vignettes throughout this study, and in detail in cases of Farina's (healthy) and Daniel's (unhealthy) dissociation.

The history of dissociation in psychoanalysis: Freud's and Janet's views

Freud and Janet had differences on the matter of dissociation as the mechanism underlying unconscious mental processes observed in patients' psychopathology. Janet was of the opinion that repression is a type of dissociation, covering those instances when the disruption of conscious access is motivated by defensive concerns. Freud's argument was that dissociation was trivial.

But I think it is important to look at their views and to see how they might be related to each other. There are repressive barriers which have the function of preventing direct access to the contents of the unconscious system. In terms of contemporary memory theory, the contents of the system covered by the horizontal, repressive barrier would be described as unavailable to introspective access or voluntary control under any circumstances. The contents of this system can be known only indirectly, through patients' affects and observable behaviour that are not accessible consciously, and, therefore, not controlled by patients.

Van Der Hart and Horst (1989) suggested that in

> 1887, the concept of dissociation is encountered in the work of Frederic Myers, in England, and of Charcot, Gilles de la Tourette and Pierre Janet, in France. Myers (1887) sought to show how far the dissociation of memories, faculties, and sensibilities could go in multiple personalities without resulting in chaos. Charcot remarked that 'by reason of the easy dissociation of mental unity, certain centers may be put into play without the other regions of the psychic organ being made aware of it and called upon to take part in the processes' (p. 455). Gilles de la Tourette (1887) used the concept to describe the abolition of certain senses in hysterical patients: they are dissociated from the patients' normal mental state. Janet (1887) used the term in the same sense as Charcot and Gilles de la Tourette did, to describe a variety of phenomena which characterized his hysterical subject Lucie and which could also be evoked in her under hypnosis. [p. 401]

To compare Janet with Freud regarding their theories about dissociation, it is possible to distinguish that Janet explains how, scientifically, the dissociation is happening for the patient, while Freud was interested in looking at it from the point of explaining why it happens. So, in a sense, Janet was keen to deal with facts, while Freud was interested in facts and their meanings.

In a very simplistic way, I argue that, as pioneering theories, neither the theory of Freud nor that of Janet explains fully today how the dissociated or repressed memories exist, how the traumatic memories are encoded by patients, and how people can manage; how traumatic memories affect emotion and cognition of the patients, and how the therapist can identify this in the processes of therapeutic intervention. Indeed, how it is possible to denote those functional problems that are part of patients' traumatic experiences, and how traumatized patients perceive and recall their unwanted experiences.

Janet systematically argued that dissociation is the most direct psychological defence against overwhelming traumatic experiences. He suggested that dissociative phenomena play an important role in widely divergent post traumatic stress responses, which he included under the nineteenth-century diagnosis of hysteria. His based his studies of trauma on concepts such as: psychological automatism, consciousness, subconsciousness, narrowed field of consciousness, dissociation, amnesia, suggestibility, fixed ideas, and emotion.

It is, therefore, possible to see that although there have been similarities to begin with, as their theories progressed further, Freud and Janet have differences. Janet believed minds dissociated under trauma only if predisposed to do so through some form of mental weakness, either innate or acquired. Freud argued that a weakened mind was not a necessary precondition for dissociation, but that consciousness could fragment whenever instinctual conflict resulted in the disruptive action of other mental forces working to banish such conflict from consciousness. For Freud, dissociation, therefore, was not the mark of a failing, but of a mind at work on other matters at that particular moment, more vital than consciousness. Freud acknowledged that psychoanalytic theory does not fail to point out that neuroses have an organic basis, but his view was that whatever their organic bases, psychopathologic states represent universal human traits taken to extremes. Keeping both these points in mind, Freud was able to extend the clinical practice of psychoanalysis beyond clinical phenomenology towards the more general theory of human psychology. Freud distinguishes drives from consciousness, and his theory on the process of repression (a term he chose in preference to dissociation) is that he believed it occurred not in a mind lacking in integrity, but in one falling apart under stress, in contrast to Janet's hypothesis. Freud's therapeutic dimension of psychoanalysis suggests that if repressing conflict creates dissociation, then retracing the conflict and finding a way to resolve it offers the prospect of a psychoanalytic recovery.

Having said this, it is important to note that Janet's principal legacy may prove to be the first systematic understanding of how the mind can dissociate in the face of overwhelming threat. He hypothesized a biologically-based trauma response resulting in a fragmentation of mental cohesion, causing biological, behavioural, cognitive, and emotional residues of past experience to continue to govern current behaviour. Van der Hart and Horst (1989) say that

> In presenting his model of the mind, Janet distinguished between two different ways that mind functions: activities that preserve and reproduce the past and activities which are directed towards synthesis and creation (i.e., integration). Normal thought is produced by a combination of the two acts which are interdependent and regulate each other. Integrative activity 'reunites more or less numerous given phenomena into a new phenomenon different from its elements. At every moment of life, this activity effectuates new combinations which are necessary to maintain the organism in equilibrium with the changes of the surroundings.' In short, this function organizes the present. Reproductive activities only manifest integrations that were created in the past. [p. 403]

The term dissociation historically is used inequitably, so, it is important to look at history. Freud's (1919d) notion of trauma fits into an economic perspective as an experience which, within a short period of time, presents the mind with an increase of stimulus too powerful to be dealt with or worked off in the normal way. This can result in permanent disturbances of the way the energy activates and operates. Freud's view of dissociation was the removal of ideas from one compartment to another. His earliest notion of hysterical symptoms was based on his hypothesis of the importance of trauma dissociation, upon which he began to construct his first theory of neurosis. (In this period, dissociation was discussed as unconscious). Soon, Freud's (1896a) conception of trauma narrowed to apply only to sexual trauma, and later only to childhood experiences of sexual abuse that may be the result of an actual sexual trauma that has been accrued or the phantasy of a sexual scene due to the instinctual derives. He devised the term "repression" to account for a patient's resistance to improvement, and used the term both loosely to mean any ego defence (1905e), and specifically to refer to the defence in which the idea is pushed into unconsciousness to be forgotten. He indicated that the associated apprehension of such an experience remains in the consciousness; that is, the conscious ego consigns undesirable thoughts and memories to the realm of the unconscious as a way of surviving knowledge of the unacceptable material. For example, in Anna O's case, she developed an occasional stiffening of her arm as the result of her phantasy of her arm not being able to protect her father from a snake. Anna O's bodily symptom spoke of a relationship to her father and her death wish towards him that she was fearful to admit. According to Freud (1915b), repression is a normal part of human development; he also indicates that the analysis of dreams, literature, jokes, and slips of tongue illustrate the route via which our desires continue to find outlets. Freud (1917e) discussed a precursor of repression proper, and referred to trauma as the cause of the mental organization. He later (Freud, 1923b) refers to the superego as an additional agent for securing the repression of id material by the ego and thereby inhibiting part of the self, the id, by another part, the superego. So, repression, from his point of view, is an active process and the model depends on a straight split between consciousness and unconsciousness in the process of development and in dealing with internal trauma.

In the cases of people who are faced with obstacles due to external reality combined with fixation on earlier phases of development, there is a conflict between libido and the ego and/or between the ego and the superego. The combination of these experiences may result in vulnerability and the lack of resilience in adulthood. Freud's concept of repression and his theory of the unconscious, although offering insights to the use of language and discourse, are not enough to explain the types of dissociation discussed in this study. He is clear in his classic case histories such as "Dora" and the "Rat Man" but, seems to fail to examine how people actually repress fearful, shameful, or other unbearable thoughts.

However, neither Freud's original theory nor his later develop-ment of repression is enough to explain the types of dissociation I am discussing in relation to trauma. There is a gap within psycho-analysis. Freud's (1895a) active idea of repression has been and still is very useful, but it misses the conscious aspect of dissocia-tion for good mental functioning, which I call healthy dissociation. This concept also postulates an unhealthy dissociation. Although dissociation has been discussed historically, there is an element of the dissociating act that is missed by clinicians. That is where a person who has endured trauma, in order to stay functional and not break down, consciously decides to dissociate his or her self from the experiences and memory of the traumatic occurrence. Although there is an unconscious connotation in this act, the conscious dissociation is a healthy action to keep the person func-tioning.

The dissociation (healthy and unhealthy) I am referring to is neither perception nor affect, but it is the thinking about experi-ences pertaining to perceptions; the thoughts to which affect is attached. In healthy dissociation, a resilient person can sublimate through positive action, while in unhealthy dissociation, a vulnera-ble person may be fragmented. This fragmentation can lead to destructiveness towards self and others. These types of dissocia-tions are quite different from repression, which works by actively severing affect and thought, so that the affect can remain when the thought to which it is linked is repressed. For example, in hys-teria, affect persists when thought has supposedly been forgotten, and in obsession, the thought, as it pertains to a childhood event, can be accessible to consciousness, but the affect is not.

The theories of resistance, repression, and the importance of infantile experiences are principles that constitute the theoretical structure of psychoanalysis, and that are all related to internal trauma, conflicts, and splits to contain and balance one's wishes, will, and desire, but it lacks explanation of external trauma in adult-hood.

One of the differences I am positing is that between helplessness and passivity and an active defensiveness. In other words, traumas which can be dealt with by psychic activity (healthy disassociation or association) and trauma that cannot be dealt with actively, which results in unhealthy dissociation. Once having fallen apart (passively), some people can re-associate to integrate, while others remain passively unintegrated. What makes the difference between these two is early object-relations. So, for the sake of clarity, the difference between Janet and Freud is less important here, because Janet's passivity is due to inherited ego weakness and Freud's is due to actual helplessness in the real actuality.

Different forms of dissociation

Dissociation, especially from a relational perspective, is a form of psychical organization in which psychical conflicts and threats to self-preservation are regulated in the mind and can be considered as a mechanism of defence when the mind cannot cope any more. The dissociative communication is not necessarily a characteristic of disposition, but it can be a warning sign that supplements and enhances the pseudo integration of psychological being, rather than true personality integration. Unhealthy dissociation I consider to be the foundation of creating a false self for those who have lost a part or the whole of themselves due to environmental impingements. With healthy dissociation, the person skilfully creates a line of defence to forming resilient constructions, which can transform the experience with some level of elasticity. This is beyond the immediate conscious mind, although it has some level of consciousness. In my work with traumatized patients, I have observed over and over how individuals seem to have an unusual capacity to dissociate (healthy and unhealthy) in order to control their mental functions such as perception, memory, and attention, as well as somatic functions, especially in certain systems available to awareness, and to reflect not so much on being in or out of the conscious state of mind. One clear example is a patient such as Daniel, who is discussed in detail in the second part of this book. Daniel is skilled at obstructing perception of a stimulus, using his persuasive phantasm. At the right moment and with the right interpretation, changes can be made in response to those stimuli that help a patient like Daniel to learn to increase or decrease the flow of his unhealthy dissociation to a manageable level of association and thinking. In contrast to Daniel, a less pathological dissociation, characteristic of a resilient patient such as Farina, who also is presented in detail later, seems to provide enhanced access to control systems that interconnect in the mind to foster a healthier function. In both types of dissociation, there is an unconscious element of functioning, and more so in unhealthy dissociation, which is driven by unconscious forces.

The notion of healthy dissociation that relates to resilience involves alterations in consciousness in which the person becomes aware of being in a state of ailment, seeking help when there is need. I hypothesize that healthy dissociation is the resilient person's response to a trauma of adult life that is due to the impact of healthy object relations in the developmental process and early personality formation.

These types of dissociation and their relation to resilience and vulnerability are distinguished from ordinary problem-solving and a matter of the ego functioning to decide what to attend to (such as whether to read a book or to watch a film in one's spare time), which Freud (1896b) discussed in terms of the two biological rules and functions of attention. Healthy dissociation and its relation to resilience is the result of a conscious choice as a coping mechanism in relation to external trauma, which also has unconscious connotations and functions.

To summarize, the notion of dissociation I am discussing is distinguished from *repression* as a neurotic process between conscious and unconscious that is determined by the need to avoid emotional pain (including specific trauma). According to Freud (1915d), repression is simply the process that attempts to turn something away from consciousness. It is the mental content that becomes unconscious and turns up in substitute forms, which could be unconscious mental representations or specific mental contents such as images, phantasies, and dream symbols. They are permanently stored in the unconscious, from where they keep manifesting themselves to consciousness in a range of transformed and disguised ways as a sublimated creative product. Freud's (1896b) earlier explanation about repression was in terms of the two biological rules and functions of attention. However, this discussion is distinguished from Freud's theory of *repression* in the 1890s, which was related to the specific notion of unconscious repression.

With regard to dissociation, and specifically in relation to Janet's dissociation, Freud (1910a) said,

> ... alongside these phenomena of diminished capacity, examples are also to be observed of a partial increase in efficiency, as though by way of compensation. At the time when Breuer's patient had forgotten her mother tongue and every other language but English, her grasp of English reached such heights that, if she was handed a German book, she was able straight away to read out a correct and fluent translation of it ... When, later on, I set about continuing on my own account the investigations that had been begun by Breuer, I soon arrived at another view of the origin of hysterical dissociation (the splitting of consciousness). [p. 22]

Freud gives an example of Breuer's patient, who, alongside of her normal state, presented a number of mental peculiarities: conditions of absence, confusion, and alternations of her character. In her normal state, she knew nothing of the pathogenic scenes or their connection with her symptoms. She had forgotten the scenes, or, at all events, had severed the pathogenic link. But, when she was hypnotized she was able to recall her memory, and, through recollection, her symptoms were removed. Freud believed the study of hypnotic phenomena helped us to understand that in one and the same individual there can be several mental groupings, which can remain more or less independent of one another, which can "know nothing" of one another and which can alternate with one another in their hold upon consciousness (ibid., p. 19). Furthermore, Freud (1915b) suggested that "the sense of repression lies simply in the function of rejection and keeping something out of consciousness" (ibid.). He expanded on this and said, "The theory of repression became the foundation-stone of our understanding of the neuroses ... It is possible to take repression as a centre and to bring all the elements of psychoanalytic theory into relation with it" (ibid., p. 300).

The type of dissociation I am discussing is also distinguished from *splitting*, which means the division of the mind into separate parts which do not communicate with one another. This is a more psychotic process, which Klein (1946) described as fragmentation and annihilation. Splitting as described by Freud (1926d) in the case of fetishism suggests the use of separate defence mechanisms to cope with the same disturbance. These explanations are also distinct from both the healthy and unhealthy dissociations I am discussing.

My discussion and assertions on dissociations (healthy and unhealthy) are also distinct from those of Sinason's (2002) work on disability and abuse, in which she addresses the dissociative phenomenon from a different angle. She has written widely on the subject of dissociative identity disorder (DID) and explains the phenomenon as conflicting models of the human mind. However, she sees dissociation as a disorder rather than a state of mind, and suggests that it is "the Mad Cow Disease of the mind" (1994, p. 4), which differs from my point of view.

My clinical observations confirm that a resilient person has the ability to experience severe trauma or neglect without a collapse of psychological functioning, and although the person may develop signs of depression and anxiety, there will be no evidence of PTSD. So, a successful act of dissociation from the unbearable memory of trauma is preventing psychological collapse. This I call a normal post trauma dissociation, which can be considered as an alteration in the extent of awareness in the context of a particular traumatic experience in adult life. For this reason, the discussion here challenges the notion that a linear relationship always exists in dissociation and psychiatric morbidity.

An overview of the historical and current conceptualizations of dissociation, methodological approaches to studying this type of dissociation, and the distinction between dissociative reactions and PTSD, is important. In psychiatry, dissociative disorders are acute or gradual, transient, or persistent disruptions of consciousness, perception, memory, or awareness. The *DSM-IV* criteria specify that DID is the presence of two or more distinct identities or personality states (each with its own relatively enduring pattern of perceiving, relating to, and thinking about the environment and the self). At least two of these identities or personality states recurrently take control of the person's behaviour, in which the person is unable to recall important personal information that is too extensive to be explained by ordinary forgetfulness and is not due to the direct effects of a substance (e.g., blackouts or chaotic behaviour during alcohol intoxication) or a general medical condition (e.g., complex partial seizures). Four types of pathological dissociative phenomena are described in *DSM-IV*, and there is a miscellaneous fifth group in Table 27–1.

The distinction between these types of dissociations is blurred, particularly when patients exhibit symptoms from more than one type. However, from a psychoanalytical viewpoint, dissociation can be considered as an unconscious separation of a group of mental processes from the rest of the psychic functions, resulting in an independent functioning of these processes and a loss of the usual associations. Dissociative identity disorder that is considered pathological in psychiatry is, in psychoanalysis, the separation of affect from cognition. It is a state of acute mental compensation in which certain thoughts, emotions, sensations, and memories may be compartmentalized because they are too overwhelming for the conscious mind to amalgamate or assimilate.

Psychoanalysis acknowledges the conjectures of disassociation in the unconscious, but relates them differently to each other and traces mental life back to the interplay between forces that prefer or hold back from one another. For example:

1. If one group of ideas remains in the unconscious, but there are conscious connotations, psychoanalysis does not conjecture that there is a constitutional incapacity for fusion which may lead to the particular types of dissociation that I am discussing.
2. Psychoanalysis also maintains that isolation and the state of unconsciousness have been caused by active opposition by other elements, such as repression. This is an unaccommodating judgement when working with the types of trauma and types of dissociation that may be employed by a traumatized patient.
3. Psychoanalysis uses concepts of repression which play important part in mental life. However, repression as a precondition of the formation of symptoms presented by patients is not enough, as it can frequently fail in the assessment and treatment of patients who have experienced trauma in adult life.

The goal of psychoanalytic treatment is to provide freedom to be curious, and to break significant defences, such as denial, disavowal, and dissociation, that defend against the fear of one's thoughts if one allowed oneself the freedom to think. In psychoanalysis, there are relationships between two fundamental experiences:

(1) the verbal reflection and non-verbal experience, and (2) the experience that has not been reflected on, and not verbalized yet. I am particularly interested in the process of the unformulated experience which is deeply felt and needed: psychic space, a sense of wonder, curiosity, the sense of explicit verbal experience as it continuously emerges and constructs, which can lead to dialogue between dissociation (both healthy and unhealthy), conjecture, and imagination. The unconscious aspects of experience can, of course, be reconceptualized by having a listening other and within transference and countertransference in the interpersonal therapeutic relationship, with continuous movement between the therapist and the patient together and the kind of relatedness which they are in.

Psychoanalytic constructivism is important, as it posits that the therapist is unavoidably embedded in, and unconsciously participates in, the therapeutic process. The clinical consequences of working with a patient who has endured trauma and reflecting on the traumatic experience within transference–countertransference interpretations helps the patient to gain insight about what persists in preventing them from knowing, and what knowing something means. Unconscious experience, interpretation, and meaning are not easily accessible to be revealed or articulated, and can at times be dissociated from. It could be material that has never been brought into consciousness, and not material that has been ejected from it. The experience is not in the foreground, but rather is unclear, uncertain, ambiguous, and created in interaction. Understanding this needs a level of language for verbalizing and communicating the understanding of the happening, and reflecting on experiences needs some psychic space. A patient with limited or lack of psychic space is unable to use vocabulary for her or his experience, and needs more time for such therapeutic interaction. But in the process, the therapist, as a good listening other, provides a containing space in which the unformed raw material of conscious and reflective experience can eventually be assigned to patients' verbal interpretations and, thereby, brings the narrative experience into an articulated form, including the seeds of words and of emotions that help to put feelings into words in a coherent language. This will result in the development of the patient's psychic space for thinking, reflecting, and relating; indeed, building a good "sense of self". Therefore, the nature of what it is possible to formulate very much

depends on creativity and limitations in the interpersonal therapeutic relationship and the power of communication. Defensively
motivated unhealthy dissociation and unformulated experience is
distinct from the repression that is keeping unconscious thoughts
out of awareness, but is coping with the anxiety of having awareness and knowledge of the traumatic experience without being able
to articulate and formulate the trauma endured.

Progress in therapy, therefore, is not simply the removal of
distortion to reveal pre-existing memories, but, rather, is a reflection
of an increased willingness and ability to interpret new experience,
and to have greater curiosity and freedom of thought. In a sense,
one could surrender and allow language to permit vague embryonic and developing senses to take their own meaningful form,
rather than forcing them in a particular direction because it is familiar and, therefore, safer for the therapist. Within the therapeutic
intervention, the patient's sense of safety can only be established by
the development of a relationship with the therapist, which will be
the beginning of a collaborative relation and process. In such a therapeutic encounter, it is probable that the therapist's countertransference is also embedded and entrenched in the realm of experience
that is not often directly held, but can be left unattended, and the
patient will find that kind of authentic experience without the therapist knowing how to make authenticity happen. By just being
there for the patient as a listening other, the therapist is humaniz-
ing the uncertain feelings regarding the most inhuman atrocities
that many patients have suffered. Following the lead of the
patient's dissociations (healthy or unhealthy) the therapist as a
listening other can create safety for the patient to develop enough
psychic space to bring what has been hurtful into a meaningful relation and develop or redevelop the patient's sense of self, which may
temporarily have been lost due to the trauma in adult life. This also
applies in the therapeutic relationship with patients whose early
environment may have been destructive and who never had the
opportunity to develop a sense of self to begin with.

Early development and healthy/unhealthy dissociation

We know that it is within a secure relationship that children begin
to regulate and integrate a distinct sense of self, which is directed

by various emotional systems. This can remain structurally dissociated due to the neglect and trauma a child may suffer. In a context of chronic traumatization, these basic developmental processes will be disturbed and eventually lead to degrees of dissociation, which is heavily dependent on the emotional systems directing them. Dissociation, therefore, becomes the defensive system of a child who is chronically affected by neglect and trauma. Such a child may adopt a simultaneous or proximate alternation of defence and emotional vulnerability, manifesting in an inability to relate to others, and also developing an intense disavowal of any relationships because of constant mistrust. The earlier and the more chronic the trauma is, the more extreme and maladaptive unhealthy dissociative behaviours will be for the individual in adult life. Secure object relations and appropriate care in childhood enables the individual to alternate between good relationships, while being autonomous and resilient, and having the ability to healthily dissociate from an unbearable traumatic situation in adult life.

For a patient who comes from a neglectful early environment, the progression of the series of disruptive intrusions, discarding the psychic space and the function of integration, prevents the development of a sense of self. The disruption of self at the level of primary affect and the consequent unhealthy dissociation can, therefore, be at a high level. It could be as if the person has enslaved and eliminated his or her own psychic space. To bring out the underlying truth that represents what the psyche does to itself when it dissociates in this way and resists reality, brings home the consequence of the lost attainment of a psychic structure that has poisoned anything within.

Healthy dissociation, in contrast, is a healthy defence, as the person consciously redirects attention away from something traumatic which might otherwise interfere with or overwhelm the psychic structure and functions. So, healthy dissociation is result of having a sense of self and enough psychic space for thinking. Healthy dissociation, therefore, is an adaptive and effective defence mechanism used to cope with the pain and fear of overwhelming trauma in which the traumatic experience is temporarily dispelled from immediate and active consciousness. By dissociating healthily from a particular experience temporarily, the person gives the psyche a break to process and digest the occurrences within a safe and sound psychic space.

This is different from normal and day-to-day dissociation, where we can separate a particular cluster of usually connected mental processes, such as our emotion and understanding, from the rest of our mind as a defence mechanism to survive a certain experience/s. For example, if in a morning before I go to work, I have a serious disagreement with a member of my family and leave home angry, sad, or disappointed, or all of these feelings together, when I go to work, as a responsible professional, I need to leave these emotions connected with my private life aside and engage fully with my work, whether clinical or otherwise. This is a conscious decision I make to dissociate myself from the upsetting situation in the morning, in order to engage with others that I have a responsibility to relate to in the professional setting. So, if I have reasonably healthy defences, I can easily dissociate myself from the morning experience in order to carry on with my daily routine because I know that if I do not do this I will have a bad day, and perhaps cause others to suffer, and, indeed, cause myself further stress, by not attending to my work and responsibilities. This does not necessarily mean that when I go back home I am not thinking about, or feeling the effects of, the incident in the morning. So, the experience, the knowledge, and the feeling of it is there, but I make a conscious decision not to prioritize it as I have other things to attend to.

I present here a vignette of unhealthy dissociation as a result of vulnerability.

Mohammed

A patient I shall call Mohammed had a big fight with his wife because he forgot their child's birthday. In part of one session, in response to a question from me, he said, "The reason is because I am deeply fearful of making close connections. I become frustrated when I get close to people. Whenever I try to have close relations with my child I get very scared, and I decide not to. I wanted to remember my child's birthday, but this would bring too much emotional connecting with my child, and when I feel connected I feel paralysed with anxiety and fear. Then I get angry and hate my wife for demanding that of me, and if she carries on like this, I get out of control with rage and I want to strangle her, to kill her . . . I hated her . . . then she starts crying . . . I really could kill her when she cries . . . I get so scared of my rage, I bit her . . . then I feel bad about it . . . then, I stop thinking about my child and my family all together."

This passage is an example of unhealthy dissociation as a result of a traumatic experience in Mohammed's early life, and specifically trauma he endured during his developmental process, which was mainly driven by the unconscious and lacks partial or total connection with reality in the here and now. The lack of sufficient psychic space prevents him from using his mental energy productively, which results in the weakening of his perception and, therefore, affects his integrative functioning. In this context, Janet's (1892–1907) reality function, as an ability to utilize the senses and mind to connect with reality, is a more relevant concept than Freud's distortion of reality principle (1895a). In contrast to unhealthy dissociation, which is cutting off from emotion, denying and disavowing feeling and reality, healthy dissociation is temporarily turning away from one's unbearable emotion consciously, with both conscious and unconscious defence mechanisms.

To demonstrate both unhealthy and healthy types of dissociation, I bring another three vignettes here: (1) an aid worker whom I call Amine, (2) a patient whom I call Ayan—both are vulnerable, (3) a resilient patient whom I call Zara. I will be brief with the first two vignettes of unhealthy dissociation, as it is easier to show this type of dissociation. Zara's vignette will be longer to maintain integrity and demonstrate the process and the healthy dissociation.

Amine

Amine came to work after having an argument with her husband and asking him to leave the house. She was agitated, and this was not the first time that her behaviour influenced other staff members' morale. She had a history of not being able to cope with her relationship and with her partner; they had had many periods of separation that she would tell her colleagues about in detail. She also, on occasions, would get into arguments with colleagues over minor misunderstandings on her part, but which she always interpreted as being victimized. Amine came from a traumatic background and had witnessed severe atrocities. However, on that specific day, in the regular weekly team meeting, she started arguing with her line manager, shouting and using abusive language. When she was asked to stop, she left the room aggressively and left the building. She did not come back to work for four weeks, sending in sick notes. Upon her return, in response to my question about how she felt, she said, "The reason I become so angry is because I feel my line manager has no ability to relate to me. She doesn't care about me and she doesn't understand me. She is deeply controlling and wants me to be fearful of her. She doesn't try to make any connection with me. She should know when I am so angry, I had a fight with my husband and she should leave me alone, but she didn't care—she has to change."

I asked Amine if she could give me an example of when she thinks her line manager does not care about her. She responded, "I don't care about an example. This is the way I feel and if you really want to help me as you are saying, you should believe me. I just don't like this woman; I can't even look at her. She makes me feel sick . . . and, I know what you are doing, although you are telling me you want to support me, you are taking her side. I don't want to carry on with this meeting."

She left the room. I arranged another meeting and she started talking about her personal life and how she was struggling and explained in detail what was devastating for her. We agreed that I would join their team meeting for a while and I suggested that in order to continue with her work in a peaceful way and be able to separate and deal with her personal and private life, she might consider seeing a therapist to discuss her issue in confidence, which she accepted.

This is a clear example of turning away from one's unbearable thoughts and emotions. Suffering from great anxiety and fear, this woman refused to accept that she was having problems and that her behaviour with her manager and her other colleagues in the team at work was not acceptable. In her personal life, she denied her children a relationship with their father as and when she wished, without any consideration for her children and her partner. She was frightened that if she allowed her partner to see her vulnerability, he would think of her as a weak woman and a bad mother, and she might lose her children.

In both situations there was a row; in the argument with her husband Amine asked *him* to leave. In the second scenario, Amine developed serious persecutory anxiety and, as a result, experienced uncontrollable anger, frustration, and fragmentation and *she* left. Amine denied her emotion and projected her feelings to her partner and to her colleagues in an intellectualizing manner. Instead of focusing on her own function and behaviour, she tried to keep her distance from others through aggression. By intellectualizing her behaviour, even some time after the event, Amine deluded herself into believing that she was right and everyone around her was at fault, colluding with the role of herself as victim. This is an example of unhealthy dissociation driven by unconscious processes, yet considered by the person concerned as a conscious decision.

Ayan

Ayan's asylum application was refused by the immigration authorities, she lost her right of appeal, and was not entitled to benefits, housing, or health services. As a destitute failed asylum seeker, she was on the street. She was raped by two men while she was sleeping in parks. Two helpful community police officers found her sitting on the street and crying (she did not speak any English). They decided to take her to the Refugee Therapy Centre with the hope that we might have someone able to communicate with her in her language. After a lengthy process involving many different members of staff, I, with one of the Community Development Workers, saw this young woman for an assessment. She was quite hysterical and at times in tears and unable to sit still. As she calmed down, she was able to disclose that she was raped the day before. She could not sit comfortably on the chair. I thought she might have been hurt badly. I asked her whether the man who raped her was aggressive and whether she was badly hurt and she was in pain. She responded, in short saying, "No, I am not in pain as such ..." I then asked the reason that she was in such physical discomfort. In tears, she said, "I am bleeding and I do not have a sanitary towel; I am worried about staining your beautiful and comfortable chair."

Ayan's presentation fully corresponds with her feeling of homelessness and her helplessness. This culminated in her lack of psychic space, and psychotic loss of her inner world, which was full of horror and violence. She lost the capacity to cope and deal with her experience. She lost the experience of possessing her body and, consequently, her inner and outer world were fragmented. Although in tears, she could not relate to the memory of her experience of being raped after her asylum application had been rejected by the Home Office. She had no sense of self and no psychic space to process her experience. Her psyche was filled with emptiness, fused with a void—a psychotic state of mind.

What was particularly significant in Ayan's account was her focus on her immediate needs regarding her bodily processes; with my question about her physical discomfort, she became increasingly preoccupied with her need for a sanitary towel. This suggests that the way she symbolized her own bodily rhythms and functions is implicated in the way she conceptualized the workings of her body and its processes, and this in turn influenced the way she related to her psychic pain. She did not have the ability to focus on her experience of rape, but just enough psychic space to have some level of connection and to talk about her bleeding. Her bleeding was her way of dissociating herself from her whole experience of rape, and, in transference, she projected her feelings to me—her listening other—through her bombshell pattern of communicating, and telling me that we had beautiful and comfortable chairs, while she was homeless and destitute. When I asked her whether she wanted to talk about what had happened to her the day before, she said, "There is nothing to talk about . . . I was raped . . . by two men . . . that is all . . . I am bleeding now and I need a sanitary towel."

This is another typical presentation of an unhealthy dissociation which results from vulnerability that is driven by the unconscious and disables Ayan from healthy dissociation of the trauma she endured. She developed an immediate and unusual attachment to me and my colleague. She lost her sense of self and did not have enough psychic space to accept that I, as her listening other, despite not breaking down at the severity of her unimaginable traumatic experience, did not have a magic touch to help her, so, she could only work on projection. Although she was able to cry, she did not have sufficient psychic space to hold on to her memory and needed me to feel her pain, her anger, and her sense of injustice, which, in countertransference, I was feeling quite strongly.

Zara

Zara came to therapy with an aspect of resilience that she felt she had lost. From the beginning, her psychopathology led her to alternate between relatively stable defences and masochistic tendencies. The principal objective for my therapeutic approach with Zara was to assess the intensity of her trauma, her age when it occurred, her level of resilience, and the pattern of her dissociations, indeed, her sense of self and current level of psychic space. I observed a clear pattern of splitting in her, which was to protect her sense of self from being irreparably attacked, hence, a healthy part and a sado-masochistic, attacking, internalized object part.

In transference, she desired closeness, but when she felt a bond between us, she would become terrified and withdraw. She would then feel cut off and rejected, and begin to yearn for attachment again. These transferential fears and re-enactments provided the opportunity to look at Zara's past object relations. This helped her, and she began to understand that the closer she felt to someone, the more she had the phantasy of being dominated. She had a tendency to minimize the devastating possibilities of the pain of rejection, pain of disharmony and of being attacked, but, at that stage of therapy, she could not refer to any particular memory. In the therapeutic process, she gained insight to the fact that any closeness represented to her deprivation and loss of autonomy, yet the lack of connectedness raised the phantom of rejection, abandonment, and banishment. She gradually realized that her need for fulfilment led her to take refuge in a political party, campaigning against inequality, working for, and giving to, charities, being a good mother, sister, daughter, partner, and friend, but never feeling comfortable in making or engaging in a meaningful relationship. By this stage (four months into therapy), I was using confrontational interpretation, which was experienced by Zara as attacking, so she considered ending therapy, but she felt guilty and decided to continue.

In one session, I said,

"I can see the thought of me criticizing you makes you feel exposed and brings a lot of conflict to your mind. Your understanding is that if I care about you, I should always be able to share your thoughts and feelings and understand what is going on in your mind and how you feel. When I don't, you are anxious as to whether we are having a relationship or not, and, more importantly, whether you are in control, and this conflict is very uncomfortable for you . . ."

She interrupted, "The point is that I am afraid when the possibility of talking becomes real . . . because I can't cope any more . . . I can't do it . . . and that is disturbing to my normal being . . . I don't know who I am any more . . . I can't afford to be disturbed and depressed like this . . . you don't take my feelings into account when you question me like this . . . I feel I am being attacked instead of being helped . . ."

I decided not to respond to her complaint about my confrontational interpretation and to continue the process, so I said,

"I can see that our discussion of your personal feelings and concerns has affected you painfully. But I wonder if you realize that you focus on your responsibilities, which is certainly related to all of this, but not so closely to your pain. It sounds to me as though you think of your success of being a good mother or good worker or a good friend as more important than your need and wish to be happy and comfortable. Could it be that you are fulfilling your responsibilities and enjoying being needed, rather than enjoying what you do?"

She said, "You are right. I can be in the middle of some enjoyment, and be caught up in confusion . . . of thinking . . . am I right or wrong? I sometimes feel I'm like an abandoned innocent little girl. When I am here, I don't mind this, but life cannot be all therapy. I know for sure that I don't like confrontation or argument. Sometimes I feel misunderstood by people and then I feel the way they have interpreted me is not even close to what I meant to say. Sometimes I think this may be a language barrier, and I try to improve my English. But here is so different. I feel understood here . . . and that scares me, it makes me feel so lonely . . . Do you understand what I am trying to say?"

This was a point at which, with her honesty, Zara began to discover what kind of stress had damaged her resilience. Through this insight she developed more psychic space. She realized that when she feels abandoned she is unable to listen fully or attend to other people's needs, or express herself clearly, and this made her feel lonely and isolated.

I said, "If I understood you correctly, you feel tormented and fearful as you are not able to integrate into your new environment. Although, as you have said many times, you feel privileged in comparison with other refugee women, in communication with others you dare not to say anything to clarify your position when there is disagreement. You are afraid of being wrong or misunderstood because of the constraints you feel about expressing yourself. All your worries about your relationships with others are taking place internally in your mind, so it is not surprising that you feel so stressed, confused, and lonely."

Zara gave an example of an incident in detail and the pain she had been through. At the time, she had hidden her feelings and pretended that she was all right, because she had "self-respect" and did not want to be bullied any more by the person she was referring to.

I said, "My guess is that you tried to protect your integrity by hiding how deeply painful the experience was for you. It seems to me that when you feel so strongly in your encounters, you find it hard to imagine that the other person could not know how you feel, since the experience to you is total pain and despair at that particular time."

She said, "Yes, but I'm sure people know. People I am talking about are not stupid and they know I am not stupid. I know how vindictive people can be. The way people talk about refugees, asylum seekers, and black people, and the way they say 'I don't mean you or people like you' make me feel sick to my stomach."

After this statement, Zara was silent for a long time, and in tears. Although I was aware that my interpretation might be painful for her, this time I assessed that she had sufficient psychic space and I decided to continue to throw doubt on her belief that others knew what she felt, in the hope that she would be able to focus on what others might think and feel out of her phantasy. She did not respond to my interpretation with insight, but we revisited this theme on several occasions until the reflection was made and she realized that others cannot read her mind and that it is helpful for her not to try to do so either.

Reflecting on Zara's presentation, it is possible to see that she might at times have felt my intervention to be confrontational, so she would shift her thoughts to confrontational experiences repeated in transference for her due to the trauma she had endured. In one session, I returned to an issue that she had started to talk about three times before. (This was related to a man who had housed her and paid for all her needs since her asylum application was rejected. After a month of being in his house, the man went to her bed, and, due to her circumstances, she felt unable to say no to him.) Initially, she showed interest, and engaged in communicating her feelings, but she stopped and switched to a different issue, holding herself together and controlling her tears by straightening her back against the chair and taking very deep breaths, starting to talk in a calm and contented manner about learning English. Here, she was clearly dissociating herself from the unbearable memory of her experience. Her dissociation here is healthy, and a sign of her resilience. This was evidence that she possessed a good sense of self and the ability to control her emotion without falling apart. She knew that she needed to work on that particular traumatic experience and to engage with it, but was able to stop herself from remembering it when became too unbearable for her.

Zara reverted to a discussion about others' treatment of her, and to the belief that people wanted to harm her deliberately. I ignored this, and instead interpreted what she had said in terms of her fear leading her to keep her dialogue inside herself. Zara's response was to describe another incident in which she was afraid to engage others outwardly, in what sounded to me like the schizoid distortion of reality that goes with a lack of insight and lack of resilience. This, I thought, was related to her persecutory anxiety related to thinking and reflecting on the man who was her rescuer but became her abuser.

Focusing on our clinical encounter above, my interventions were intended to clarify what had actually happened between Zara and the man in question, and what had happened in Zara's mind. I asked Zara two questions, and offered the clarifying comment that this person and other people she referred to were probably unaware of her pain and her emotions resulting from how she perceived their behaviour. Although she did not respond to this directly, she did respond to my acknowledgement of the deep pain she felt.

Assuming she had not taken in my clarification because she felt criticized by it, I then took the sting out of my comment by interpreting for her why she did not realize the person she was talking about was unaware of the depth of her feelings. This time her response was more accepting; she took in and expanded upon my interpretation. By sublimating that, she stopped her unhealthy and, indeed, unconscious dissociation, and as a result was able to reclaim some of her resilience, which had been lost as the result of her "environmental impingements".

In many sessions before and after this process, we focused on Zara's experiences as a working professional in London and the prejudice and racist attitudes that she felt she encountered as a result. However, in this particular session, I did not bring in this aspect of her beliefs, as I wanted to turn her attention to her relationship with others and away from what others thought of her. I was hoping that she could feel connected again. I thought it would be useful for her to gain insight into her feelings and thoughts in that particular kind of relationship and into her inability to express her feelings and thoughts before getting extremely frustrated and angry and becoming severely confrontational. In a much later session, as Zara reclaimed her lost resilience, she talked about the profound effect of kindness she had received from this very person she was complaining of as being racist. She said that this type of recognition and understanding has been very helpful for her, enabling her to accept limitations in relationships. She felt that with this insight her confidence and self-esteem increased and she developed a better sense of self and better capacity to relate to people.

Zara's feedback and assessment of herself and changes she has made in relating to others is evidence that my continuing with interpretations that confronted her false beliefs and presecutory anxiety was the right clinical intervention. She was able to realize and verbalize aspects of her internalized object relations, her defences, and the way they affected her identification systems. Her ability to reclaim her lost resilience was the result of good early object relations. Zara's presentation and the changes she made is evidence which implies that a stable personality trait might be temporarily weakened or lost due to traumatic experiences, but can be reclaimed. For example, the man Zara trusted became her object relation at the time that she needed him, but he betrayed her trust.

However, her good enough past object relation was there, helping her to seek therapeutic help and pick herself up again. Zara herself indicated that in therapy she felt she had a listening other who helped her to think, reflect, and build her sense of self and regain her lost resilient self.

In another session, referring to her vulnerability and her need for closeness she said,

> "See, when I am talking about things here, together we can make sense of them, but I know I can't grasp that by myself and do it. Sometimes I know what I need to do, but I just can't make myself do it, I can't trust myself."

> I fed back to her, "We both know you used to be able to do this, and without realizing it, you are referring to the time before you lost part of your self."

> Zara agreed with this, felt relieved and said she now understood what I had meant when I was talking about her childhood and the effect of not having her mother emotionally available to her in her adolescence, even though she had her strong, healthy presence in her childhood.

Here, I employed two modes of intervention. The first was to simply point out Zara's maladaptive patterns of behaviour. I relied on her to do the rest, as I hypothesized that she only had to recover some of her resilience in order to observe her own behaviour and modify it in her own interests. This proved to be an accurate prediction. I also attempted to legitimize and validate Zara's pulling back and waiting for reassurance, while at the same time noting her self-protective, defensive nature. I was aware that pointing out her defences with a confrontational interpretation would have been felt as hostile, but I hypothesized that it was a necessary course of intervention. However, I was still concerned that she would not be able to make use of it, and instead of sublimation, it might drive her to dissociation and emotional withdrawal from treatment in order to protect herself, but she engaged with it and, therefore, my hypothesis proved right.

Zara's meaningful silences became more present in the process. On occasions, her silence was an expression of dependency, an active attempt to get me to help her, to save her the unpleasantness of having to think back and try to remember. I would not comply with her expectation. This, indeed, was helpful, and encouraged Zara to make the necessary change and feel confident about recalling the information herself. In one long silence, she attempted to get me to take a more active role. She said "I realized something", and then waited for me to ask about it. I decided not to respond and leave the space to her. This encouraged her to work on her thoughts without depending on me or needing my reassurance and encouragement. This result in further changes and enhanced her autonomy and resilience.

For a period, the focus of our work was on Zara's obsessions, which induced her anxiety and disposed her to a sense of guilt, gratifying her ideas of punishment for phantasies about having intimacy with her father and feeling guilty. It became apparent that the foundation of this lay in her relationship with her mother, who was unresponsive to Zara's emotional needs in her adolescence. Whenever we succeeded in Zara identifying an example of irrational behaviour and thought that was destructive, a pattern in which she had lived for so long, she usually reacted with surprise and curiosity, and showed interest in further exploration. She would bring, and make associations with, dreams and memories, the effects of which she was previously unaware. She would come to a session still concerned about a question left unanswered or unresolved in the previous session, report her dreams and recent experiences and thoughts, shedding new light on the issue.

In the transference, Zara sometimes wanted me to be a nurturing mother, to make her feel good and at peace, and to protect her from the bad world, and not as her therapist and her listening other, helping her grow by exploring uncomfortable areas of her experiences. This was related to her internal representation of her parents. Sometimes, she saw me as an indulgent but repressive object, rather than a therapist whose job it was to support her to gain insight, autonomy, and resilience. My countertransference did not match her internal representation of her parents. However, we were able to reach the stage when I could safely assume a sense that she and I were partners, working together in an exploratory process within a therapeutic alliance. As a result, Zara's new-found calm led to a reintegration of herself and a better understanding of her object world. Moreover, she was calmed by her discovery of the possibility of her split object relation, rather than combined invasion. This discovery evolved from her experience of preserving herself in the transference with me. She was able to recover what belonged to her as something of her own, but this was now combined with my containing function as her listening other. She could identify with this in order to contain herself, and, through this process, regain her autonomy and resilience. Through interpretation of her projection in transference, I presented myself as a good object, as I felt that she needed to own and internalize a good object, rather than feeling empty and lonely. I also made use of other aspects of her object world, which she presented in transference: for example, interpretations of the invading or persecutory object, her mother as she had experienced her in her early adolescence. This helped Zara to discover her identification with the little girl whom she had projected on to me, and began to withdraw the projection, achieve a better sense of self, and to feel more integrated. With those feelings, she came to recognize her hostility towards her depressed mother. Since her love was no less strong than her hatred, a violent defensive conflict resulted, and her negative impulses were slowly replaced by more psychic space and peacefulness, thus enabling her to regain her resilience. She realized that as a little girl she was not deprived of her mother's love. She realized that torturing herself with self-accusations and feeling bad and inferior throughout her adolescence was, to a great extent, part of her development, and she did not need to feel guilty about it now.

We reached a stage where she gained a solid sense of self and enough psychic space and resilience to be able to love part of her mother and to feel that a great part of her was loved by her mother. Following this insight and changes of this kind, Zara began to distance herself further from the object world, becoming more alive and dynamic in the process. She became able to see how she had been using the mechanisms of introjections and projection. She began to reflect, identifying processes of introjection, projection, and projective identification. In the transference, the relationship she established with me, like any other object relationship, was made up of a never-ending complementary movement of introjections and projection. When the introjected object tended to occupy too much space in her, I considered that consciousness of her capacity to project part of herself on to me would help her to differ-entiate and separate herself from the object—she would dissociate healthily.

For, when separation anxiety became excessive for her, her projective identification tended to increase, and she would move towards unhealthy dissociation. Having me as her listening other, who interpreted her projections, created insight in her, which contributed to her abandoning her masochistic and narcissistic identification. Interpretations of projective identification encour-aged the formation of stronger ego structures in her, by means of gathering together the essential aspects of her ego, with continuous reorganization, representing changes in her ego structure, con-stantly seeking realization and unification. This allowed her further psychic space, something that is central for healthy dissociation and, therefore, resilience.

Conclusion

This chapter centres on the concept of dissociation. The argument is based around the notion of there being healthy and unhealthy forms of dissociation employed by traumatized people, resulting in resilience and vulnerability, respectively. It is proposed that trau-matized people who avoid psychological collapse (such as PTSD) after a traumatic experience do so through a successful act of healthy dissociation. I am also making the case that the old nine-teenth-century concept and defence mechanism of dissociation, is, and always has been, very useful. Based on my clinical experience, this is especially the case for those who have suffered external trauma in adult life. I described the concept of dissociation (healthy and unhealthy) as distinct from definitions offered by the *DSM-IV*, as discussion is consistent with psychoanalysis. I also make a distinction from the psychoanalytic term of repression, and split-ting is outlined.

Vignettes provide substance for testing the hypotheses as part of the empirical study, which links back to the chapter on method-ology. To support the hypotheses and to further develop the theory, the illustrations and outcomes in this chapter provide evidence of how, by having a therapist as a listening other, patients are

more able to develop a better sense of self, develop more psychic space, and the ability to use healthy dissociation, and, by
doing so, gain or regain some resilience, thus becoming less vulnerable.

CHAPTER SEVEN

A non-clinical encounter

Boris

Here, I write about a meeting with a person whom I shall call Boris, who had been in power in the running of an African country. I mainly focus on the aftermath of trauma in his unhealthy dissociative manner. He and much of his family had suffered tremendous trauma prior to him coming into power. This is not a clinical vignette; it is an observation based on a discussion with this man. I would like to emphasize that at the time, I was not fully aware of the negative effect this man had on me. I was clearly disassociating from the unpleasant experience I was having and the anger and frustration that I felt. I listened to his entire narrative, much as a therapist or supervisor would, looking for those features in which I could be guided by psychoanalytic concepts. I could see that his portrayal of humanity was false and that he was aware of this.

I will give a few brief factual presentations that I encountered with him. I use the sense of self here as an existential function that is connected to object relations, which depends on the socio-cultural circumstances, and the central aspects of the loss of a socio-cultural environment. I also use the term psychic space, but it is less experiential or existential, being based instead on one's identity and ability to have a sense of the self, rather as the psychic structure is correlated with sense of self, but in a different conceptual framework. I use both terms, equating a coherent psychic space as a structure of the mind with having a sense of self, and use the terms interchangeably.

I will explore the loss of psychic space and the forces that gave rise to some atrocious hardships going on under his authority and his inability or helplessness to see these. The dissociative discussion here is a descriptive model of a traumatic experience in adult life, the persistence of traumatic memories, and the general characteristics of post traumatic dissociation. I look at Boris's inner images of himself and others, from an object relations perspective, and how this man and others with similar experiences manifest themselves in interpersonal situations. Although object relation theoretical stances concerning idealization, persecutory anxiety, and their effects on the integration of the ego are the foundation of the inner object, I assert that the types of dissociation in response to trauma have generally been ignored. I observed that the structure of Boris's ego was full of fragmentation that signalled the possibility of implosion. His psychic structure resulted from the external pressure, which was much greater than his internal resources. As the result of his destructiveness, he was unhealthily dissociating himself from part of reality and part of himself in order to escape that which haunted him from within, seeking a repetition of the trauma he had endured by projecting it out without any identification or insight at the conscious level. Through this mechanism, he, in his mind, was perfecting his thinking and protecting himself from any knowledge of his motives and of his actual, devastating, unconscious intentions.

As I listened to Boris, I was struck by the distinct twist with which he gave evidence of himself and others without affect, but with tension and tolerance. It became clear that Boris was not able to connect with his objects from the past or present, imaginary or real, and displayed a lack of any engagement as if this had nothing to do with what he was saying, resulting from enactment and unhealthy dissociation. He was able to recall the content of memories, but no reflection of moral judgement—just his horror and his reaction. There were definite and unique indications of intellectual reflective functioning leading him to enactment and dissociation. Boris's object representations were very limited and restricted, and any interpretations were completely disavowed by him. I noted how difficult it was for me not respond to him as his therapist. I also felt in many instances that I was making judgements and wanted to show my disagreement with his narratives. This was a projection of dissociated parts of him into me, specifically, the function of moral judgement.

The type of dissociation between his conscious claims and his unconscious was important, but I could not measure it clinically. In line with object relations theory and his patterns of coping, I observed him to have two different functions: (1) insecure regulatory strategies in reacting to separation reminders, and (2) inability to maintain proximity in order to relate to others in a meaningful way. This reflects a failure of his anxious hyper-activated strategy that was so catastrophic for him that it was unconsciously associated with personal death. However, since he was not my patient and the case is not clinical, it is important to emphasize that my analysis is purely speculative and for the purpose of illustration. With this proviso, I now bring example of our encounters.

In a meeting, I said to him, "I know how angry you are with your enemy and this has a background to it. Could you please take a minute to think about what happened to your mother and tell me about it?"

He responded well, but only for two minutes, and then drifted away again. It was clear that he adopts a dissociative strategy to distance himself from a stressful, lethargic memory by diverting his attention, thus restraining and deeply inhibiting it. His avoidance of reality and his deactivation strategies for dealing with separation reminders provided strong evidence of unhealthy dissociation. In his presentation, he elaborated encoding information rather than actively repressing it from memory. In other words, the regulatory strategy Boris used was to hold distressing material outside of his awareness and memory right from the start, not thinking about and relating to his experience, but thinking that what people did was wrong and he should put it right.

I asked him about peace and justice for all (which is something he claimed and constantly insisted that he believed in). He said,

"People like you in the western world have only seen one-sided justice, and a great number of these crimes have not been investigated and some perpetrators and guilty parties not prosecuted, and you want to accuse us of not respecting justice."

I said, "For all you said, you don't see it as important to call upon all your community members to step up and work towards ending the culture of impunity that is widespread in your country."

Boris said, "Impunity has been granted and these atrocities happened to *us*, which delays voluntary repatriation and undermines any efforts at national reconciliation."

I said, "Do you think it is likely that this contributed to a new escalation in the cycle of violence?"

He nodded and continued, "I was very disturbed by the very substantial document I received stating complicity with the greatest killer since Hitler. They are now accusing our state of perpetuating the universal theory of the genocide which, according to my people, might not be as simple as the way it has been explained on the airwaves in the west."

I said, "Look, I understand that we cannot go into all the details, some of which makes me shudder with horror, but if it is true and such crimes against humanity have remained unpunished because of complicity, it is necessary to ask questions, and also to demand an impartial investigation. Do you agree with this and do you think it is possible, and will you support it—tell me please?"

He said, "Two strangers came to my house. One of them was in military uniform and was carrying an automatic gun; the other was wearing civilian dress, but was carrying a revolver under his shirt; he was a higher ranking officer. They requested to see my father in person by name, but our guard was smart enough to say that he was not there. They said they would be back later in the afternoon . . . There was no time to waste; we assembled a few items in rush, and managed to run away, but on the way they stopped our vehicle . . . they carried my father in a most inhuman way across the road. I thought my mother and I had just escaped from death, knowing that my father would be murdered. That was the moment that my father lost his life . . . my last memory of him was him howling in his own blood in pain . . . blood was everywhere . . . Many people witnessed the most atrocious acts done to their families, and they suffered more than any human should . . . they had seen so much with their very eyes . . . I told you before what they did to my mother and how she died in front of me, so, you tell me, how can we forget . . . you tell me how you would feel."

I was not prepared for this question, while I was feeling so appalled and sickened by his narratives about his "enemy". As I was thinking about how to respond to him, I realized that I was not able to dissociate myself immediately; I had developed a headache and physically was feeling sick as I listened to his detailed descriptive account. Although I was very careful not to treat him as my patient, I could not stop myself from making a comment about my headache on hearing what had happened to him and about his lack of emotional engagement with his own memory.

He was less defensive now, and said, "My emotions have been under the strain of my attempted self-control in order to do my job and do well for my community. I have to harden myself for others. I cannot do my job if I am emotional."

I said, "I am sure you are aware that you never forget, but I wonder how you deal with your memory."

He responded with vivid details. I will not go into detail about the events that related to his history, as they include extremely disturbing factual information that I have observed personally. Given the sensitive nature of these facts, the reader will understand that they cannot be fully revealed because of the necessity to protect Boris's anonymity as well as the psychological protection of readers of his account.

However, leaving that part of his narrative aside, Boris continued, saying, "Since the beginning of the conflict, there have been discrepancies concerning the number of people still present in this area. The reports state that many returned home; the only people who failed to return are those who have been involved with the genocide and it is therefore legitimate for them to be chased cross the border."

As we continued talking, I observed that the dissociative nature of his traumatic memories and the value of his abreaction in resolving them were related to his own terrifying experiences. It was clear that he was really trying to control himself. I asked him whether he was all right. He said that his memories were recurring with hallucinatory vividness without him being able to end it, and it is this that triggers his powers of action and speech, and not the direct suggestion of killing for revenge. He saw this as an ordinary method of healing.

I added, "And perhaps healing from the wounds of such atrocities that you have experienced." (To my surprise, I found myself for the first time feeling sympathetic towards him, but I decided that I did not want to think about it at that moment as I did not want to divide my attention.)

Boris said, "I have no time to be sentimental and this type of sentimentality is for people who don't have anything else to do. We have lots of work to do here."

Putting emphasis on his remembering and his dissociation, I thought Boris was generalizing his pain as his community's issue, so I asked him whether he remembered clearly all that had happened to him and his family. There was no emotional expression as he went through more of his severe traumatic experiences in great detail. In the process of recalling his memories, although he was becoming tearful, he held himself back and I wondered whether these memories could ever be relived with emotional vividness and whether he could ever stay with them, deal with them reflectively, and become able to dissociate more healthily, and perhaps have control over his behaviour and actions.

I said, "I can see you do not wish to talk about you, but rather about your community as a whole. However, coming to the issue of people in the region, the huge loss of human life is a tragedy. I hear, on the one hand, that you are saying that your policy is aimed at preventing any foreign intervention in favour of those who remain here; on the other hand, you want to attract the maximum of foreign aid, and you also said that you are in favour of community reconstruction and reconciliation. How this is possible while you are still of the view that all these people are perpetrators and it is for that reason that they still remain in the camp around the borders, bearing in mind that we are talking about well over a million people? To my knowledge, most of the men lost their lives, and the majority of those remaining are women and young children."

He said, "What do you know—you don't know anything—you don't know what they have done to us . . . you don't know what they would do, if we let them once again . . ."

I said, "I know that in comparison to you, my knowledge is very limited. Of course it is. But I saw many wounded people in a relatively serious condition, some with shotgun wounds, others injured by bomb fragments. It is impossible accurately to state their numbers, but incidents seem to be increasing. I only visited one centre and I saw more than a hundred wounded, so it is difficult to say, and I assume no one knows, how many people are injured, how many are dead, and how many are dying. In explaining the situation, you referred to rebels. In my visits, I did not see rebels, but very deprived, simple families. I did not see anyone who wished to pursue conflict. The great number of mass graves that I came across attests to a systematic intent to annihilate those people, and it is a fact that they have been considered as a military target by army. These mass graves are everywhere, but they are carefully hidden and located in areas that are difficult to access. I was told that it is extremely dangerous for people to be found in an area where mass graves are located and to be caught there leads to the person's immediate execution."

He stopped me and asked, "How many mass graves have you seen?"

I said, "I saw three mass graves. Bodies included women carrying babies on their backs, children, and elderly people. Each person had a bullet in the head, even the babies. I saw at the far end of the camp, on the border, in the small wood which serves as the borderline, piles of skeletons. There, too, the bodies had one bullet in the head . . . there are people who have been feeding themselves with plants, and drinking rainwater. I met a young woman exhausted from dehydration, and despite our efforts to help her, she died in our hands. Walking back to the car, I saw the body of another woman dead from exhaustion while giving birth, with a half-born baby and the body of another child of approximately four years old lying next to her. No doubt her child died of hunger and loneliness. Helping those people is considered by your people as helping the enemy and actively supporting perpetrators. It is difficult for me to understand, having been there and witnessed who they are, how one can consider a vulnerable child as a perpetrator. I understand you may say the child allegedly is the child of a perpetrator. Do you agree with me that this type of generalization is false, and a child is a child, just as you were a child who had to survive the many traumatic events you encountered?

"I also saw a dying man, abandoned on the road. This man had deep wounds from a machete on his head and body. Through one open wound, I could see his brain. He was left there, dying. I asked him who did that to him, and he said, the army men. I asked whether he has his family to take care of him and if he wanted us to take him home. He answered that his wife, all his children and his siblings had been killed, apart from his brother, who is psychologically not well and could not care for himself. He said that his brother was there, but abandoned him on the road to save his own life."

Suddenly, and out of control, Boris cried, "Bastard . . . he escaped . . ."

I was shocked by his reaction, as Boris claimed to be a man who has the capacity for ethical reflection in a robust manner which is based on his vigorous belief in human rights. As this is not a clinical case, I can only speculate that his view of his beliefs tends to collapse through his unhealthy dissociation, and in relation to his enemy, he dissociates himself from his own beliefs in human rights. One assumes that his dissociation can be considered as an ordinary human response in the given circumstances, and a way of dealing with his pain and his guilt about surviving. However, in my observation, I thought that he was triggered more by a regressive slide into states of mind that are endemically defensive by constant processes of dissociation while his distorted mental states were co-existing for him behind the façades of routine, stable, day-to-day functioning and "doing good for the community", as he put it. The extreme destructiveness and the conjoining of his psyche with the minds of his group converge with the progressive dismantling of the subjectivity of the other, which led to social disturbances in which he, in his mind, on behalf of his group, lost any internal cohesion. This is a clear example of unhealthy dissociative reactions. It is characterized by fluctuating back and forth, affecting others, and transmitting the possibility of him and his group rapidly regressing into unhealthy dissociative modes, dissociating themselves from the reality of becoming perpetrators as the result of the trauma and humiliation they have suffered.

However, at this point I was boiling with anger and frustration. I gathered my thoughts as much as I could and said, "I was under the impression that you do not agree with violence, but you don't seem to be disagreeing with a vulnerable wounded man dying in the street under your authority . . ."

He said, "You and people like you were not here to see what they did . . ."

I said, "Can't you see that you are doing the same?"

He said, "No—you are blind to the reality. You are closing your eyes on what they have done . . ."

I said, "I condemn what 'they' may have done. I condemn and am very sorry about what happened to you and your family, indeed to your community. It is difficult for me even to read the evidence of trauma and atrocities inflicted on your community. No, I am not blind to seeing the reality. I do not agree with what 'they' have done, but I am asking you, and I beg for an answer, why you are doing something that you know is inhuman. You yourself have been on the receiving end of it; you know its hurt; you know it is unbearable; you know it is wrong; you know—even after all these years have passed—you still cannot stop thinking about how you lost your father and your mother . . . why are you doing it to others when you are a man who believe in human rights? Please help me to understand your situation."

He said, "You need to know the history of what happened to us the way we are experiencing it, not the glamorized western model presented by American, British, French, German, and Dutch journalists . . . Do you think I like this?"

I said calmly, but with conviction and sincerity, "I don't know. Do you? . . . Is it helping you, not thinking about your mother and how you lost her? Is it helping you not to feel guilty for surviving your father? Is it helping you to deal with your inability to grieve for your losses? Is it helping you to dissociate yourself from reality and the meaning of reality that you are creating? Is it making you feel a better or a happier person to kill a member of the community who killed your loved ones? You are the only one who can tell me."

He broke down, weeping for a long time. He then apologized for crying, and said, "A man, and especially a man in power, cannot and should not cry. This is the first time I have cried in my adult life, and I hope it will be the last time."

This was a very important moment because he had integrated again to the point of having an overwhelming affect, in spite of the fact that he was mostly detaching himself from feeling. He associated himself with his reality, which he did not like.

He said, "Cutting myself off from emotions in some way provided me with a great liberation."

This confirmed that his constant unhealthy dissociation is a prime result of post trauma. The restoration of his emotional expression seemed to be the most important element of his acting out as the consequence of his traumatic memory of the scene that he so desperately needed to dissociate from.

In this meeting, we had almost five hours of conversation, to the point that I felt totally drained and did not have the energy to continue any longer, although he seemed keen to continue talking. This man clearly displayed predictable signs of malignant narcissistic dissociation, with a strong illusion of believing in peace and justice, denying his instinctive impulses and those flare-ups of violence. His perception of reality and the collapse of his psychic space was the foundation of losing his sense of self, his flexibility of thinking, his ability for empathic understanding, his tolerance for ambiguity and his capacity for mourning his traumatic losses. He let himself become fixated by an increasingly concrete, simplistic, rationalistic and paranoid search for answers and the illusion of safety by creating an unsafe environment for others. He presented three important aspects: unhealthy dissociation consciously, the loss of his sense of self as an individual, and not having the listening other to deal with his traumatic experience and his unmourned losses. Despite his questionable manner and level of abreaction, I dared asking him to help me to understand his situation and his way of thinking. His explanation and his conception of his emotional memory were attached to the existence of a separate and distinct explosive energy in his mind, which was connected to his memory, and discharged by his political function: while he was part of the killing, he dissociated himself from being killed and, indeed, of being the killer.

In contrast to a healthy dissociation of the traumatic memory, which can help a return to health and integration, the unhealthy dissociation needs the recollection of the traumatic experience in all of its details, including the emotional component, which Boris would not allow himself to do. So, the essential step for integration is the removal of the unhealthy dissociation to the traumatic memories, which then creates the possibility of overcoming violent tendencies that were maintaining Boris's ongoing unhealthy dissociation.

In contrast to Boris, many resilient people that I work with who are able to dissociate healthily present much less fragmentation, less anxiety and avoidance dimensions, are less threatened by potentially distressing situations, and function better. They can experience and express emotions and not become lost in a precipitation of negative memories and worries. They seek support when they are under too much stress and use constructive means of healthy dissociation as a coping strategy. As they dissociate healthily, they feel comfortable exploring new stimuli and are not hostile; indeed they are more empathic towards people in need. People with unhealthy dissociation, like this man, exhibit no affects compatible with the notion of resilience and healthy dissociation strategies, including exclusion of painful thoughts and memories of trauma they have endured that they are not able to deal with. Instead, one of the features of their dissociation is the extreme depersonalization of objects, which are simply not considered as persons, as demonstrated by Boris, who had no moral or ethical response to them as persons. Although these types of dissociation have unconscious connotations, they are made at conscious levels of responding to unbearable thoughts and feelings. People like Boris, who present high levels of unhealthy dissociation, also exhibit defensive projections, fail to notice or acknowledge their own hostility, and consciously deny their anxiety about their own death and annihilation. They exhibit a variety of affects, including projective identification, and are eager to give narratives rather than accessing painful memories; those have the content of their memories, but not the affect. Freud (1894) described this kind of separation in the content of memory from the affect, especially in relation to obsessional states, indicating that the person with this type of memory function, or, rather, dysfunction, has the potential to spread negative thoughts from one remembered incident to another in paradoxical cognitive closures in response to a positive affect induction, and is not able to regulate negative emotional memories, although he remains preoccupied with the memory of events, only able to think that these things should not happen and to act on this thought.

My encounter with Boris is based on an in-depth interview rather than clinical intervention; I gathered that making any changes at that stage of his life seemed to be difficult for him. As this was not a clinical example, I decline to make further comments or to draw a conclusion.

PART II
CASE STUDIES

CHAPTER EIGHT

Introduction to case studies

H ere, in the second part, the cases of two patients are presented in detail: Farina, who came to therapy with some resilience, and Daniel, who came with great vulnerability, and the characteristics they both brought to the treatment and their transference relations are explored. They both used dissociation as a defence to keep themselves functional in their social setting. The focus in both cases is around how the human mind develops resilience and how psychoanalytic intervention can enhance resilience in patients. It is challenging, but I look at the clinical material as evidence and my focus is on the feasibility of using transference and countertransference as a test, experienced in phantasies, a partial idealization, and in aggression, which was conveyed through the way patients presented and how they built up in transference in different ways. I clarify what changes take place in the process (the outcome), and how those changes come about through the interactions of certain factors in the patient, the therapist, the therapeutic alliance (transference and countertransference), and the evolving life situation (the process). This method generates hypotheses but does not test its tenets experimentally against competing hypotheses. This is partly because the methodology of psychoanalysis does not allow controlled conditions or quantitatively varying stimuli, and partly because analysis of each patient is unique, not exactly repeatable as a standard testing model. I am using the concept of transference in clinical work as a framework, in which something is always going on, where there is always movement and activity as an essential tool of the analytic process, observing how the patient's relationship to their objects is transferred, in all its richness, to the therapist. An example is how patients try to draw the therapist into their defensive systems, how they unconsciously act out with the therapist in the transference, trying to get the therapist to act out with them, and how they convey aspects of their inner world built up from infancy to childhood and adulthood. These experiences are often beyond the use of words, which the therapist can often only capture through the feelings aroused in the countertransference, an important and essential tool of the analytic process. The notion of therapist being used, and something constantly going on in the patient–therapist dyad, both consciously and unconsciously, opens up many other aspects in transference–countertransference. It is this ongoing movement that provides the possibility for change. I give specific attention to how these are linked with patients' past history and its effects on their present behaviour, their conscious, unconscious, and their way of dissociating. I also demonstrate how and when these idealizations and/or initial aggression broke down, and how primitive aspects of early object relationships and defences emerge and live out in the transference, as well as how the patients attempt to draw the therapist into acting out, and how working on these can lead to changes in patients' internal objects.

I hypothesize and make a general assertion that those patients more resilient to trauma exhibit, in psychotherapy, the four key characteristics I discussed in detail in the first part of this study. Resilient people can manage their traumatic experience by successfully dissociating as and when necessary, in order to pursue the business of their lives, while vulnerable people have certain unconscious mechanisms that interrupt and disable that necessary healthy dissociation. I suggest that healthy dissociations links with the idea of an inner psychic space, which can be fostered by having a listening other in therapy, and that both contribute to a coherent and relatively robust sense of self that is the foundation of resilience and that results in the ability for healthy dissociations. To test the research question, and establish the foundations of resilience and vulnerability, the discussion centres on dissociation (healthy and unhealthy). The listening other, the psychic space, a sense of self, and resilience are referred to throughout as elements of the overall hypothesis on resilience and healthy dissociation as well as vulnerability and unhealthy dissociation.

In the first part of this study, with vignettes, I relate these four features to the patients' experiences. In this second part, I present fragments of the process of a resilient patient (Farina) who shows all four features, and then present the vulnerable patient (Daniel), who does not show these features. To test this, I will be using material to demonstrate where I would expect Daniel to be different if he were resilient, whereas, being vulnerable, he shows malfunctioned reactions in transference with negative and mistrusting thoughts. I then demonstrate how these features begin to change *as a result of therapy*, and Daniel shows signs of gaining resilience. Farina, in contrast to Daniel, I present as the resilient patient, and she displays strong resilient features to her personality throughout the course of her therapy, although she shows aspects of vulnerability in the beginning and it was that which brought her to therapy, due to the trauma she had endured. Her innate resilience could not have remained unaffected by her experience of trauma, but it was restored through the process of therapy with the use of transference and countertransference. Both patients' progress was monitored against the four factors mentioned above.

I test my hypothesis by focusing on these two patients' ways of surviving the trauma they endured, and what this means about their ability to dissociate and what drives this ability, specifically at an unconscious level. The improvement in Daniel as the result of therapeutic intervention evidently links with his increased ability to get in touch with his past and reconstruct his life, in (a) allowing himself to use the process and to develop some psychic space and to think and to feel about his experience; (b) having me, his therapist, as his 'listening other', which helped him to develop some sense of self; (c) learning to dissociate more healthily when not able to cope with his memories of the trauma he endured and his feelings about it. Farina's improvement evidently links to the idea of being able to seek help in the first place and (a) to use me as her listening other from the beginning in order to reconnect to her inner psychic space, and (b) regain a stronger sense of self, which had been partly lost due to the trauma she had endured.

It is important to clarify that the two cases presented are not intended as clinical illustrations: they are used as evidence to support the general points I am making about trauma and dissociation. The methodology, as described in the first part of the book, is psychoanalytic theory; looking at factors influencing why and when some people use healthy dissociation and others use unhealthy dissociation, and shows that the four variable features, psychic space, sense of self, a listening other, and healthy dissociation are found in resilient cases and not in vulnerable cases. I relate this to early developmental influences, early containments, and the development of sense of self (or failure of it). The relevant data here are drawn from the clinical material and is analysed for research purposes. Thus, the empirical material from the cases is used to show the points I am making in this part and in Part I through clinical vignettes. As there are debates about the question of illustration *vs.* evidence in clinical research (the distinction between case illustrations and data as clinical evidence is discussed in the methodology section), it is important to emphasize that the cases here are not intended as case illustrations, but are purposefully presented as empirical evidence based on the research design outlined above. It is important to note that respect has been paid to the patients' confidentiality, which is an essential prerequisite for the focus on, and the use of, clinical data in this study. This is considered to be absolutely central to psychoanalytic psychotherapy. The need for confidentiality in psychoanalytic work goes well beyond any ethical codes of other professional groups' statements about confidentiality relevant to their practice.

CHAPTER NINE

Case one: Farina

C linical data presented here is a fraction of four years' therapeutic encounter with a patient whom I call Farina, who had made satisfactory progress. Farina is from Middle-East, in her thirties, and the single parent of two children. She referred herself for therapy. This ability to seek help presaged the likelihood of some resilient quality. The presentation of her case provides clinical data and details of the technical treatment of a resilient patient, whose psychopathology led her to alternate between relatively stable defences and a tendency for masochistic aggression. Central to the psychoanalytic approach is the exploration of interpersonal processes, with attention paid to underlying unconscious activity; our interplay in the transference–countertransference is the core of our therapeutic work. At the start, my principal objective was to assess the importance of Farina's experience of external trauma, its intensity, her age at its occurrence, her level of resilience, and these concepts: her sense of her self, her psychic space, her ability, or lack of it, for healthy dissociations, and using me as her listening other in transference. Referring herself, and specifically asking for psychoanalytic treatment, confirmed her ability to seek a listening other. Data gathered in the process also focused on measuring her social function, her capacity to relate, and her object relationship in transference.

Background

Farina's father was an academic who had always had problems with depression, and had been on medication on and off as far back as Farina could remember. She described her mother as a depressed but "energetic", loving mother, much engaged with her career and politics. Farina was the elder of two, with a brother four years her junior. She described her childhood as "OK" and her family as "a very respectable functional family in society". Her problem in early adolescence was mainly her drinking, before she became involved with politics. However, she stopped drinking after starting her political activity. She remembered that she never had a close relationship with her father, but always felt close to her mother, and missed her when she was not there. Farina achieved well academically without putting in too much effort. She had two children at the start of our work, a thirteen-year-old daughter and a ten-year-old son. Her partner had been executed because of his political activities. She said that she felt lost, and found it difficult to have the sole responsibility for her children's upbringing, and more so since she became a refugee in London. In her country, she had a good support system from her family and friends when she needed it. She said that she respected her partner's political stand, which led to his execution, and she was proud of his way of life, but she felt a great sadness because her children had lost the opportunity to have their father. Farina and her partner had both been involved in political activity in her country and were under surveillance, interrogation, and persecution, and both had been in prison. Her husband was killed after two years' imprisonment and she was released. Despite all this, it was not until her arrival in London that she felt deeply that she had lost her social world: her partner, family, friends, home, work, and her social status.

In countertransference, I liked Farina. Her considerable resilience was evident from our initial meeting. She had an incredible ability to present her horrific life history with affects, but without any sign of collapsing psychologically. She was insightful about her feelings and, although tearful, had the ability to stop when the feeling was unbearable for her, and she would tell me so. I identified that something was missing in her presentation of her past; I assumed this was something she was not proud of. I had the impression that she relied on her defences of having high academic and career success, and felt pleased to be competent in her political and professional life as well as being a good mother. I also had the sense of a little girl whose trusting environment had been disrupted and who never had an opportunity to work through this issue. I suspected this might be related to her father, as she indicated that she had never been close to him, never missed him, although he was a respected man in society. I decided to raise this with her, and I put a question to her gently. She denied it, and immediately changed the subject to her experience in prison. Her response confirmed my inkling. My hypothesis was later supported by evidence from clinical data, when Farina confirmed her experience of childhood disruption.

In the process, there were occasions that I felt totally helpless and lost in her presenting material. I kept silent on those occasions, as I realized that I had to carefully monitor Farina's unconscious processes as well as my own. I had to ensure that my helplessness was not becoming disruptive to our work. I found myself being very interested to discover the inner dynamics of her masochistic personality, which involved her level of dissociation, serving to protect herself and her object from being attacked beyond repair. This came from both the healthy part of herself and also from her sadistic, attacking, internal object. However, she showed a great ability to dissociate healthily. For example, although she experienced trauma in prison and through the execution of her husband, she did not present herself as a victim, displaying a strong sense of self and the ability to have insight into her psychic space, but acknowledging that she was being punished for her beliefs and political convictions.

Farina referred herself to deal with her anxiety and depression, which seemed to have arisen in connection with ambivalent object-relations, her unmourned losses, and her guilt. There appeared to be a dimension of her personality characterized by regression, which needed to be understood in terms of her ego-splitting, arrested ego development, her lack of self-fulfilment, and her apathy. She also presented schizoid processes of withdrawal to her inner world under the impact of her primitive fears. Farina was able to say that she was not capable of maintaining a loving relationship, as all her relationships had led to impasses, and the only successful one had ended with her partner being killed.

In one of our assessment meetings, in response to a question, she said, "I want to have psychoanalytic therapy to help me to feel I am alive."

Farina presented as a very accomplished and sharp thinker. On many occasions, without a second thought, she would cut the links I tried to suggest in transference interpretation and change the subject to something equally important, thus employing healthy dissociation as a method of defence from subject matter she would otherwise have found difficult to relate to. On occasions, she talked to me as if I was a useless object, unable to understand her despair. The way she expressed her wishes seemed to me as if, for her, life had never begun. She increasingly appeared to be two-sided. On the one hand, there was a lively and generous side to her, which was perfectly visible to those around her, and on the other, a dead and masochistic side; for example, after the loss of her husband, she believed that she should not be in any other intimate relationship in her life and devoted her life to her politics/work and her children, which I perceived as an aspect of unhealthy dissociation, cutting herself off from her needs and desires. In order to dissociate from her unbearable emotional pain, she had a way of talking factually, which I perceived as healthy dissociation. Although she knew better, she acted as if she had no awareness of the meaning of transference and my role in that. She could, therefore, become quite resistant to, or dismissive of, my interpretations. In contrast, some of our sessions became quite meaningful, filled with accounts impregnated with her unconscious phantasies and dreams involving the presence of others whom she felt close to and loved by, but who in reality were far away. I give an example when she came to a session and started to talk about her dream.

> I had a strange dream. I was in a confined space covered in blood . . . there was a large man being beaten, with many wounds. He was in the corner very close to me. I looked into his eyes, which were full of pain . . . and looked at him again and saw he had an unfocused look. It

seemed as if he was going to die. I was left feeling helpless and very angry. Although I didn't know him, I couldn't let this man die like that . . . it was not fair . . . I wanted to shout and scream for help, but I couldn't . . .

She finished fully reporting her dream, then immediately started talking about her association and continued, "When I was in prison, I saw many tortured prisoners dying under the sadistic attitudes of prison officers and the prison authority in general. I would have liked to complain and shout at them, but I couldn't speak as I knew I would be killed, too."

I listened to the account of the dream and her associations. The intensity of Farina's dream and of her associations was at the time too overwhelming to stay with in countertransference, but I heard her plea for help, indeed, her fear and her unconscious wish to drag me into the deadly prison that she felt she was in. I thought that seeing a tortured man in the dream was helpful for Farina to associate with the look in her mother's (very depressed but energetic, as she portrayed her) eyes, but also with her beloved lost partner, whom she has not mourned properly and was not yet able to fully associate with. We explored and discussed her dream further. This opened some needed psychic space for Farina to make further associations, which helped her to regain some of her resilience that had been lost to the trauma, and so she developed a stronger sense of self.

I found it a relief to be able to stay with her by thinking positively about the fact that Farina became able to recall some of her memories that she had dissociated from through her dream and through having a listening other in therapy making associations. It became apparent that she had reached a stage where she could elaborate on the conflict between her moral stand and her wishes and desires. Through gaining more of her psychic space, part of her that had been dead was coming to life. As therapy progressed further, this part of Farina became more and more present and permanent as she was able to move on from the intensity of her horrific, traumatic memories. But, unexpectedly, she went into a period of distant and despairing attitude to therapy. In one session. she arrived in a gloomy and miserable mood and said, "The whole therapy is useless to me, it's just words; it doesn't take my awful feeling away. It is useless. If anything, if I am honest, I am suffering more than before I started this. I have been going round and round for months, I don't know what I am doing . . ."

This implied that Farina at that stage was no longer willing or able to make use of me as her listening other in the therapeutic process. I was overwhelmed by her statement, as it represented a sudden shift. My feeling was of numbness, void, and fear of collapsing. I experienced a sudden strong feeling of undesirable helplessness. On reflection, I thought my collapsed feeling was my projective counter-identification, linked to, and corresponding with, the projective identification used by Farina. My assessment of this sudden change was that Farina had an unconscious need to communicate her earlier experiences to me so that I could help her to find meaning. I felt her communication here was not related to her experience in adult life. However, as at the time I could not gather my thoughts, I kept silent to give myself time to think and reflect more on this encounter as well as consult on the issue in supervision.

I thought that Farina unconsciously projected into me her feeling of being trapped, just as in the therapy she felt that she had "been going round and round for months", and while there was no doubt in my mind that I could help her make sense of it, I could not do it at that particular session. I felt that I had lost the moment. I became aware that Farina had the tendency to act out instead of representing her conflicts mentally, which I had not thought of before. Farina projected into me her feeling of desperate helplessness (as in the prison), and I felt it in an overwhelming way that disabled me for the moment. This is relevant here, as it seemed to be a moment when she felt that she did not have a listening other, and that was true: there was no psychic space inside her (or outside her, in me) to reflect on what was going on. So, here she clearly exhibited some of the features of vulnerability and I became lost in it. I am saying this to show how a resilient patient such as Farina can also have and demonstrate the presence of vulnerability that I, as the listening other, her therapist, needed to attend to. This is despite the fact that in the process, the four key features of resilience central to this study were evident in Farina's presentations. So, although she had the ability to dissociate in a healthy way by making a conscious decision, there were also unconscious processes, linked to unconscious projection and then unconscious phantasy about the fate of the object. I had hypothesized that healthy dissociation is a conscious act to prevent suffering (e.g., helplessness) and turning away from it consciously and temporarily, thus helping the person to carry on without collapsing psychologically, but there always exists an unconscious connotation that is beyond one's conscious choices.

However, due to the fact that I was indecisive in this particular session, my judgement not to make any interpretation was the right decision. On reflection and discussion in supervision, it became more apparent that Farina was projecting her emptiness outside to avoid feeling it in herself, and unconsciously she wanted someone to "kill" her to confirm the presence of the awful external world she lived in; in her conscience, this made her feel empty. By making a displacement to a big tortured man in her dream, whom she would have liked to have rescued, she had unconsciously protected me as her listening other, her object. I had to think about how Farina could be helped to feel that she had unconsciously projected her deadly emptiness outside of herself in order to avoid feeling it. I thought that at this stage of therapy Farina did not have enough inner psychic space to hold on to her disturbing thought. She dissociated herself from her unbearable memory and projected her helplessness and uselessness to me, further separating herself from her reality, which resulted in weakening her sense of self. Although part of her unconsciously projected that to me, another unconscious part of her wanted to keep me alive as she knew somewhere in her mind (unconscious or subconscious) that she needed me to stay alive for her as her listening other and a person who could contain her without dying on her. Her need to keep me alive was evidence of her resilience, indeed, her desire to stay alive herself, although she was using projection to deal with the part of herself affected by the trauma she had endured.

I imagined that, even though she had always denied it because she had no direct memory of it, she must have already experienced this emptiness when she was very young; that is, when she had had to be separated from her mother repeatedly for different reasons, and because of her father, who was unable to take care of her and was perhaps threatening to her. (Although I still had doubt and uncertainty about Farina's relationship with her father in childhood and whether her childhood was disrupted by him, there was no communication from Farina confirming this. But there were signs of her having knowledge about it, as she always changed the subject when talking about her father, thus healthily dissociating.) I was aware that she may have unconsciously put into me what was causing her anxiety, but I refrained from interpreting her projection directly, as I felt such an interpretation could be experienced by Farina as extremely intrusive, and be perceived as me telling her that I knew what she was feeling better than she did. I reserved the interpretation for when Farina would be ready and interested in gaining insight into her psychic functioning, allowing me to be her listening other. In order to clarify, as mentioned in the introduction section, Farina displayed some vulnerability, which was a result of trauma. Although it was clear that her resilience had been affected by the experience of trauma, whether at an early stage or more recently, her resilience was evident in her projection of her helplessness on to me, as her listening other, as and when she felt vulnerable, thus enabling herself to dissociate from the unbearable external situation and not to feel emptiness.

It seemed to me at that particular time that Farina needed me to help her to become able to picture the bad internal object that was present in the depressed side of her, not the missing good object, her listening other. In these instances in transference, this was not the absent good m/other, but the presence of the bad object in her. I set myself the task of finding a way to help her to express her feeling in transference, which would provide us with an opportunity for interpretations of transference, as a representation of her unrepresentable internal part-object. By doing so, the absence of her good object had become present in transference and opened up more psychic space, and as a result she developed a better sense of self that enabled her to associate and dissociate healthily as and when she had the capacity. I present a fragment of a session where Farina says,

"I'm really wondering whether you are any use to me in this process."

I replied with deep conviction, "Perhaps I am the container."

Farina gave a start, and said disbelievingly, "What?"

I added, "Yes, a container who could hold good things but instead brings you the confinement of prison in your mind, making you feel as if you are under torture and drowning."

Farina remained silent and calm, concentrating hard. It seemed obvious to me that if I offered myself to Farina as an object, she would be able to experience the corresponding affect. To help Farina discover what was happening inside her, I tried to start with a gesture she had made, so that, through rediscovering sensation, she could then discover its emotional significance. I added,

"And by turning your head away you are telling me about your feelings of sadness and anger and how much I disappoint you by not responding to your helpless feeling."

She asked, "I turn my head away?"

I replied, "When you tell me that I can't help you, it's a bit like turning your head away from me, rather than communicating with me."

I thought it was difficult for Farina to experience the transference, as she could not associate with her feelings of being imprisoned by her listening other, who is persecuting her with her interpretations. There was a silence, and then Farina said emotionally,

"No, I have a sense that I really have a big hole at the bottom of my heart . . . I think that is why I cannot take care of myself properly; I do it out of a sense of duty. Before I started therapy, no one ever knew that there was this sadness within me. My mother, as we have spoken about before, has always been the presence of an absence—if this makes any sense . . ."

I was very pleased. It had worked. I had offered myself as the "negative" of a part-object in the transference. I was the breast that was lacking, the hollow breast, as it were, the "presence of an absent mother", as she put it. Here, she felt able to articulate her experience, thus displaying more psychic space that had somehow been opened up by having and making use of her listening other.

In the following session, Farina started by saying, "After the last session, I don't know why, I felt like vomiting and had a very bad dream."

This opened another dimension in our work. It was clear that Farina was finding a better sense of self and becoming able to talk about her life experience before the external trauma of becoming a refugee. She thought about separations that had occurred in her life. On reflecting on her feelings in the session, she had become aware that she had enough psychic space to think about what it was unthinkable to her before. She then associated with another part of her and talked about sexual differences and conflicts of sibling rivalry with her brother, showing her potential for thinking about what had been unthinkable for her. This provided evidence that she had the potential for more psychic space when she met me as her object, which sufficed as her listening other, and opened up the possibility that together we could create more psychic space. These things were situated at a secondary level of her associations that were affected, and had repercussions throughout. The significant change happened. After this session, the phantasy construction of Farina's love-life and relating was no longer invasive for her.

We now reached the stage where I had to rethink my counter-transference feelings in relation to Farina's material. I realized my rather gratifying experience must correspond to an inner conviction on Farina's part that whatever I said in my interpretations, she was somehow always right. Whatever difficult or even tormenting qualities she showed during our work, there was an inner certainty that she had some very special place, and that my interpretations remained, as it were, only my interpretations: in her view, I was just doing my job. She, however, seemed to be content that her place was secure and that she had no need to change. Even though we were working successfully on her unconscious, and to a great extent helping her to deal with many issues related to her past and present, she was evidently not yet ready to look at particular issues she was holding back from her early developmental period. It was possible to confront her by making interpretations, opening exploration, but her deeper unconscious remained closed to investigation and analysis, and as a result the integral progression of her treatment could have become falsified. The certainty of her special space and not wanting to change had an added quality. It included the notion that I, her therapist, had a special attachment to, and love for, her, and that for my own sake I would not wish to let her down or let her go; I experienced this, and constantly had to re-examine myself. Farina's feeling of being my special patient and the elusive nature of much of our work, her perception of my love for her, was an unconscious phantasy that she needed to survive the pain of change, and the pain of reconstruction of her past. It would be much more comfortable to link this part of her with her past experience; being the elder child, the special love and attention that she had with her mother as her favourite child, and her relationship with her father, whom at that stage she could portray as "A significantly unkind man, whose manner at times could be inappropriate."

I made an interpretation, but Farina regressed again and said, "You are making interpretations to do your job. You do not really believe what you were saying yourself, how can you know my life better than I do? I think you are speculating . . ."

I realized I had made a mistake. I should leave her more time and not jump to interpretation on the subject that she was sensitive about and resistant to discussing, thus revealing her vulnerability. She was still in denial and did not want to admit, or, rather, even to believe that her father's behaviour to her was not acceptable and it was all right to say that. Her denial was the sign of her vulnerability, the fear of losing her sense of self. So, I decided not to push on this. I observed that even the pain of suppressing her feelings was debilitating for her. While I was aware that my prediction was based on Farina's hints in her expression, I felt baffled and without an answer again. I realized that I should not use confrontational interpretations about this issue, and not make her more vulnerable. My task was to increase her vulnerability with the awareness that she was a single mother of two young children without any family and social support. In my view, the important point was to first get the underlying assumptions into the open, to be experienced in the transference, and create necessary psychic space for Farina to face her reality by just being her listening other and helping her to build a stronger sense of self, until we reached the point where she would be able to bear and associate with her memories and her feelings about them, and be able to link the transferential encounters with her past experiences. This helped us to reach the stage where Farina's omnipotence and her special place of phantasies were no longer prominent in the transference. Her early anxieties and the living out of further psychic conflict came into the transference, through her dream. The substance of her dream was lived out in the transference, so we were able to make shifts. Despite gaining insight, it was still possible for Farina to get caught up in a kind of passive, despairing masochism. To give an example, I present a fraction of a session focused on one of her dreams. She reported:

I was in a place during a war. I was in an important meeting full of other people sitting round a table ... we heard an aeroplane outside and knew from the sound that there was something wrong ... I could not focus on the discussion in the meeting any more ... without asking the chair or other members of the meeting, I left the table and went to the window to look out. The plane was in danger. Watching the aeroplane, I saw ... it was so high up and looked extremely small ... I felt unable to do anything to help ... I left, wondering whether I could save them and whether people were dead ... I wanted to rescue and see who the pilot was ... the plane was so far away and so small ... I wanted to reach them ... but I could not ...

I based my interpretations of this fragment of the dream on the war that was continuously waged between Farina and I, shown in the way she had turned her back on the other members of the meeting in her dream. I made a link with our therapeutic encounter and her lack of engagement: while the meeting was going on at the table in her dream, she decided to go and look for something outside, employing her dissociation in the dream similar to the way she did in work going on from session to session between us, to avoid the pain of what happened to her as a little girl. I said,

"I am wondering whether in your mind the war seems to be continuously intense between you and me. This dream, like many of your other dreams, shows the way you need to turn your back when you are not able to bear the thought of something I say. In your dream you acted as you do here with me—while the meeting was going on at the table, you decided to go and look for something outside. It is similar to the work going on from session to session between us, isn't it? When you need to avoid the pain of what happened to you as a little girl, instead of saying you are not able to deal with it right now, you change the subject with anger and turn your head away. Between the sessions, you focus your attention on helping others, as you have done in the past and are still doing, rather than thinking about yourself and how together we can help you to overcome your unbearable experiences. I wonder whether the people in the plane that you wished to help, but couldn't, are representative of yourself in your dream. I know part of you wants to focus on what is in your mind that you cannot yet share with me, but you find it difficult. You know you are fading away, like the passengers in the plane while you are out of reach. And, you know, it doesn't matter how much as your therapist I want to be helpful to you, if you are unreachable, I will be left with the desire of being able to help you rather than the actuality."

I was thinking that there was a psychic space, but she closed it by dissociating and looking elsewhere. But her psychic space still exists, even if it was unusable at that particular moment. She responded to this interpretation surprisingly well, and said,

"When I looked out, knowing that something was wrong with the aeroplane, it was something strange, but I could not connect it to therapy and our relationship." (It is important to note that this was the first time Farina referred to us and a relationship between us. This is evidence that with the interpretation of this dream, a psychic space opened up for Farina to have a sense of herself and relate to me as her listening other, while she was still unable to talk about her actual experience. But she rediscovered her resilience to dissociate healthily with her unbearable memory.) She continued, "But, this morning I was thinking about coming here and from my behaviour in the last session I could see that you are a therapist who is trying to help me, but I am absorbed in looking at the other aspects of my life and making excuses that they are important . . . I can see that I am avoiding looking at the part of me that is in trouble and the thought of it making me fall apart, die . . . Looking at my dream, it does make sense, instead of sitting at the table and being engaged in what I set myself as a task of being in that meeting— I mean in therapy—I leave the meeting and want to reach something out of control . . . So, in therapy, although you constantly remind me that I enjoy my space, I show my preference for getting absorbed in situations of painful collapse rather than turning to and enjoying help and the progress that I can make with your help. This is deep . . . lots of thinking to do . . . what you are indicating is that in my dream I was you, and the people in the plane were me . . . wow . . . it does make every sense . . ."

Here, there is evidence that although Farina was defensive before, as our therapeutic relationship progressed, and as the result of transference and dream interpretation, she got more in touch with her feelings and her psychic function, indeed her unconscious, by making use of me as her listening other, developing a better and stronger sense of self, and enabling more psychic space. Her dream and interpretations of it were helping her to reclaim some of her resilience that had been lost as the result of trauma, and with more psychic space for reflection and insight, she began to feel the existence of her masochistic part.

In the session after the one in which we focused on her dream, she came in without greeting (she had a polite way of greeting on entry and departure from each session, no matter how difficult the session was, so I observed a massive change in her behaviour) saying,

> "I felt disturbed after the last session and the discussion we had about my dream."

At my request, she talked about her concern, and said,

> "I felt awful. . . . Whatever is going on in therapy . . . seems somehow to get me caught up in this rejection and fighting . . . I was thinking why is it that I almost always fight with you and reject anything you say, and after fighting, I start thinking about what you said. . . . My thinking is that I am terrified of becoming dependent on you, or anyone in fact . . . and I am so frightened of some of my emotions . . . and I think I am so fearful of you not being real . . . in a sense what I am saying is I fear losing you . . . these thoughts are quite confusing and frightening . . . I almost didn't come today . . . I am scared, very scared . . ."

We explored these feelings further and she was able to speak about her awareness of the importance of the excitement she gets when involved in this way. Although this was quite insightful, from the tone of her voice I had the impression that she was complaining that the insight was being used against progress in the session, and a kind of war against me was still going on. I felt the need to relay this to her. To her dismay, I interpreted this to her. In a depressed voice she said,

> "According to your interpretations there seems to be no part of me that really wants to work, and I am not co-operative at all . . . is this what you are saying? You must be sick and tired of me nagging and complaining like a little girl . . ."

I felt myself wanting to say "NO" and to tell her that this could not be quite true, since she actually came to sessions and we had done a lot of important work. I then realized, of course, that my immediate feeling in reaction was the outcome of projection. I was introjecting, and wanted to act as a part of Farina who needs to be positive, as if the part of her that was capable of knowing and working had been projected into me. I felt trapped. I *was* trapped. On the one hand, my countertransference existence was in the positive part, so that she was not responsible for all of this acting out or I need not recognize it; on the other hand, living out of the positive part meant I had to agree that there was no part of her that really wanted to work. Although she was waiting for my response, as I felt stuck, I decided to stay silent, so as not to say something unthoughtful.

She thought there was no way out of this for her, as she felt that there was nothing she could do about it, and she felt depressed, as she could see what I meant in the session that she was referring to. I said what she could not say. I was referring to her father's behaviour towards her in her childhood, the out-of-the-ordinary unhappiness she experienced in her early adolescence, her drinking problem at such a young age, before she became involved with politics (she started drinking secretly at the age of twelve, and she is from a country where drinking is not acceptable, especially for a woman). However, we agreed that she was not yet ready to discuss this aspect of her life, although she had conscious knowledge about it. I did tell her that I did not see that she had enough psychic space to work on this now, but she understood that we needed to work on that part of her life experience. This was a great change, but, more and more, the sessions became locked into the notion of her understanding, while not being able to do anything about it, or with it.

In one session I used one of her recurring aeroplane dreams and reminded her that she became concerned about watching the pilot and wondering whether he had died, and connected this to the possibility of this being a representation of her beloved partner, the only man she could love, trust, and feel safe with, and there was nothing she could do about it when he was killed, and now, here with me, how removed she felt I was from her and how frustrated she felt by not being able to reach me. I was trying to encourage Farina to become aware of her psychic space by providing an interpretation of why she was not making use of her listening other. I was unable to help or protect her, so, in her mind, she was now left on her own with the feeling that I might be dead.

She said, "Although I understood, I couldn't help being helpless . . . that is why I feel frustrated and sometimes angry and feel therapy is not helping . . . I feel trapped."

I said, "You are feeling that I am not helping you?"

She said, "Yes."

I said, "I wonder whether you realize that you are actively trapping me by this kind of remark, which is your way of demonstrating the war that is going on between us. I also wonder if you are aware that when you feel safe enough to accept that I am your listening other, without judgement or condition, your fear of rejection or feeling of losing me increases. I am saying this because for a while you were referring to me as a person, as your therapist, and now you regress to referring to me as 'therapy'."

She said, "I know you are right on both counts, yet again . . . but . . . why . . . why does it have to be this way . . . can you do anything about it?"

She started crying at that point, and continued until the end of session, while occasionally observing me.

Here again, it is evident that Farina's dream was now lived out in the transference. She was able to see that she was constantly and actively trapping me, by her remarks, which were in themselves a demonstration of her violent feeling that was projected to the war going on between us. She was able to gain insight into her psychic space and at times think reflectively about her relationship with me as her listening other and how this was affecting her sense of self, but then she felt too close, and she would pull back and start regressing.

Through this process, she gained insight of her psychic function and she gradually started to open up. Although she did not know why, almost halfway through one of our sessions, she suddenly remembered about a special water flask she had in her adolescence while she was in secondary school and felt despondent and miserable about it. She said,

"I would take the flask and fill it with whisky, cover it carefully, put it in my picnic bag, and go to the end of our very large garden alone, sit behind a tree—always in the same spot—and drink. This was the beginning of my drinking . . . there was no real pleasure in drinking, but I would feel less miserable, sad, and lonely and that felt good."

I said, "I am thinking this might lie in your response to the fact that I told you that part of you is trapping me with remarks such as 'I do not see any part in you that wants to co-operate', and together we are breaking that part."

In her response, she confirmed this. "I realize this actually ... I feel some kind of satisfaction in the fight with you and I could sense and see that you feel trapped, but part of me is pleased. As stupid it may sound, I enjoyed it."

After further exploration, a small change happened and this manifestation of her masochistic satisfaction began to lessen. Farina changed and became less obsessed with being in total control. She was dissociating more frequently, related to me in her conversation as a person, but she could not give up control entirely yet. For her, giving up meant giving in to authority, which she was not able to do.

The transference at this stage was not so much that she got pleasure from the excitement of making me feel trapped by her projection, but that the problem lay in the recognition and acknowledgement of her improvement, which would also mean her decision to be willing to give up some of the pleasure in defeating me (or herself). She regretted her behaviour in transference and became quite keen to talk about how "bad" and dismissive she had been to "me" in our relationship, but she was not yet able to acknowledge or celebrate her improvement.

I said to her, "I am thinking about the reason that you are not willing to give up focusing on the "bad" rather than focusing on and enjoying the fact that you have made tremendous changes; indeed, by your own admission, you are feeling much better. I wonder whether clinging to the "bad" is linked to your fear of losing the "good" that you have achieved again. Perhaps it is a reminder that there are issues that you are not ready to associate with, but that we need to deal with."

She agreed with this and said, "Things have changed. My mood has definitely altered and stabilized, my sense of being lost and fragmented has totally gone. Now, more often, I feel sad, sometimes resentful, sometimes offended that you as my therapist have not given sufficient attention to my actual memory, which seemed to me vivid and important, but I cannot finish it and I get angry with you. I know I have to recall and talk about it, but I can't. And, I think you don't help me. I know you know—but you don't say it."

I said, "I can hear that you are saying your good feeling about the good work has gone away from your memory too quickly, because you feel

I should know exactly what is going on in your mind. You think that I, instead of you, should visit and talk about your experience. When you feel safe with me, you see me as part of you, rather than another person . . . but I am still wondering about what it is that is stopping us from revisiting your memory."

She agreed with this. But she switched to another memory of her adolescence, much less important. She wanted us to look at her feelings, which, in her view, had been missed or dismissed by me, despite her considering them to be of importance. This healthy way of dissociating was helpful in allowing her to see the dismissal of the feelings as my limitation and not as having a reflection on her.

I reminded her of the stress she had put up with and her dissatisfactions, while I was thinking that a lot of pleasure had really gone out of this now, as in the non-pleasure in her starting to drink in her adolescence. I also was thinking about her resentment and said,

"It is important to note that your feelings have shifted, and you have lost the uncomfortable blocked mood, but yet you still cannot own your new ways of thinking completely, and it is therefore easier for you to think in term of my dismissing them, rather than you resisting them."

I immediately regretted saying this, as I realized that I had made a mistake and that I had been defensive about, and resentful, of her feeling that she was dismissed by me.

However, Farina said that she agreed, but complained, "I feel left behind with you. Sometimes I think you are going too quickly for my way of thinking and I never can catch up with you."

I thought, it is true. I should have been more patient. I felt I jump to interpretation in a moment of excitement without that much reflection, based on my positive countertransference. I apologized for making her feel this way. However, despite my shortcoming here, she could accept, displaying clear features of a resilient characteristic, that part of her resentment might be connected to not yet being able to fully connect with the changes she had made—"my new self", she called it—and that our encounter in transference had enabled her to help herself to undo the fragmented feelings she had and to have further realizations of her sense of self, but this had been too fast for her and challenging.

She explained, "You, as my therapist, have become an unrealistic promiser that I have allowed myself to be pulled along by . . . but there is a hollow . . . a sense of a void or emptiness . . . I don't know how to explain . . . Sometimes I really feel I cannot catch up with you . . . sometimes I feel I am sinking in an unknown territory . . . I feel so close to you . . . then I feel terrified."

I pointed out to her, "It sounds as if you feel that I have not really analysed your problem about being stuck and fragmented, but have pulled you out of your comfort zone that you were so used to. I am referring to your depressive position and your feeling of being stuck mechanically, which you have been used to for such a long time."

After a brief silence, I continued, "It seems to me that you may feel it was my inventiveness that pulled you out, similar to when you felt that you had been seduced by your father if he was being nice to you as a child and not treating you the way he was treating your mother."

She stopped me and added, "There was also the other fear at that moment, the fear of getting caught up into excited warm feelings that I had with my unkind father."

We were able to establish that her anxieties and her thoughts of my leading her out of her previous state of mind (her comfort zone), and her fear of her own positive, excited, infantile feelings both needed further consideration. I put this to her. She nodded in agreement. This led us to talk about her unresolved anxieties from her past that had come up before as important, but she did not at times have enough psychic space to face them and needed to project her anxieties to me. In order to avoid thinking about them, she led herself not to have contained feelings, not to experience and express the good feelings, particularly the warmth and gratitude which had been emerging in her. This was a break-through, and smoothed our working relationship.

Evidently, there had been a clear shift in Farina. She developed a better sense of herself as a result of more psychic space. The changes in Farina manifested as follows:

1. A significant change of her affect.
2. Something had been deeply touched, which, although embarrassing to her, provided her with the warmth and depth of feeling that she had reached; a different depth, which was distinct from the infant–mother relationship.
3. Her attitudes in transference changed. She started talking to me as a therapist with whom she had a relationship, rather

than referring to me as "therapy", which was initially her way of addressing me.

4. She became able to see how the changes she had made in her way of listening and relating to me helped her to feel safe with other people, and led her to enjoy her encounter with others. As a result, she was not constantly frustrated by others around her.

5. Her anxiety had shifted to quite a high degree and she became contained.

6. Her depression lifted, which reflected in her not wanting to be left alone.

7. She started talking about her children with love, joy, and affection, rather than guilt, sadness, and responsibility. She started reporting and celebrating her children's successes, proud of being their mother. She started having family dinners, sitting with her children rather than putting food on the table for them and going and reading her book, which she had always done before.

8. She reported that she had started going to the theatre, and had seen one of Shakespeare's plays at the Globe, which she thoroughly enjoyed. She loved theatre, but since her arrival in London, had never been to a play.

These changes, which remained with Farina, are evidence. It is confirmation that psychoanalysis, as theory and therapy, is appropriate for the treatment of traumatized patients, as a unique activity of psychoanalysis is centred on an intersubjective relationship. The phenomena of transference and countertransference between Farina and me allowed the emergence of a generative interplay between creative impulses struggling for expression, and a persistent search for clarity through appropriate analytic interpretations of dreams and transference interpretations that culminated in constructions of what had taken place. The fraction of this clinical work presented here produced self-evident psychoanalytic substance and clinical implications for those who may want to use it. The material is an intersubjective product of two minds. It provides evidence that the strength of the psychoanalytic method, if applied appropriately and on time, guards against the possible weakness shown in interpretations in the process. It also confirms that it is important to understand that evidence of psychoanalysis comes from within, and it cannot fit within quantitative methods. Furthermore, this work provides evidence about mistakes I made in analysis and provides verification that, as the therapist, one may face the danger of not accepting one's limitations and may develop omnipotent beliefs derived from a conceptual system in one.

On reflection and further thought about this process, it is possible to clearly substantiate that the struggle between Farina and me progressed and moved from one level of interaction to another. The transference, instead of being a medium with respect to her recovery of memory and an aid to working through, on occasions disappeared from my view. It disappeared into an unseen but faithful repetition of the child–mother relationship, especially as, on reflection, I realized that in my countertransference I became the overprotective or over-compensating mother, which followed an over-projection of the immediate transference confrontation. This, however, helped me to see where I was going wrong and brought to light the fact that my interventions were unintentionally educational and moralistic, rather than analytical, although, at times, I still regarded them as analytical interaction. I was making a mistake and, without realizing it at the time, I could be faced with the possibility of adopting the position of mother substitute to Farina, wishing to be a better mother than Farina's actual mother was. Therefore, although I was monitoring my countertransference as much as I was consciously aware, on momentary occasions, in response to her projection, I would slip away from psychoanalytic interactions, and, like her mother, I would become paralysed and unable to see the nature of my involvement and interaction with her. On those occasions, our therapeutic alliances were lost. On reflection, I realized I had to keep my professionalism intact, and be constantly alert to how I was affected by Farina. Although her age was very close to mine, too often I found myself feeling maternal towards her. Thinking about what was happening at this second level of transference, at the time, it was the fact that Farina was being too defensive and resistant. In countertransference, my defensiveness to her negative and attacking transference momentarily shifted to thinking that she had a negative therapeutic reaction and was not a suitable patient (an unanalysable patient) and, as a result, unconsciously I would turn into an educationalist rather than an analyst.

Although difficult, it is very important to mention that my countertransference reaction to Farina on occasions was wrong. On
consideration, I accepted that in some parts of our therapeutic work
the difficulties were arising from my side and the change required
at first was in me (the therapist) rather than in Farina (the patient)
in order for appropriate work to continue. So, in reality, on those
occasions Farina did not have her listening other in the consulting
room. My supervisor had been outstandingly helpful, but had not
spared me in pointing out this type of situation with Farina, or
other similar patients. My own resistance, shared by my way of
thinking, showed itself in externally directed, determined defences.
I also thought the difficulty in retaining flexibility of mind was complicated by the fact that the conceptual and clinical psychoanalytic
viewpoint, like any school of thought, is a function of personal
dedication, but when one commits oneself fully to a particular viewpoint there is always the danger of thinking that there is
no other way, and also of finding safety in selective denial and
disavowals of reality. These then become a triangular pattern of
transference–countertransference between Farina, me, and my
supervisor. I was becoming aware that I could not be as analytical
as I would have liked to be with Farina. My warm, maternal feelings towards her were preventing me from doing my job properly.
My supervisor was of the opinion that I was too critical of myself
because Farina was not a suitable patient for psychoanalytical intervention, but I was not convinced.

I was aware of my fault and determined to rectify my approach,
which I did. As a result, our work started progressing further and
some of Farina's masochism and grandiosity decreased. She was
depressed, but said, "I feel more real without needing to act out."
This opened up the opportunity for her perverse sadomasochistic
phantasies to emerge, as did her delusion of her omnipotent control. The analysis of the position of her being, and her actual existence in private as well as public space, led to her emergence from
depression and the exploration of her loneliness, and exposed her
vulnerable part, which she was so afraid to face. Further, this
opened up the emergence of her homosexuality and penis envy,
together with the failure of her manic-like masturbation, which led
her to suicidal depressed feelings that she so much needed to
discover in her suicidal mother. These occasioned the change to real

psychic space, where some of her emptiness was lifted. This phase of our work took quite some time. Progress either was very slow or, at times, close to none. This particular period was characterized and corresponds with Kernberg's (1976) depressive emptiness rather than Klein's (1946) depressive position.

My countertransference had changed, and in transference I become more of a therapist rather than a mother. This confirmed that Farina's depressive emptiness was clearly equivalent in many ways to her lack of real psychic space. Then it became apparent that, at an unconscious level, I was lending her some space by not challenging her and feeling like an over-protective but vulnerable mother. I thought that the discovery of feelings and ideas about her mother being extremely depressed and empty had awakened her depressive concern for her mother, rather than a schizoid hatred for her mother and her father, who spoiled her childhood. I considered this type of emptiness and changes in the process as signs of resilience. To demonstrate this, I focused on Farina's imaginative use of phantasies. One was her way of gathering people she cared for in her phantasy to fill her real inner space. From an object relations point of view, her emptiness was related to defects in her ego and her masochistic surroundings, which combined with the increased suffering from disturbances in her sense of self. Her emptiness could also be studied from instinct theory with the primary cause being due to an oral hunger, a longing for emotional supplies from the good object that was not available; indeed, from defences against her phantasy formation and, indirectly, the formation of her sense of self. The success in this process became clear when Farina reported that she was able to experience her mother as a real person for the first time. This experience was the psychic food that filled her emptiness and enabled her inner psychic space and her ability to be herself. This was evidenced by Farina's significant change of affect, which became apparent and sustainable. She became aware of, and touched by, facing her embarrassment and humiliation, rather than avoiding it. By doing this, she reached a different depth of feeling, allowing herself to have positive feelings, and to make distinctions between her feelings now as an adult and her feelings in her childhood. This was soon followed by further changes as the result of Farina getting in touch with her emptiness positively, which was "before starting to fill up" and reached to "A

considerable maturity . . . needed for this state to be meaningful",
as Winnicott (1974) put it.

Farina became aware that she had abandoned herself, although
she had longings for emotional supplies from a good object/
m/other. She was evidently defended against her absent mother in
her infancy. The substantial data here is that Farina's schizoid reaction was her defence against her depressive emptiness. This describes the relationship between her resilience and her vulnerability,
the experiential aspects of the concepts of her psychic space and of
her emptiness. This is based on the change of inner experience of
Farina's masochism during her therapy, and from one of empty
space to one of real space. The pattern of intervention I used here
describes the relationship of inner psychic space to schizoid and
depressive emptiness, together with the emergence of her healthy
inner psychic space—her resilience.

I am presenting this simple material to stress a number of points
about the use of transference, indeed, the use of interpretations of
her dream and their relation to Farina's dissociation. These reveal
meanings of the therapeutic encounter in a fairly precise way by
being lived out in the session. This was shown in Farina's specific
participation, which was problematic and with misery rather than
meeting up with her hopeful and lively objects. This was evident on
the many occasions that she turned away from my interpretations,
dissociating herself from the issue, specifically when she did not
want to work on that particular issue. For example, in a session in
the second year in therapy, I used an interpretation of her dream in
connection with her relationship with her father. She could not deal
with it and said, "I clearly recognize them as unnecessary and
unhelpful. I told you many times that he was a very unkind man.
He happened to be my father and I loved him—I loved him dearly.
I longed for him and I cannot change it now—so, please can we stop
talking about it . . ."

With further discussion and interpretation, however, she would
relate to the memory of events that she was dissociating from in an
intellectual way, but not connecting with emotionally. She would
agree with me, indeed, would recognize the helpfulness, but not be
able to relate to her memory emotionally. This she called "not a
satisfactory reason to get emotional". I could clearly see the positive
aspects of her personality, but her own capacity to move warmly

towards her object and internalize it was at the time quickly dissociated from, distorted, and projected into me. It was on those occasions that I had to be the one who pulled and led her.

In a session she said, "I can see how much you changed me, I
am a different person, since I have been coming here, I realized a
lot of things about myself. I know I can enjoy myself, I can smile, I
can relax, I can love . . . it is all down to you . . ."

Here, there is specific meaning of the symbols that we can locate
in the transference. Farina obtained insight into what was almost
a choice between moving towards a helpful object or colluding
in despair. Her defences were mobilized and she went towards
colluding in despair (by not owning her work on changes she has
made) and tried to draw me into criticizing and reproaching her
masochistic defensive organization. But my hunch was that she
was giving me all these positive remarks to charm me not to challenge her undivided dissociation with a certain painful event.
However, she really had the knowledge that she did not get the
pleasure in life that she could have while not associating and
working on those hidden areas: she knew that we had to work on
them.

It is, thus, evidence of Farina's earliest fusion of her instincts,
which, by a kind of assimilation, binds the essential core of her
death instinct, which continually threatens her existence. This, I
thought, must be present in all developmental phases of her libido,
but especially in the phallic and genital stages, which traces back to
disavowed castration in her masochistic phantasies of being
castrated, indeed, copulated with, giving birth to a baby that she
did not want. As Freud (1905d) specified in the case of masochistic
pain, "it may well be that nothing of considerable importance can
occur in the organism without contributing some component to the
excitation of the sexual instinct" (p. 204). In "The economic problem
of masochism", he discussed that in masochism "pleasure in pain"
subverts the pleasure principle, which would "otherwise tend
toward the zero excitation characteristics of the Nirvana principle
and would be entirely in the service of the death instincts" (Freud,
1924c, p. 160). Farina's portion of the death instinct and that of her
libido has not diverted outward towards objects and remains inside
her organism. Freud (1905d), in this regard, suggests that "with the
help of the accompanying sexual excitation . . . becomes libidinally

bound there. It is in this portion that we have come to recognize the original, erotogenic masochism" (pp. 163–164).

As our work progressed further, Farina's defences lessened to the degree that she become able to acknowledge relief and warmth. She became able to acknowledge a helpful object, her ability to relate in the transference increased, and she could internalize her relationships, which led her to further internal shifts and psychic change. The transference became more meaningful to her, and histories of how she turned away from her good feeding objects became clear to her. This indicates that by projecting her love into her abusive father and twisting it, she helped to consolidate the picture of him as a powerful and seductive man. It was this that was causing her anxiety. Farina's choice of men in general reflected the extent of her anxiety that was still operative, but she dissociated herself from it. Her father may well have been seductive towards his daughter, but it was clear to see how this had been used by Farina as a defence.

The question of whether to interpret this material, and if so when, was something I had to think about carefully. I decided to focus on the transference in our relationship as something that was going on all the time and was tangible for her. I was aware that this was something essentially based on Farina's past and the relationship with her internal objects, indeed, her belief about them and what they were like, but she was not yet ready to face the reality completely. However, transference interpretations in the here and now and their relation to her past provided her with the opportunity to make links. This helped Farina to make associations with her painful and shameful memories, and this helped her to build a sense of her own continuity and individuality. As a result, she achieved a healthy relationship, which helped to free her from the earlier, more distorted sense of herself. She began to have a clearer sense of self and, therefore, to gain more autonomy and resilience.

CHAPTER TEN

Case two: Daniel

aniel, a twenty-seven-year-old, married man with one child, was referred by his psychiatrist, who felt at a loss as to what to do with him. Daniel came to the UK as an unaccompanied minor when he was fourteen, due to the loss of his entire family. In the referral letter, the psychiatrist reported that medication had no effect on Daniel's level of anxiety, and in their face-to-face sessions, Daniel had been unable to speak about himself and that they had many occasions when he was completely blocked. He was referred for assessment and possible treatment for anxiety attacks and his increased outbursts of anger, which led to physical violence, directed at the walls and furniture, and destructive behaviour towards his wife in front of his child. While his rages never led to physical attacks on his wife and child, the provocations were severe; shouting, nagging, taunting, mocking, baiting, and so on. He raised a concern that he was neglecting his little girl while he was in his "dark mood".

In our initial assessments, Daniel gave only sparse information about his early development and spoke little about his father. His father was a doctor and an important man in society; he was involved with politics and commanded great respect in the community. He spoke highly of his father, but also mentioned that he had been violent at home. At this stage, he did not tell me that his father had been killed by the authorities. His mother was a nurse; a loving, caring mother, of whom he said, "I had a great relationship with my mother as she was always there for me."

Daniel had witnessed his mother being raped and killed when he was thirteen years old; he had recurrent flashbacks about the incident, but could never finish his thought. Later in the process, Daniel said, "From the age of four months I was looked after by my maternal grandmother, and later cared for in a nursery, when my mother was hospitalized for some months."

He remembered that after her return from hospital, his mother was unable to hold him, and he was told that was due to her having had an operation. He recalled, "My mother had described herself as being devoted to me and was telling others about her deep distress at not being able to hug or hold me, and at having to leave me."

She told Daniel that, for her, separating from Daniel felt like part of her was dead, so much so, that she had discharged herself from hospital early, and the grandmother stayed with them to ensure that she would not have to pick him up. When he was three years old, the family moved to another city, where Daniel was left with a servant while his mother was at work. He was told that he became very distressed and agitated as a result of the separation from his grandmother and his usual nanny, so his mother decided to give up her work to stay home and look after him.

Although initially Daniel talked about his parents with love and respect, he later said with bitterness that his parents had been overprotective of him and he felt lost without them. During his adolescence, when he was pushed towards independence, his ability was minimal and the idea of independence also felt deeply menacing and threatening for him. In relation to girls, when I asked, he said that he felt ridiculed by them and always felt that they suspected he would be impotent. This idea had been dramatically reinforced when his first sexual encounter with his wife ended in abject failure, an event that probably precipitated his acute deterioration, preoccupied thoughts, and subsequent behaviour, resorting to dissociation, much of which was not healthy. Daniel worked as an engineer; his job was quite important to him, and he was worried about losing it, as he constantly felt anxious, especially when having to communicate with his staff. In response to my question about his anxiety, he concretely said, "When I think about my wife, my anxiety reaches high levels." It was difficult to gather a coherent history from him, as he was quite limited and aggressive in responding. I perceived this as unhealthy dissociation and not having enough "psychic space", related to the trauma that he had endured. I had the impression that beneath Daniel's controlling, superior, and rigid obsessional structure (which was explained in detail in his referral letter and I was getting a taste of it), there was a phobic organization. Instead of telling me about himself, Daniel spoke about his wife and others, such as his colleagues, neighbours, and politicians.

My assessment of Daniel was that he was an extremely vulnerable patient, whose obsessional personality was causing him severe limitations in his life. He said concretely that although he did not believe in it, he came to see me because he felt things were not going well for him and his doctor told him that therapy would help him (compare to Farina, who referred herself). Daniel's presentation was coherent and interesting when talking about others. He would become livelier and talked without intensity. But he became silent if I turned the direction of the conversation to him. I took these things as evidence of his vulnerability, his unhealthy dissociation, lack of psychic space to deal with his emotional pain, not having a clear sense of self, and, indeed, his inability to relate to me as his listening other. I present a fragment of the material to illustrate this.

In a session, Daniel was talking intensely about a member of his staff, a woman, who makes him extremely unhappy with her lack of competence, but he cannot dismiss her. I asked him how he feels about this woman. After some silence he said, "You see, I am blocked, I'm not able to speak about myself . . . why don't you want to understand this? . . . My wife can be very harsh to me sometimes . . ."

Here, Daniel said nothing in response to my questions, but told me in detail that he was attending his outpatient psychiatric appointments regularly, as he could see no other option but to keep on seeing his psychiatrist, always with the hope of being able to talk. This was his way of warning me of his inability to communicate his feelings and to relate to, or cope with, having a listening other. This showed his intense absence of psychic space for a real relationship. (This hypothesis was later confirmed in the process, as he was not allowing himself to have, and was not allowing me to acknowledge, any psychic space.) However, I was pleased that he was able to tell me much more in two sessions than he could tell his psychiatrist, with great difficulty, over years (this was reported in the referral letter by his psychiatrist). For example, he was able to talk about his father and his involvement with politics. He was killed when Daniel was only nine years old (the psychiatric team were not aware of these facts). He had a vivid memory of saying goodbye to his father for the last time. I understood this to signify that the listening other in our relationship had to some level begun, allowing Daniel to reveal sides of him that other potential listening others had not been permitted to see, due to his unhealthy dissociation, which had the effect that the reality of him ceased to exist, as if there was nothing real about him to be acknowledged.

With my encouragement, he continued to talk about his childhood experience of his father, and said,

> "I will never forget that day. I was upset with my dad, because he was supposed to take me to football the day before but he had a meeting to go to and told me we could not go to football that week and would go next weekend. The next day, when he was driving me to school, I was quiet and did not talk to him. He asked me, 'Are you still sleepy?', and I said yes. When we arrived at school, I reluctantly gave him a kiss on his cheek, but not as warm as usual—that was my last kiss—I never saw him again."

I observed that Daniel started this revelation quite calmly, but was becoming quite tense, revealed by his body movement and the change of his affects in his face. I thought the emotions might be too much for him and felt that I had to do something. I said,

> "Although you are trying so hard to control your sadness, it must be horrible to lose your father this way. It is OK to feel sad about it."

He said, "I do not want to talk about this—just do not ask me about him any more. Do you understand?"

Yet, for me, this was a ray of hope. Daniel's disturbed psychical world, with the right intervention, could begin to take shape for change. He felt he existed not where he was, but elsewhere, through others, especially those who were dead (his father, mother, and maybe his sister and many other relatives and people he knew in childhood, but had no idea where they were and whether they were alive). I could easily imagine that he would feel empty, as he projected his ego so much into others, unhealthily dissociating. With conviction, in our third session, I used quite a simple interpretation, which had a very powerful meaning for Daniel. I said, "When you were telling me that your wife can be a bit harsh, don't you think you were also telling me about yourself?"

From his expression and his physical movement (leaning forward towards me with interest), I felt that a door had opened a crack. I had a sense that it was the first time he had discovered this, and, indeed, was interested to see how he was projecting his feelings to his wife. I put this question to him gently, to test his insight. I was right—it touched upon his projection and his identification, and gave him a glimpse of a world that he wanted to know, so he immediately showed interest, but could not stay with it for long. He changed the subject slightly, but was able to stay with himself, showing the beginning of being able to allow himself to use some of his psychic space positively. Without attaching any importance to it he said, "I had a very happy childhood and my problems started when I left my home country when I was only fourteen."

In our fourth session, we agreed to make a decision on whether to start working together, or if he needed time to think about this type of treatment. Without encouragement, he started telling me about his childhood. He said,

"I lived with my parents from birth, who loved me a lot, and I didn't experience any separation in my early childhood" (later in the process he remembered that he had had a period of separation from his mother, and he had already told me that in his very early life his mother had had an operation). "My maternal grandmother, my aunt and uncle, with the help of my nanny, took care of me whenever my parents needed it. I was never left with a childminder. My mother, like my father, had been very involved with her career and politics, but she had always made sure she had time for me, and always said to me that she would have liked to spend more time with me."

Then he stopped, and there was a long silence. This narrative was offered by Daniel after I told him that we needed to make a decision.

Here, Daniel was talking about an unhappy childhood, which he reported as happy (later in the process it became apparent that his mother was not actually very well, and had limited involvement with Daniel's care), which is not uncommon in adults who have been exposed to trauma in childhood.

I felt this young man realized that he desperately needed help, but did not know how to use it, and how to make use of me as his listening other, while he had acted as a listening other to others in order to avoid being listened to. He was trying so hard to talk and make a case for being my patient and not being rejected. I put that to him. He said,

"I would be very interested in coming to see you, this is really interesting, . . . but I am so tied up both professionally and with family commitments and have so little time that I would never find the time to come and see you three times a week as you are asking me to . . . I don't know what to say."

I told him, "I see, although you can see the need, you are not sure about it. I understand it is an important decision for you to make. Why don't you think about it and let me know your decision later? If you decide to go ahead, we can arrange a regular time to meet, and if you decide it is not for you just now, the door will always be open if you change your mind. In case you decide to go ahead, I propose that we should meet three times a week, but initially we start with twice a week, as I do not have room in my diary for the third session yet, increasing to three sessions in couple of months time."

I thought he needed me to be firm with him and set the boundary from the beginning. However, although I offered this to him, knowing he needed help, part of me wished that he would say no, as I found him quite challenging. I then suddenly felt infused by feelings of sadness and disappointment, and I wondered whether this might be due to projective counter-identification. This could be the sadness that Daniel as a child had and dissociated from and totally disavowed; something he could not yet speak about or, perhaps, could not admit to himself. I felt that through projections he was sharing this feeling with me unconsciously. I thought of an interpretation and said to him, in a tone that reflected the sadness I had felt,

"Your mother was very interested in looking after you when you were a child, but she was so involved with her profession and with her political beliefs, indeed with being ill as the result of her operation, that it was impossible for her to look after you the way both you and she wished for. So here, because I said that I don't yet have time to fit in our third session, but we can start with two sessions initially, then increase to three in two months, I scared you by not being here for you."

A heavy silence set in, charged with emotion and quite unusual affect for Daniel. After a long, but calm and thoughtful silence, Daniel spoke with sadness in his tone for the first time,

"I agree to undertake the therapy sessions you are able to offer me, I mean initially limited to twice a week, which was not what I had in mind and not what you said I needed."

This was very good. It seemed to me that Daniel had recognized his mother's discourse in what he had said to me, and he had also recognized in the tone of my response what he had never been able to admit to himself. He experienced what could happen in the transference and therapeutic relationship between us. We had experienced an exchange that reminded him of the exchanges that he had once experienced with his mother, so that these now acquired new meaning. A door had begun to open for Daniel into the world of the unconscious. He said, "I am now convinced that with this new dimension in my life there must be a way forward."

Here, the transference interpretations opened a window for Daniel to get in touch with his sadness for the first time (he confirmed this). It is my experience that in order to move forward with this type of patient, just being there is an important factor. The focus, therefore, has to be in being a listening other and paying attention to small changes without too much interpretation.

So, we started working. In the process, Daniel's resistance gave way to thoughts and impulses about which he felt ashamed, embarrassed, excited, or guilty. Further details of his sexual life soon appeared to be a serious issue that he had not been able to disclose before. He had started masturbating in his sister's room at the age of ten, after his father was executed, holding his sister's underwear, both fearing and wishing to be seen. He related these events with shame, embarrassment, and self-disgust, hence, there was still a tinge of excitement as he was talking about it. Thus, it was easy to hypothesize that his disgust was a reaction formation to his libidinal excitement. Slowly, he revealed a catalogue of sadistic interests and phantasies. Things to do with death, dying, or ghastly and horrid situations that attracted, pleased, and satisfied him; for example, watching reports of rape or people being tortured, learning about people in concentration camps, and sexual murders filled him with excitement. His ultimate wish was to have sex with a corpse. Following further explorations of his phantasy regarding the creation of exaggerated mental images in response to his ungratified needs, it emerged these were related to his mother. He recalled that her breasts and genitals had fascinated him. He became aroused by talking about witnessing his mother being raped and killed by officials.

Although I did agree to work with Daniel (with hesitation), I could not even imagine his level of disturbances. My hesitation was based on the fact that I did not like this angry man who talked *at* me rather than *to* me and would reject anything I suggested. Here I was, being constantly shocked by his reports of perversion, and he did not show any interest in hearing my interpretations and would dismiss them as rubbish in an aggressive manner. However, the interpretation of my countertransference feelings put me in touch with the part of Daniel that felt dead to him.

In a session in which Daniel was presenting with bizarre behaviour, I put to him,

"I wonder if with your behaviour you wish to drive me 'mad'—wanting me to scream and shout at you, to reject you, as you see it in your phantasy."

In response to this interpretation he calmed down, and was able to talk about his mother's panic attacks in his childhood. He said,

"She would scream, lying on the floor, kicking, swearing, and having to be restrained by my father or other male family members. There were occasions when my mother would lock herself in the bathroom, falling with a thump, and then lying silently. I would be wondering if she was dead. I despised her for this in the most extreme way. I have told you this, but, please do not tell me anything about it. OK?"

I listened to him and did not say anything. Regrettably, it has not been possible to ascertain the exact nature of the mother's mental state, and to examine whether this was due to her personality problem or *her* trauma, with related symptoms of post traumatic stress disorder. The latter seems to be more likely, as there was no history of mental illness in the family or, in fact, physical illness, except as a result of her being tortured badly (although Daniel initially told me his mother was in hospital, later he said he was able to speak to his extended family in his country of origin, and was informed that his mother was, in fact, in prison and not in hospital, and that she could not hold him because she had been severely tortured).

On my announcement of our first break, Daniel's anger and violent feelings towards me became more real and apparent (by this time, we had been meeting for almost four months, initially twice weekly for two months, then three times weekly). He had overcome some resistance, with my help, and had reported details of his private world. I indicated my awareness of how courageous he had been to trust our relationship. He could, at times, react with acute paranoia and contempt. In transference, he went back to the initial stage of our meetings, experiencing me quite concretely as hating him, disrespecting him, and being annoyed with him. He truly felt and believed that I had contemptuous feelings towards him; he felt humiliated and deeply distressed. In transference, I had become his mother, who rejected and humiliated him for his powerlessness. At this stage, any form of interpretative intervention, transference, or otherwise could barely subdue his hatred, resentment, and rage towards me. At times, I was bored by his remarks, and on occasions, I was frightened; for example, once when his rage was explicit and threatening he said with contempt, "I would smash your eyes if you are making me a laughing matter."

After the break (two weeks), he missed another two weeks' sessions (twelve sequential sessions) without either phoning or writing, and came back without prior announcement or response to my letters (I wrote two letters in his absence to say that I was sorry to not see or hear from him, and to remind him of the date and time of our sessions). On his return he said he could not bring himself to come, and could not make contact with the Centre either. He felt that I had told everyone about his phantasies and about what he wished to do to his wife (he had not mentioned anything about a phantasy about his wife before, but his feelings and beliefs were quite real to him). I was keen to know where all these phantasies were coming from. With exploration, it became apparent that his perception arose from the fact that a new member of the office staff had smiled, welcoming him when she opened the front door to him, and had asked him who he had an appointment with. I explained that she was new and her question was genuine, as she was not aware of whom he was seeing. But he was suspicious and his rage about this encounter subsequently continued to quite a worrying level. After a few occasions on which he showed this kind of rage, I explained to him that if he felt this way, and if coming to see me caused him so much extra pain, worry, and anger, we might have to make a decision to suspend his therapy for the time being. This provided further substance for his rage. He resentfully complained, "If my parents were alive, they would support me no matter what, why can't you?"

Both wonder and scepticism were reflected in his omnipotent feeling that if I really meant to help him, I should allow him to do and say whatever he wanted in whatever manner he wanted; otherwise I was, he said, "A pretentious liar, like all the others, pretending to care."

My fear and anxiety about his aggression increased further when he angrily reported that he had murderous feelings and that he saw young woman laughing at him, which I took to mean staff in the office. It became clear to me that during our separation in the break he had lost any psychic space that we had managed to build during the previous four months, and thus he had no sense of self and no sense of reality. He was in a state of total paranoia. His anxiety was increasing massively, to a debilitating and unmanageable extent. So, I made the decision that I had to manage this situation, which was perceived as very real to him, and that it should not be through use of transference interpretations. It had to be concrete and accessible to him, in a form that he could not dissociate from easily. I talked to him about this, and we made an agreement that if he came exactly on time, I would personally open the door for him, so he would not need to face anybody else in the Centre. Daniel settled for this agreement and kept to it for a long time without fail. I was relieved, and could conduct the sessions with some degree of comfort, although he was still displayed extreme anger towards me and would speak in a hostile way, making rumbling noises when I made interpretations or asked him a question, thus not allowing me into his thought and feelings.

On one occasion, I noticed that the sound he directed at me sounded both like a dog aggressively barking and the bark of guns.

I realized that I had unconsciously identified this in him before, but could not make sense of it. This suddenly dawned on me and helped me to locate that this was how he felt he was being treated, in his inner world, in general, and in his transference with me, especially when I gave him warnings about suspending his therapy. I realized that, in the transference, Daniel's cruel and relentless hatred, anger, and disgust towards me, his wish to attack me and kill me, and his contempt and denigration, represented his attack on his mother, aimed at triumphing over her, seeing her break down, go mad, feel castrated and helpless, which corresponded clearly with his image of wanting to be intimate with a female corpse. He was hoping to achieve this with me; he would come to sessions in a state of excitement and full of expectation and hope that I would attack him if he behaved badly to me. Consequently, in his phantasy, he could experience me having a panic attack in the consulting room with him, hence, as a grown man, he would now not be scared as he was as a little boy witnessing his mother having such an attack. So, in his mind, that is what he strove for. If he could cause me to have an attack, he could hold me, hug me, comfort and rescue me, which he had not been able to do with his mother, and when he was disappointed, he felt attacked and humiliated and wanted me to die. If I was dead and he did not have a relationship with me, he would not need to go through this disappointment, and, thus, he did not fear harming me or losing me. On the other hand, his dependency on me was growing dramatically, painfully forcing the realization that he needed me, which represented his need for his mother. He hated this, and reacted with rage and fear. So, for this reason, our breaks became catastrophic for him. However, despite all these things, we reached a stage where he was starting to gather a sense of self, and could verbalize how the absence of the listening other felt to him, and he could see how this affected him and blocked his psychic space to think about himself and to gain insight into his experiences and its effect on his daily functioning. Ending each session was becoming more and more unbearable for him and would create strong feelings of rejection, abandonment, helplessness, and the fear of losing me, and he left with the feeling of wondering whether I would be alive for our next session. He was patently suffering when the sessions came to end, resulting in intense feelings and his paranoid ideas of my hatred and contempt for him. In turn, he became increasingly appalled and revolted by my interpretations, in particular those focusing on his wish to be loved, admired, and held by me. This was coupled with the underlying terror he had had to go through when realizing that his mother would never come back again, and responding to the feelings underlying his hatred, which were reflections of the wish for permanent union with her, about which he felt deeply ashamed and humiliated. However, as expression of his feelings now unquestionably existed in transference, he gradually became responsive to transference interpretations. However, although there was clear evidence of improvement, I was concerned that he was still not reporting any dreams.

In this process, he began to get in touch with his feeling of hatred towards his mother for leaving him as a baby, and repeated reminiscences of her panic attacks, during which he was terrified of her dying. He became able to approach his deeper feelings that his mother had hated him, and it was at such times that he experienced himself as dead. This evidently was repeated with me in the transference, through his provocations to get me to attack him, to react to his aggression and fear him, responses that would make him feel alive and competent. This was less of a paradox than it at first appears to be. In view of the fact that if he could leave a session feeling aroused or alive, the objects at risk outside the consulting room—the girls in the office, representing his mother or perhaps the absent sister, whom he might murder—were temporarily protected (in this period he told me about his only sister, two years his senior, being taken by soldiers on the same occasion that they raped and killed his mother, and this was the first time he had talked about his sister).

Here, it is evident that Daniel's early broken and, therefore, unresolved relationship with his mother was re-enacted in the transference, especially his attempt to assume control over the abandoning m/other, which was constantly present in here and now. He felt that as his therapist, I was making him feel bad and dead, so, in his mind, he was attempting a role reversal to feel in control. Daniel wanted the gratification of leaving me feeling dead, useless, an incompetent and inadequate therapist, so that he could remain unaware of the underlying feelings of envy and admiration which filled him with despair and self-hatred. Thus, despite his continuous determination to attack me and "make me suffer", as he put it, a distinct pattern had been established and clarified, which was helpful in allowing him to talk further. He became more able to feel safe with me. This was reflected in his comment, "You know, when I leave the sessions frustrated at not having succeeded in killing you by my 'badness', I act this out by murdering you at home in my phantasy, so, for me, you are dead until our next session anyway."

After this, Daniel became quite obsessed with the idea that I was attracted to him and that I wished to see his penis, but could not ask him. When I challenged his thoughts through interpretation, he felt rejected, and acted this out by starting to come late for sessions and avoiding participating in treatment. We had a few sessions in total silence. When this was challenged, he perceived it as if I needed his attention all the time, and was fearful of losing him: in his mind, he was the love of my life. Although this was a challenging process, he had made some changes, for example, his delusional projection of his sexual preoccupations was beginning to decrease with his assuming an unwilling ownership and understanding of himself; this had the potential to open some psychic space for him, enabling him to make sense of himself to some extent. This, however, was a problem. On the one hand, if he saw me as accepting him as my patient and as being able to contain his projections, he would feel disgusting, while on the other hand, if he felt rejected by me, it meant to him that I hated him, was disgusted by him, and wished him to die. The concept of me trying to help him as his therapist was not one he yet could relate to. He would respond to my comments with phrases such as, "This is rubbish", "This is nonsense", and "Don't give me this rubbish".

So, achievement of a therapeutic alliance and bonding at the conscious level with him was evidently not possible, or was very minimal, at that stage of our work. He reached a less paranoid state and could have some sense of himself as separate from me, his potential listening other, so we managed to make some progress with transference interpretation.

In one session, in a little boy voice, he acknowledged positive feelings towards me and said, "I do sometimes miss you, you know . . . I wish to kiss you and to be kissed by you, touch you and hug you, I wish you could hold me . . . I know you can't, even if you wanted to."

This immediately overwhelmed him with self-hatred.

I said, "It is quite sad that you are not able to stay with your warm feeling of wanting to be close to me as you wanted as a little boy to be close to your mother."

The moment was lost. He could not stay with his feeling. He shifted and started telling me about his masturbation. I did not attend to his perversion, as I wanted to try to stay with his feeling of wanting to be close. I continued with transference interpretations and, through further explorations, he responded well. He discovered his wish to unite with me, as a person representing the parental couple, in a state of permanent non-separation. This discovery was confirmed by Daniel to be good for him and he could, on reflection, now relate to and understand his compulsive anal masturbation between sessions, at weekends and excessively during our breaks, which he was regularly reporting. Through this discovery he became able to verbalize some of his feelings. He said, "Within the sessions I experienced you as someone or something I merge with and feel comfortable with, but when the sessions end, I see you as a horrible person, attacking me, and the only recourse I had to keep myself contained was to use my finger for anal masturbation. It is like a substitute."

This was a sign that by having me as his listening other he was gradually gaining more psychic space for reflection and developing a bit clearer sense of himself and insight to his mind and, therefore, some resilience. Although it was not an easy task to deal with him in the way he presented his feelings, my sympathetic responses were felt by him, but only when he was able to hear and relate to interpretation without feeling attacked.

With Daniel I had to learn that when he was in paranoid state of mind, insight was not achievable for him at all. I also learnt that I had to monitor my countertransference feelings very carefully and constantly remind myself how much Daniel had suffered and how ill he was. My awareness of this, and of the spiteful and complex ways in which he constantly attempted to ask for my collusion in his destructive attacks on the treatment and on me (representative of his powerless relationship with his mother, to whom he was so intensely and primitively attached), served to remind me of my role, and of the importance of not giving up on him. It became evident that when he was not in a paranoid state of mind, with associated contempt and rage, further exploration and transference interpretations would bring insight and comfort to him and enable him to talk about his fears. Thus, Daniel gained some insight about his relationship with his wife. He was able to express that the reason he was impotent was because he was deeply fearful of women's genitals. He was very scared of hurting his wife. He was able to talk about how frustrated he got when he attempted sexual relations with his wife and failed; in response to my question, he said,

> "I get mildly excited while my wife's clothes are on, but upon their removal I would feel paralysed with anxiety, I get scared and angry and because of my impotence I get in an out-of-control rage. I fear I may strangle her, I want to bite her, I want to squeeze the life out of her, I want to kill her . . . I hate it when she looks at me with pity . . . and when I tell her 'Don't look at me that way' . . . she starts crying . . . I really could kill her . . . you know . . . then I get so scared . . . thinking this is my child's mother . . . it is really scary . . ."

> I said, "It is frustrating not to be able to have a loving, intimate relationship with your wife . . . and you wish her dead rather than seeing that you are upsetting her. It seems to me that because your opportunity to build a loving relationship with your mother was taken away from you, it left you very vulnerable . . . and makes it very hard for you to even imagine that you are able to build a relationship with another woman. I cannot help wondering whether those soldiers killed part of you by killing your mother. . . . We never actually talked about whether your wife is aware of what happened to you and your family."

> He said, "No, I never discussed my past or these feelings with my wife and I never will . . . are you mad?"

This brief material aims to present a clear descriptive account of Daniel's disturbances and in particular the detail of the transference manifestations. Therefore, a fairly typical session posits that this unusually and perhaps exceptionally kind therapeutic intervention is specifically appropriate in working with patients who have suffered severe external trauma. I have attempted to portray methodically the repetitive quality of Daniel's remorseless attacks on me, and how this continued over long periods of time. He was reacting to feelings of dependence, need, and vulnerability, so he became tough, abusive, and potentially murderous towards the objects he depended on, and feared (as did I) that he would lose control and act out this aggression on me, his wife, and others he depended on. It became evident to me, in the process, that this was clearly related to his childhood disturbances of attachment to and separation from his m/others, which continued and culminated in him becoming a refugee child. So, he grew up with complete cultural alienation, and alienated himself further by not talking to anybody about what had happened to him, in the hope of forgetting and getting on with life like other adolescents of his age. However, although he focused on his studies and was academically, and later professionally, very successful, he was not able to stop the horror inside him, the nightmares, and the flashbacks, which he was never able to complete, and which were eating away his sanity. Here, I present another example.

In a session, Daniel told me that he had seen me in the street earlier that morning and was stunned that I was really alive and that the thought of me being alive was shocking and unbearable for him. He said,

> "I only feel safe if I know that you are here with me and dead after I am gone, that is why when I thought about you outside the sessions I could not cope . . . I never thought about it before. It was shocking to see you. It was so real . . . so scary, I froze up . . . I don't know why, but this is very disturbing to me."

I said, "Perhaps for this reason, between the sessions you needed to use your finger for anal masturbation and imagine that I was with you, even as a piece of shit, so you could feel close, warm, and in control of me and yourself. So, seeing me in the street is, in a sense, the loss of your phantasy of keeping me in control over your finger . . ."

He demonstrated growing murderous rage, which I interpreted as his attempt to reverse his feelings of deadness in himself after having seen me alive in the street earlier. I said,

> "My being alive impinged on your phantasy that you had left a session with me dead, and you lost the power to place me inside your anus, which could help you in your phantasy to re-establish your aliveness by trying to have me inside your body, even dead. This is perhaps linked with the time when you experienced your screams as not being heard by anyone around when your mother was raped and killed by soldiers and you could do nothing."

He immediately calmed down and responded reasonably well. This helped us to reach the stage where he was able to talk from beginning to end about his disturbing memories and flashbacks without experiencing a mental block. This effected a change, and he became close to his feelings related to the time when he experienced himself as dead with his mother.

The reconstruction was such that Daniel was able to experience a sense of triumphant aliveness through manipulation of his column of faeces, into which he could project his feelings of deadness and so overcome them. This was re-enacted in his sexual phantasy about the dead, in which the corpse was identified with the faeces, which in turn confirmed his aliveness and enabled him to feel safe and intact. I had to take constant hammering from him for being alive, and then he would continue his attack with contempt and disgust for himself for needing me to be inside him dead. He initially imposed a penalty and told me that I was incompetent, useless, disgusting, and disgraceful. He wished to make me suffer; he made hostile sounds and spoke in a hostile way with hatred, at times threatening to stop the treatment or kill himself. We moved from this stage, reaching the stage that, in his phantasy, he could kill me and keep me inside himself between sessions and that kept him going. During this period, he had a real relationship with me for three hours a week, alive and real. So, this relationship, with its challenges for him, led to the point where he was able to express hopelessness at his dependency on me, into which he by now had the insight to link it to his losses and view his compulsive anal masturbation as an unhealthy dissociation.

This, although not much, was a great therapeutic achievement. However, in my countertransference I was experiencing difficulties, often feeling distressed and uncomfortable and having to watch my self-protective mechanisms very carefully, so as to obviate the possibility of a countertransference acting out. Sometimes I felt dead, with no energy to continue, and at times, as the result of introjections, I did not wish to continue. With this background, I now present a fragment of a session.

At the beginning of this session, Daniel made rumbling noises of frustration and disgust when he entered the room and lay on the couch. He expressed his hatred of me for making him need me and he snarled bitterly at me because he felt dependent. He started by saying,

"You disgust me; just sitting there, without saying anything . . . I know you are not going to answer . . . why don't you talk to me? I hate you for making me need you . . . you enjoy this . . . you enjoy seeing me needy and seeing me vulnerable . . ."

I did not respond. After a few moments of silence, he said,

"I am just talking to the wall and I can't believe that I can't get up and leave . . . I wish I could make you suffer as I did with my parents, but it doesn't work with you. They reacted, but you refuse to react. You say that I get sexually excited if I can get you to talk, but you are not going to give in like they did. I want to make you suffer. I hear my mother calling me . . . I wish she was here . . . no, no, I don't . . ."

He became silent for a few minutes. I interpreted his suffering about a forthcoming break, and said,

"Your pain, your sense of loss, and your feeling that I am leaving you alone with your 'madness', indeed your murderous feelings towards your mother . . ."

He interrupted me with a grumble of contempt. I continued,

"Despite your grumbles, we both know that there is a longing for closeness, a wish to possess me, a wish to have me in a way that I would never leave you, like the feeling you wanted to have with your mother."

He again responded with a snarl and a contemptuous noise and said,

"Why do I have to listen to the rubbish you say about you and your breaks . . . always it is you who decides about breaks without even asking me . . . I have to take it or leave it, even if I feel like shit about it . . . yes, it disgusts me that I need you so much and I want you to talk to me and to consult me first before making decisions about your bloody breaks . . . It is no good telling me four months or six months in advance . . . It is still not my decision . . . Still, it shows that you don't care about me and you have to be in control. You are just doing your job and you will be happy if I die . . . you go and spend your time with your family . . . I hope . . ."

I interpreted by suggesting,

"I can see how frightened you are about the break and how much you wish me to know these feelings that you have for me, how much you feel that you need me, how much part of you wants me to love you and part of you needs me to hate you in the way that you hated yourself for having needs and feelings. You are in rage with me, because without me you don't need to think about yourself . . . I can see that you are like a little lost boy who needs his mother and so much wants me to be your mother—it seems unbearable for the little boy in you to think of his mother leaving little Daniel to spend time with her family . . ."

He calmed down and became tearful. I continued, "The dreadful ill will that consumed you and with which you are compelled to attack me. You think if you were to show me the sweet little boy part of you or anything other than spitefulness, you would be terrified of how vulnerable you would be. You are scared that I would ridicule you just as you ridicule yourself when you feel there is something special between us. There is a relationship, and it is a relationship that you want to have and, despite your denial, you are longing for. My integrity lies in considering how to look after you and this is hard for you to believe. I imagine, although you feel that there is a relationship between us, you don't want to accept that you can relate to me safely and to learn how to relate to others outside here."

Once again, although he was listening, he went back to his aggressive manner and responded with contempt, saying,

"What are you talking about—this is rubbish . . . All I want is to make you suffer, like my mother . . . And what drives me mad is that I can't do it. I can't get to you . . . I want to captivate you. I know I irritate you. I can see from your face and from the tone of your voice . . . well, you wouldn't be human if you were not getting irritated with me . . . I want to kill you, I want you dead. I can't think of you alive. It disgusts me if I think that you see other people and to think of your husband and son . . . I wish them dead. I really wish them dead, even I die with them. I wish your son dead if you have one. I wish him dead."

I said, "It is clear that you want to treat me like a piece of shit, and you want me to feel that I am a piece of shit; but you also want me to be dead, then you would not have a relationship with me, rather you could have control and manipulate you feelings as you wish, doing to me what you want in your phantasy without fear of my retaliation. On the other hand, part of you wants me to stay alive and to teach you how to build relationships and you wish to kill my son in your phantasy, if I have a son, because that gives you hope of becoming my only son."

I interpreted that on the one hand, Daniel was telling me that he could not bear the thought of me belonging to anyone else other than him, just as I die in between sessions, so did everything else that he related to me. On the other hand, he was indicating that the existence of other preoccupations with his mother, of whom I was a representation, caused him to experience death.

He responded well to this interpretation and said,

"You are right this time . . . Yes, it disturbs me every time that I think of you alive. Although it is frightening me to death, I want to kill you; I want to smash your head in here and now. But, I also want to kill your son. You are right; I do want to be your only son. Do you have a son? Sorry, if you have one. I shouldn't say what I said. But, he is a very lucky man if you have one. I think what is happening is that the way I love you or I need you is quite a strange feeling for me and I don't know how to deal with it."

I said, "I am pleased to hear that you do know these are more your thoughts than reality, but you feel that you do not want to get close to anyone and let yourself believe that you have no need for closeness either, but part of you knows that this is not true and our relationship has proved that. You now know you are longing for relationships, but you are scared of loss. So, if you don't have a relationship, you don't need to be terrified of losing it. The problem with our relationship seems to be that you feel that you have to love me because you need me too much, so, this makes you feel vulnerable, like a baby who needs his mother's breast but expects to be rejected and not to have his cries heard by his mother, to be abandoned and left alone, just as you now feel left by me . . . not attended to and not heard properly, as we now approach the break."

It was the end of the session, and he left with disapproving ridicule and dismay, saying, "Rubbish, rubbish, rubbish. Keep it to yourself . . . see you whenever."

Daniel, in many sessions, elaborately brushed aside my interventions as unpleasant encounters, showing no interest in the roots of his problems, effectively numbing and deadening me. He constantly expressed his wish to kill me, so that I could serve his need as a dead object over which he had complete possession and control and in comparison with whom he would feel alive. His attacks and provocations were aimed at getting me to behave indignantly and dreadfully towards him. This, in his mind, would enable him to see me as useless and empty, in order for him to deal with envious feelings towards me which he experienced very strongly when he perceived me as a person possessing a quality that he needed. I had to raise this with him on many occasions and to explore how his perversion was lived out in the transference, with little approval and mainly ridicule and disparagement in response. I, as his listening other, the denigrated therapist, represented the dead body idealized by Daniel; being castrated and dead, in his mind, and not able to offer resistance or opposition, would result in Daniel feeling alive. The perverse phantasy, although a deeply regressive manifestation, did reflect an intimate link with the Oedipus complex, in so far as the triangular relationship was reintroduced in his phantasy of vagina and castration that was avoided through his attachment to the dead body and then his perverse, uncontrollable attachment to me. The pathological nature of his superego can be in no doubt. It was also apparent to me that at this stage Daniel functioned in an extremely primitive way, but, slowly, he was gaining enough resilience and an improved sense of self to enable him to have some psychic space in which to think about himself that he did not have before.

Daniel's acute castration anxiety, his sadistic phantasies about female genitals, his phantasies of himself as a girl with his anus being penetrated, and his phallic pleasure derived from anal masturbation, I could see, in pre-Oedipal and Oedipal terms, as defences against genital strivings and dependency on his unavailable mother. Some of his phantasies also arose from his traumatic observation of his mother being raped and murdered when he was in early adolescence. His desire for the dead in his phantasy, which was stimulated by the many significant deaths in his life, seemed to be related to his wish to merge with his dead mother. Daniel's impotence, as well as his cultural inhibitions, contributed to his revolt against sexuality, which was intimately linked with his destructive phantasy. His unconscious yearning for his mother, which stemmed from his infancy, before she was killed, created his phantasy of a dead woman's body, coupled with the notion of being a frightened and castrated little boy with the hope that the dead mother would not get ill, would not have panic attacks, and would not get raped or murdered. So, in his phantasy, he would be safe with the dead mother. Castration and death, for him, were the supreme threats against which his deeply wounded narcissism rebelled, and his unsafe desirability was replaced by disgust, which maintained his life. Hence, the reason he insisted on his wife being a passive, help-less, and inert partner who gave him a sense of power and the secu-rity that he would not be castrated. He became able to allow himself to say that any movement from his wife to get close to him would make him extremely frightened and to feel the need to eliminate the risk of rejection and retaliation. I made the interpretation that his wife brings back the fear he had in adolescence when his mother had panic attacks. He felt really offended by this comparison.

Daniel's dread of annihilation and castration was projected on to the object, which led to his sense of being alive and unharmed. His attachment to, and identification with, the object as his solitary source of narcissistic supply, meant that he experienced the trau-matic memory that he so much wanted to avoid—when he is faced with object loss. He experienced this with me in the transference, while his compelling attempts to destroy me ground away his awareness of his need for me, initially resulting in catastrophic separation anxiety reactions, a pre-genital sadistic wish to kill the love-object, and the possession of the object that only can be achieved if it is eaten up and destroyed. However, using transfer-ence interpretation and working on these issues, I provided Daniel with some insight and a little more psychic space for reflection. In one of the sessions when Daniel was threatening me, he said, "It is the only way that I could keep you to myself, and protect you. I stop you from leaving me and going away from my side to be killed in this dangerous world . . . the world is very dangerous place and you do not seem to grasp that."

Daniel's need for me here is characterized by his greedy and destructive tendencies that reflect his unsatisfactory early experi-ences. This was confirmation that his phantasy was a projection and his sexual interest, especially his compulsive wish for my dead body, betrayed his part wish to be alive, hence, the prospect of my retaliation presented him with a strong fear of relating and being in a meaningful relationship. However, after he formed sufficient attachment to me, albeit not constructively, he then became fearful of me not being there for him; this was an improvement. He was also fearful of making me ill with his stress as his mother was, so his wish to kill me was the result of his fear of loss and his help-lessness. In transference, I could be Daniel's father, who was killed by the authorities. Thus, if I were dead, he would have his triangular relationship back, and instead of dealing with the losses of his parents, he would replace them with my corpse, and in his phantasy he would be safe. For him, the object must be dead, in order for him to feel safe. I put this to him.

"I can see that you sometimes think of me of your mother and sometimes as your father, but, both are uncomfortable as you are so fearful of losing me. It seems to me that in your mind, if I was dead, I would be safe in your possession and you would never lose me again and no one could rape me, kill me and take me away from you."

He found this helpful and we explored it further. As a result, he became able to enact a reversal of the image of his mother's killing and her abandonment of him. That was a great shift in Daniel's psyche and helped him to move forward. This was the first time that Daniel could convert his childhood trauma into something positive as an adult. It becomes clearer to him that his phantasy was closely linked to, and stuck in, his Oedipal process as well as his pathological superego. Albeit with difficulty, he realized that in his masochistic perversions, his ego chose an activity that would please a sadistic superego and his gratification was located in the total destruction of his dead object. In his hostility to his perverse self, he could identify with a sadistic and unforgiving superego, but the dead object remained a compelling source of attraction and fulfilment to him with its possibilities of acting out his phantasies, among which was killing me in his transference feelings. The part of Daniel who hated himself and the part of him that was gratified by the perverse phantasy endorsed his parts to operate exclusively of each other, without modification.

Despite some improvement, Daniel's primitive split-off part of his ego was located at an archaic level of object relationship and consequently was more likely to be fixated with psychotic features most of the time. However, at this stage of therapy and with the increase in his understanding, he showed that he had gained some level of resilience. It became clear to me that Daniel functioned on different types of defences, those (1) of external trauma from the sadistic perversions, where it is apparent that survival of the object is paramount; (2) of the split ego that retains a good relation to reality; (3) of using denial, disavowal, and unhealthy dissociations to block his potential to use me as his listening other in order to develop some psychic space, thus resulting in him clinging to his psychotic delusional dissociation and preventing him from achieving a coherent sense of self.

His high level of anxiety and his constant unhealthy dissociation was accounting for his controlled behaviour at work and, to some level, adapted behaviour at home. His behaviour with me in the transference implied his borderline pathology and early psychosis. This was apparent from our initial meetings, but in the process we found a way that I could let him be for a while, without too much confrontational interpretation or challenge, allowing him to develop an ability to relate to himself when his psychic space allowed and it was bearable for him.

Daniel's adolescent developmental process was severely disrupted by the external traumatic events, which deeply interfered with his development and resulted in his psychic conflicts. However, through very gentle and careful interpretation, specifically focusing on his anxiety and the manner in which he dealt with it, gradually, the roots of his anxiety became clearer to him and therefore much more predictable. This achievement allowed us to move forward. I could then use interpretation more freely and he became comparatively more perceptive. As a result, the quality of his object relationships was set, and the channels for his libidinal gratification became much more specific. His perversion was manifested in the form of his primitive masturbation and phantasies, specifically, his feeling of being in a state of symbiotic union with his object. In transference manifestation and interpretations, it became known to him that his way of dealing with his unresolved trauma was not an acceptable way of dealing with his pain.

It was clear to me that standing in the way of allowing the repressive processes of his young adulthood to bury his phantasy in the unconscious may well be crucial in keeping alive some trace of hope for his integration. However, I was left with uncertainty about the danger of reconstructing his adolescent period after the loss of his father and his mother, as that could bring too much pain, too great a burden, which might result in his settling for the false solutions that came with his adulthood and leave him feeling more vulnerable and hopeless. It was too much of a risk that the little resilience he developed would get lost again, and that he may have a serious breakdown. Although I was ambivalent, I decided not go that way, as I did not think it would be productive. At this stage of therapy, although Daniel had made sufficient improvements to prevent him suffering a serious psychotic breakdown, he continued to be in a state of constant vulnerability. Aspects of his childhood memories, apart from the traumatic ones, remained unknown, which was frustrating for him. However, his obsessional paranoia was lessening, specially with me and with staff at the clinic: for example, he would say hello and goodbye to members of the office staff when he saw them, if he was going to be late, he would phone and introduce himself, leaving a message for me, and he was dealing with my break in a sensible manner, but his obsessional paranoia in general still remained one of his problematic characteristics which needed further work.

Thus, the two levels of operating, his obsessional control, and his defence against his phobia, could be seen to be lived out in transference. When the deeper layer was tackled by transference interpretation, he could sense why the gentle use of my words felt knife-like, and his anxieties re-emerged in transference. We worked on them in a meaningful manner this time, and his understanding increased. His psychic space evidently developed much further, which led to him having a better sense of himself, and he started associating with his pain in a reflective way. He developed the ability to verbalize his feelings, rather than acting them out.

This I consider a great achievement. It is the case that as a therapist, being a listening other, I had a great deal of experience of neurotic defences and could easily detect them in patients. However, special effort and attention was required to be able to detect the presence of primitive/psychotic defences in a patient like Daniel. I had to understand the link—or lack of link—that existed in his personality and, therefore, his pattern of communication, and it took some time to get it reasonably right. Although Daniel, at an intellectual level, was educated and held a professional job, he had difficulties in accessing the symbolic meaning of language and needed my discourse to awaken or reawaken his bodily phantasies to help him to find their emotional meaning in his forgotten sensory experiences. This, then, becomes a point of departure for his mental representation. I find what Freud (1924e) says not enough, but none the less helpful in this regard:

world of phantasy that the neurosis draws the material for its new
wishful constructions . . . the world of phantasy plays the same part
in psychosis and there, too, it is the storehouse from which the
materials or the pattern for building the new reality are derived.
[p. 187]

Hence, encouraging Daniel to have contact with his phantasy world
was paramount in offering a special setting to him, as someone who
fluctuated between the psychotic and the neurotic aspects of
himself without having a clear sense of self or enough psychic space
for reflection to begin with.

For any process to be established, Daniel needed to feel that I
was constantly aware of the presence of these different aspects in
him, which he himself was not able to distinguish, and that I was
listening carefully. I can illustrate this with a statement Daniel made
at our initial meeting. He said, "I was happy since my birth, before
I became a refugee." This could be understood in different ways:
(1) it could simply be a tribute to his parents' wish for him to be
happy, or (2) it could be a disavowal of the existence of the unhappiness he felt all his life. They are interrelated, and one does not
necessarily exclude the other. With that statement in that meeting,
Daniel presented simultaneously the angles of neurosis and of
psychosis.

In the beginning of the process, Daniel mostly presented a fragmented part of himself; however, as therapy progressed further and
he gained some level of resilience this changed, and I learnt how to
relate to him and when and what to interpret or not to. In my interpretation, I would focus on his more developed neurotic level, but
occasionally add something to let him know that I had not forgotten the existence of his primitive/psychotic side. When he wished
to leave an aspect of himself out, dissociating unhealthily, I would
see it as my responsibility to draw his attention to it. In a sense, I
became the guardian of Daniel's desire for integrity and resilience;
by being his listening other my aim was to help him to achieve a
good sense of self and more psychic space for reflection, and to
learn to dissociate in a healthy way when his feelings became
unbearable. This helped us to reach the stage that Daniel wished for
his ego reunification and the part of himself that felt lost to him, but
he was also frightened of discovering archaic aspects of himself that

felt mad to him. He was particularly fearful that his mad side may contaminate the rest of him and feared that he would never recover, so, as a result, he was constantly dissociating unhealthily.

Another important change made in the process was the fact that Daniel's anxiety was lessening as I interpreted the shame and guilt he felt, feelings that he could not admit to himself. He began to gain awareness of his primitive attitudes. It was helpful for him to be reminded that at work he functioned as a responsible adult, but in therapy and with his family, he was different, and surely he could not be both of these extremely differentiated characters. By doing this, I was de-dramatizing Daniel's vulnerabilities by verbalizing his experience, with the idea of Daniel getting more in touch with aspects of his unconscious.

Daniel needed to identify with me, the person who dared to verbalize his inhibited and inappropriate aspects, a person who was able to look not only at his "madness", but at all parts of him with acceptance. So, Daniel became able to make use of me as his listening other, and that enabled him to gain more psychic space and a better sense of self. I used my countertransference interpretation to show Daniel that I could accept him without falling apart or dying on him. This enabled us to begin to make connections with Daniel's anxieties concerning separation from his object/m/other. For example, in one session, I said,

> "It might be very disconcerting for you to feel like a small child who suffers so much if his mummy goes away, while at the same time you have to make such important decisions that may affect you and your family."

> He said, "I want to get this silly little boy who misses his mummy out of me!"

> His response here is evidence of the insight gained in the therapeutic process and the outcome of transference interpretation. Here, Daniel evidently developed a sense of self and enough psychic space to recognize and relate to his vulnerability, which helped him to create enough resilience to be able to identify and recognize the split parts of himself, which was consistent with his wish to deal with the oppressed and disturbing part of himself. In reality, he had always wished this unconsciously. I repeated to him what he said. On hearing it, Daniel became aware of his tendency to expel and abandon the side of himself of

which he disapproved. In order to be able to adopt and reintegrate his part, he first needed to realize that he had expelled and abandoned it. On reflection I said,

"You would like to get rid of the vulnerable child in you, as you reproach your mother for doing so when she left you."

Daniel was surprised at finding himself identified with a mother whom he both consciously and secretly believed he hated. So, this shifted our work to a different level and we began weaving back and forth between his abandoning ego and his abandoning object. At this stage of our work, his persecutory anxieties had already been diminished substantially, and he gained better knowledge of his object phantasy. He increased capacity and developed enough psychic space to put himself in his mother's place in phantasy. He began to think of his mother as an internal object with more fine distinction for him, just as in the transference. I then appeared to him as a more tolerant object and he regarded me more benevolently. Although, despite a great improvement, Daniel still had a tendency to reject an aspect of himself, I thought at this stage he needed me to remind him of acceptance in my interpretations. It was important to draw his attention to the difficulty the adult part of him had in accepting the oppressed, abandoned, and disturbed child in him.

This we did successfully and without too much challenge. Daniel was embracing a desire to get better, but sometimes dreading it. This at times was related to his fear of getting nearer to the end of his relationship with me. So, as soon as he thought of our separation, he had a tendency to trigger the part of himself that unconsciously sabotaged and incapacitated the progress he had made.

I set myself the task of challenging his behaviour that was focused on hiding his progress from himself. It was necessary to point out to him that he needed me to draw attention to his achievements so that he could gain some confidence in his capacity for reparation and resilience while viewing me as an object that treated him well. He also needed reminding that as his therapist, his listening other, I emphasized his progress, but remained aware that he had not forgotten the negative points. I explained to him that when I offered interpretations by verbalizing his disturbing and fearful thoughts, that was my attempt to hold and contain him not to act out his destructive thoughts and help him to learn that he could feel at ease with his new self.

Here, I was concentrating on what was being lived in the transference and how interpretations were rarely heard when he was anxious and heard well by him when he was near to the depressive position. His operations in transference were based on his primitive defences, and transference interpretations became reality and not his phantasy, so he used the transference differently depending on the level of his psychic space, his ego function, his perception, and his sense of self, which at times could be fragmented. Sometimes, he heard my interpretations in a more paranoid way, as a criticism and an attack on him. Therefore, I had to learn to talk to him carefully about his paranoia at this stage, rather than using confrontational interpreting which would lead him to become absorbed with contempt. Through gentle interpretation, he would still become distressed, but realize that it was all in his mind, and that what he heard was not attacking, but unconsciously understood and used by him in that negative way.

When I first met with Daniel, I was unable to contemplate a possible solution for him to reach at the end of his therapy, but I felt I should give him a chance. It was clear to me from the beginning that, to a great extent, he seemed to block interpretations. My concern was that if, at the end, Daniel remained convinced of his righteousness, in a sense it would reinforce his delusion. I thought this would show me that I was wrong in accepting this type of patient for treatment. If, on the contrary, he rediscovered some of his reality, although he would initially be in despair due to his lost object, he could develop psychic space, and own or (re)gain some resilience that he may have had and lost as the result of multiple traumatic losses and retraumatizations in his development process. I have to say that my hypothesis in the beginning was that, at the end, if our work was successful, he would most probably no longer deny and disavow his reality, end his preoccupation with perversion, and become able to adopt a healthier attitude and associate or dissociate healthily. This was confirmed by evidence in the process and, indeed, in the outcome.

I had not imagined in my initial hypothesis that Daniel would come to an agreement with me, but this become possible. In one of our final sessions, he said,

"I have accepted now, as far as it is possible, to live with the paradoxical feelings that I had for as long as I remember . . . I know that I am not dead and that I will never be able to be a dead body as long as I am living . . . this helps me to understand myself better. I also know now that I never, ever, will be able to be with my mother again to make any reparation with her. I know and accept now that as a child in such a vulnerable situation, I could not stop what happened to my mother. I also know that I have to face the feelings that I suppressed, ignored, and never wanted to think about them for all my life. With the opportunity that I have here, and with your way of coping with all my rudeness and dysfunctional attitude and behaviours, I have learnt that what I can say about myself is that I am the child of political parents, who have not been in a position to be there for me as much as I wished them to be, and, perhaps as you said, they may have wished to be. That is the reality; it is a very painful reality, but it is reality. At the same time, I can say it is beautiful, because it is the reality of my life. Thank you, it is so liberating that I am able to be a better father to my child than I was before, and enjoy it, rather than being stupidly cut off from my child, hurting my partner and criticizing her for everything. I am not confused about myself any more. I accept that I feel different from others, and that is OK. I know that I have different sides to me . . . and that is OK, too. I just have to deal with it without fear of falling apart."

Being on the road to recovery, gaining resilience and, therefore, some strong, real sense of self and insight to his situation, Daniel was meeting the part of himself that he cut off and unhealthily dissociated from for a long time. The therapeutic space and my role as his listening other facilitated an environment that allowed Daniel's phantasies to evolve. By so doing, he found a better sense of himself, enough psychic space, and realistic resilience that can become integrated parts of him, which he had been unable to gain due to the traumas that he had endured from a very early age. Evidently, psychoanalytic intervention helped Daniel to become able to see the best possible solution to the situation he had been in. I was convinced from the beginning that if his archaic phantasies and unhealthy dissociation shifted, he could develop enough resilience and psychic space to ease his psychological functioning.

I found Klein's (1923) suggestions to be compatible with Daniel's psychic structure, in that she indicates that schizophrenic children are not capable of play in the proper sense, but, rather, they operate in a particularly repetitive manner, and if, through our intervention, we can penetrate to their unconscious, we find that the wish-fulfilment associated with their repetitive manner is pre-eminently the negation of reality and the inhibition of phantasy without any direction or integration. She says,

> The idea of enlightening children in sexual matters is steadily gain-ing ground ... The knowledge obtained by psycho-analysis however indicates the necessity, if not of 'enlightening', at least of bringing up children from the tenderest years in such a fashion as will render any special enlightenment unnecessary, since it points to the completest, most natural enlightenment compatible with the rate of development of the child. The irrefutable conclusions to be drawn from psycho-analytic experience demand that children shall, whenever possible, be protected from any over-strong repression, and thus from illness or a disadvantageous development of char-acter. Alongside the certainly wise intention of countering actual and visible dangers with information, therefore, analysis aims at avoiding dangers that are equally actual, even if not visible (because not recognized as such) but which are much commoner, deeper, and therefore call much more urgently for observation. [Klein, 1923, p. 419]

Klein (1929) discussed the handling of the transference expres-sions of hate, jealousy, and envy brought in by strong persecutory feelings in the treatment of a six-year-old disturbed child, Erna, who had a severe obsessional neurosis and paranoia. She argued (Klein, 1930) that there is an early stage of mental development at which sadism becomes active at all the various sources of libidinal pleasure.

She (Klein, 1929) suggests,

> sadism reaches its zenith in this phase, which is ushered in by the oral-sadistic desire to devour the mother's breast (or the mother herself) and passes away with the earlier anal stage. At the period ... the subject's dominant aim is to possess himself of the contents of the mother's body and to destroy her by means of every weapon which sadism can command. At the same time this phase forms the introduction to the Oedipus conflict. The genital is beginning to exercise an influence, but this is as yet not evident, for the pregen-ital impulses hold the field. ... the Oedipus conflict begins at a period when sadism predominates. The child expects to find within

the mother (a) the father's penis, (b) excrement, and (c) children, and these things it equates with edible substances. According to the child's earliest phantasies (or 'sexual theories') of parental coitus, the father's penis (or his whole body) becomes incorporated in the mother during the act. Thus the child's sadistic attacks have for their object both father and mother, who is in phantasy bitten, torn, cut or stamped to bits. The attacks give rise to anxiety lest the subject should be punished by the united parents, and this anxiety also becomes internalized in consequence of the oral-sadistic intro-jection of the objects and is thus already directed towards the budding super-ego. I have found these anxiety-situations of the early phases of mental development to be the most profound and overwhelming. It is my experience that in the phantasied attack on the mother's body a considerable part is played by the urethral and anal sadism which is very soon added to the oral and muscular sadism. In phantasy the excreta are transformed into dangerous weapons: wetting. [p. 24]

However, coming back to Daniel, we reached a stage where Daniel gained enough psychic space to trace his problems back to the traumatic events he had endured from his childhood. So, I had to identify and interpret primitive, neurotic, and psychic mechan-isms, choosing a vocabulary that would touch him at a deeper level. This was because, prior to this, it was difficult to reach him through verbal symbolism. This meant that I had to be attentive to his bodily manifestations and bodily phantasies. In addition, I had to carefully monitor my countertransference feelings and give myself enough freedom to accept the mistakes that I made and to learn the paths my unconscious was using and how to recognize them.

I should mention that Freud's (1920g) description of the split-ting of the ego also was a helpful explanation for me to bear in mind. He indicated that

two psychical attitudes have been formed instead of a single one, the normal one, which takes account of reality, and another one which under the influence of the instincts detaches the ego from reality. The two exist alongside of each other. The issue depends on their relative strength. If the second is, or becomes the stronger, the necessary precondition for a psychosis is present. The view that postulates that in all psychoses there is a splitting of the ego could not call for so much notice if it did not turn out to apply to other states more like the neuroses, and finally, to the neuroses themselves. [p. 202]

Often, in my interaction with Daniel, the bad object was either not representable or it had to be repudiated. Offering a representation of the bad object helped Daniel to get in touch with his feelings. As a result, correspondence between his ego and his object started developing, helping him to desensitize the bad quality of his object, which resulted in desensationalizing the bad quality of his ego that had been limiting his psychic space. This provided him with more psychic space in which to tolerate aspects of himself that he considered bad; he could then re-own them and gain a better sense of self. Furthermore, once Daniel was able to understand and make sense of his bad object, by way of contrast, he made a clearer distinction and developed a better idea of the good object, even if this was simply to denounce its absence. Owing to the connection and association between his ego and his object, Daniel accomplished a better psychic space that helped him to have an idea of what is good in himself, which was the sign of development of having a real and solid sense of self. He also understood that when he unconsciously sets up a bad internal object within himself, he sets himself up to feel dispossessed by other people. He then began to realize that once a non-idealized and ambivalent good object has been established in him, his ego will prove competent in sharing its productivity without feeling deprived, and he began to feel gratitude towards his internalized object.

The focus on creating psychic space in the treatment of Daniel is in line with Grotstein (1978) referring to Milner's (1969) book, *The Hands of the Living God*, about inner space and its dimensions, such as emotional space, rational space, and transitional space. Milner (1969) suggests five components in the creation of inner space: (1) mouth, tongue, and nipple; (2) hands; (3) rectum; (4) mother's arms; (5) ability to separate from the mother. Milner's patient, like Daniel, was suffering from severe schizoid problems, operating on a false-self basis, and needing to be helped to find her real self and develop outer and inner space. Milner (1969) illustrates the psychoanalysis of a severely schizoid young woman in which the drawings made by that patient during her treatment were a vital part of the communications made to her analyst, because the analyst was able to use them in a distinctive way. She considered the drawings in relation to her idea of inner space and said,

> slowly, as a result of pondering on these drawings and all she had said, I was to come to formulate a central question: does what was originally the on-going background of darkness and rhythmic beat of the mother's heart and breathing become, in later states of development, the inner awareness of one's own body? And if so, how? Certainly her drawings so far had suggested that there must be a slow creating of a concept of an inner containing space, whatever may be the different materials of memory out of which it is built. [Milner, 1969, p. 122]

She further discussed these different materials of memory and said,

> I was to come to think of the experiences of that inner space that can be actively explored long before the hands can become explorers, the space that is one's mouth that can be explored with one's tongue . . . I even began to wonder whether the capacity to explore one's own inner space, by directing attention inwards to various parts of it, does not have its first bodily prototype in the exploring tongue that plays with, actively samples and relishes, the sense of the solidarity of the nipple within one's mouth. [*ibid.*, p. 123]

She changes the libidinal area, "as showing how the whole conflict could have been transferred from the inner space of the mouth to the inner space of the rectum . . ." (*ibid.*, p. 124) and says,

> Also I had been interested in more internal aspects of the frame; that is, in learning how to achieve concentrated states of mind in which one creates one's own inner frame, frame of reference, as essential in all mental productivity, whether creating ideas or works of art, a state in which one holds a kind of inner space; but I had not yet seen that one of the earliest roots of such a capacity might be the experience of being held in one's mother's arms . . . [*ibid.*, p. 250]

> But I thought that for Susan to achieve this becoming incarnate, thus separating herself off from mother-me, claiming the right to be behind her eyes again, claiming her own point of view which could not be identical with anyone else's, for her such an act of affirming and claiming her own privacy within her skin could be felt as an

ultimate selfishness, one that would bring annihilating retaliation from mother-me-the-world. What she could not see, or only intellectually, was that in fact such an affirming of her own private inner space, far from cutting her off from people, would in fact become the only basis for a true relationship to them. [*ibid.*, p. 272]

So, psychoanalytic intervention and investigation with these types of patients is associated with the method of enquiry where the recorded sentences are statements in need of interpretation and not sentences about events which, in principle, can be observed and the validity of which requires a divided system of interpretation. Diagnostic methods and opinions in psychoanalysis are the result of linking such recorded sentences to the diagnostician's pool of theoretic knowledge with specific rules of discrimination or background hypotheses. This ongoing examination and exploration is integral to, and one of the central objectives of, psychoanalytic practice and research, and does not exist in any other form of psychological therapy.

Daniel, or people who, like him, have experienced trauma, may go through a few stages:

- their perception involves feelings about what has happened;
- a stimulus is perceived as unbearable;
- perception is suspended by various processes;
- defence mechanisms spring into action.

In this context, the creation of psychic space is important. The experiences are intimately related, where a patient talks about an empty space that changes into a real space. But the question arises as to what would constitute an empty space as opposed to a real space, and whether the distinction made by the patient is simply characteristic in terms of that particular experience or whether the patient is making a genuine distinction between the two experiences of inner space. Winnicott (1971) talked about a form of space, such as potential space; Khan (1974) about dream space; Bion (1967) about the container as a component. These explanations do not distinguish between clear space, transitional space, and an experiential space. Kernberg's (1976) subjective experience of emptiness and Winnicott's (1974) fear of breakdown demonstrate the lack of psychic space which was evident in working with all the patients presented in this study, even in resilient ones such as Farina. The inner psychic space, or lack of it, and the associated emptiness which manifested itself in the therapeutic encounters with Daniel and Farina are important components of resilience and vulnerability and the level of vulnerability and resilience.

CHAPTER ELEVEN

Discussion and results

I n working with traumatized people from relational perspectives, it is important to look at the pattern of dissociation and of
mourning, or lack of it. For example, the structure of mourning
in relation to Daniel's first losses, specifically his mother, and the
introjections of his primary loss that created emptiness with no
psychic space, left him in a vulnerable position. When confronted
with the loss of the maternal breast (itself a consolation for the loss
of mother–child union), Daniel, as an infant, mourned by learning
to fill the void of his mouth with words, a successful displacement
of libido from the lost mother, and came to terms with his painful
separation. Mourning, then, was a process whereby Daniel, as a
child, negates the loss of his mother and accepts that his mother
could not be there. His sense of self and his ability to identify
himself is no longer with the lost object but with other, so his
mourning can be defined as a negation of attachments and as a condition of customary subjectivity and signification. His failure to
appropriate mourning resulted in losing his sense of self and lacking any psychic space for thinking and reflecting and, therefore, a
lack of resilience that led to his inadequate integration into unmedi-
ated relation to others.

His listening other in transference, therefore, became symbolic compensation: that is, reducing the other's exceptionality to a means of representation, internalizing the lost object into the structure of his own identity as his primary support system of mourning by introjection. The difficulty in the process arose when his traumatic memory associated with the other stopped the introjections, which continued in his later life as it had already happened to him developmentally.

Comparing Daniel's and Farina's vulnerability and resilience in relation to their developmental process, the concept of consistent object, or m/other, is helpful in consideration of resilience and its development. In the process, it was clear that in Farina's case, although her mother was not a perfect one, she was a consistent present object, while with Daniel, there never had been any consistent object. Daniel's mental state ascription with regard to his original trauma made him vulnerable and unable to deal with difficulties in life, and the smallest problem was received by him as a severe trauma. Daniel's vulnerability and his lack of resilience at the time he entered therapy was mainly related to the disadvantages in his early development for a number of reasons, such as:

1. His care-givers did not facilitate a secure relationship that sets the basis for having a listening other as the foundation of resilience.
2. He had to take care of himself, which entails an emotional disincentive, when he had not yet developed any psychic space for reflection.
3. He did not have the environment to help him develop a solid and stable sense of self and learn to relate to others, his subsequent relationships were jeopardized by the lack of a role model, and he never experienced any object as his listening other in his developmental process, or, indeed, later in his life.
4. Lack of consistency in his care affected his psychological development and functioning.
5. He never developed a sense of basic trust to project into the need-gratifying other in asserting his resilience and independence.
6. His need to initiate co-operative and collaborative relationships with others was never met.

When he entered therapy, Daniel was extremely vulnerable, and his phobia and obsessional personality were causing severe limitations in his life. His mental development was a type in which his primitive libidinal value of faeces and urine remained unaltered through his adulthood. His phantasies of projective identification with the internal parents, and loss of his parents at a young age, led him to a pseudo-maturity and denied him psychic space to develop a sense of himself and real autonomy and resilience. His phantasies mainly were accompanied by anal and genital masturbation with intense aggressive content. His significant confusion about his body's cavities led to his inability to distinguish himself from the object and his inner world from outside reality. He could only maintain limited object relations and had highly erotized excretory activities. These structured dissociative characteristics militated against his breakdown, but also provided him with temporary pleasure, as they gave him the illusion of omnipotent control of the object, which is not uncommon in this type of pathological organization. Daniel's effort to seduce me into colluding with him was his means of communication primarily, but also was a projection of his despair and disbelief in my ability to help him.

Some of Freud's cases are relevant to both Daniel's and Farina's cases. His description of the enduring bonds of love that remain long after the other has departed (Freud, 1917e), elaborate the identification process as a positive incorporation of the lost other. This is relevant to Daniel's mourning, or lack of it. Daniel's false self was adopted to defend against the unthinkable, which was related to his inability to mourn and fear of his own death. It was clear that Daniel's anxiety originated in his aggression, which was grounded in his projection of his death instinct outwards from himself. His anxiety and his internal threats of danger and the workings of his death instinct were to have important consequences for his phantasy, as well as his creativity and his intelligence.

Freud's (1914g, 1926d) distinctions of object from narcissistic ego, instincts in the service of intimacy, and interpersonal relatedness from aggressive instincts, are concepts used for the analysis of both Farina and Daniel. The fundamental distinction of primary narcissistic separation and union identifies a basic dissociation inherent in the existence of patients such as Farina and Daniel, which explains the dualistic conception of their instincts, their characters, and their life. Freud's (1926d) descriptions about two sources of anxiety are constructive: (1) deriving from guilt due to aggression and the internalization of authority in the superego; (2) deriving from social anxiety, which primarily involves the fear of loss of love and of contact with others.

Klein's (1940) point of view is helpful for identifying and analysing the primitive vulnerability of a patient like Daniel, caused by the need to recognize that the other he hates is also the other he loves. This line of thinking and reasoning confirms that although initially he was extremely disturbed, as therapy progressed, Daniel reached the depressive position and became able to take his other in as a whole object. This increased his psychic space and led him to take in and tolerate more pain, deal with his ambivalence, and learn that he can love and hate the same person and still have a relationship with them. As the result of transference interpretations, he reached the depressive position by realizing that his love and hate are directed to the same object. His unconscious impulses to repair objects felt to have been damaged by destructive attacks of hate were inherent in his depressive feeling. Daniel's mental representations of the drives came to be conceived as unconscious phantasy. Due to his environment impingement, Daniel lost his unprocessed drive, which should be orientated towards his object, not as separate from objects, but as turning to objects for gratification. He lost his object before being able to play with gratifications and developmentally internalize it for reciprocation by the self-object. Daniel's trauma, his psychic retraumatization, and his paranoid and obsessional positions were indications that, due to the traumatizing effect of his death instinct (his internal death instinct as the source of the trauma is based on his psychic organization), introjections for him then became coercive. So, his anxiety had to be deflected and projected for detoxification. His introjections of the complete object, both the loved and hated aspects of the *other*, were not felt by him as separate, which resulted in increased fear of loss and a strong feeling of guilt, a state close to actual mourning. This was due to the aggressive impulses he felt to be directed against his loved object, but was not proper mourning. In the process, as his depressive position came to the forefront, he started to understand the mechanism of his survivor's guilt.

Bion's (1959) concept of "attacks on linking" that project to cut off problematic object relationships, but which, in the end, lead to the destruction of one's good objects, and his useful concepts of "containment" of Daniel's anxiety within the relationships are relevant and useful explanations of post traumatic stress in a psychoanalytical framework. He (Bion, 1959) says that through the use of projective identification, the patient projects intolerable anxious feelings on to the therapist, who, in turn, contains and interprets back to the patient in a cohesive and manageable form.

To understand the combination of Daniel's internal and external world and his psychic space, or lack of it, I assumed that his inner psychic space, playing between unhealthy dissociations, projective identification, and persecution, on the one hand, and the integration of his depressive anxiety and reparation, on the other hand, were both important to work with. It was important to help him to learn that if his irrational thoughts and feelings went on one side of the line, and his rational thoughts and feelings went on the other, his life would be less complicated. In transference, he gradually realized his paired emotions, love and hate, were disorganized and muddled, and needed constant reordering and managing. Initially, this was alien to him and he was not able to relate to the concept, but slowly, as we reached the stage where he could relate to me as his listening other, he could relate to it.

During my work with Farina and Daniel, I revisited some of Freud's patients and the key concepts with which he tried to make sense of his patients' symptoms and their lives. I specifically found revision of Anna O (Bertha Papenheim), the Wolf Man, and the Rat Man (Ernst Lanzer) useful in understanding Farina and Daniel's dreams, their traumatic memories, and the emergence of their personalities. They also shed light on the sources and dynamics of neurotic anxiety from neurophysiological concerns, from actual predisposing and concurrent causes to interpretative investigation of their phantasies. From a psychoanalytic discipline in which the subjective meaning of experience, whether real or phantasied, is the basis for understanding the patient, the dream interpretations and experiences of transference with Farina and Daniel indicate a movement away from a causal model for the effects of the childhood trauma in the formation of adult personality.

At the age of eighty, Freud (1936) analysed an incident that had happened when he was forty-eight. In Athens, he stood before the Acropolis and experienced an unexplained sensation. He reconstructed it later, and wrote, "I had . . . a momentary feeling: What I see here is not real" (p. 244). He could not deny the attestation of his perceptions, so he transposes this uncertainty into the past and envisions a situation that had no means to happen: that as a student he had had reservation about the existence of this monument, a split within his own conscious ideas. He says, a "surprising thought suddenly entered my mind: So all this really does exist, just as we learnt at school" (*ibid.*, p. 241). He wrote of an experience when he discovered that it is possible to see that we believe in a fact, and then discover that we have been unconsciously disavowing it all along, and the fact that as a child, he both did and did not deny the existence of the Acropolis. Freud recognized that seeing the Acropolis was not only accomplishing his childhood wish, but also he discovered that from the perspective of his childhood, he was playing the part of a great hero. He wrote:

> When first one catches sight of the sea, crosses the ocean and experiences as realities cities and lands which for so long had been distant, unattainable things of desire, one feels oneself like a hero who has performed deeds of improbable greatness" [*ibid.*, p. 247]

Having reached the Acropolis, Freud compares himself with Napoleon, who, "during his coronation . . . turned to one of his brothers . . . and remarked: What would Monsieur Notre Père have said to this, if he could have been here to-day?" (*ibid.*).

Freud (1889) showed that apparent recall of early experiences may be determined by unconscious links between the memory and repressed wishes, rather than by actual events. He realized that one of the most persistent memories of his own childhood was a screen memory of playing in a field of flowers with his half-brother Emmanuel's children, John and Pauline. This allowed him to articulate his neurotic need for an intimate male friend, as well as the competitive aggression in such a friendship. Later, with Breuer in *Studies on Hysteria* (1895a), he produced a detailed account of symptoms associated with the recovery of repressed memories, focusing on treatment of Anna O. who was treated by Breuer. He described how when the hysteric experiences the illness, they sometimes overcome it by gaining insight into how it came about and the relation of phantasies to accurate memories of traumatic events. By describing her traumatic experiences and her feelings about them, Anna O seemed to gain some relief from her debilitating symptoms, such as partial paralysis and hallucinations, and, indeed, overcame them. These are both related to Daniel's presentation in therapy. In the beginning, Daniel was not able to recall and relate his childhood experiences; therefore, it was difficult to gain insight to his behaviour and his phantasies. His unhealthy dissociation, as his defence mechanism, kept the perception part unconscious, but in a way that there could be fragmentation in memory and the meaning of what had occurred. One part may acknowledge his perception, the other dissociates and disavows it. So, in the external experience of trauma, the hidden power of dissociating from reality is different from repression. Adopting an interpretative formulation and acknowledging the patient's own participation in this type of dissociation (both healthy and unhealthy) allows the patient to keep some level of psychic space and a sense of self.

Generally speaking, people with a healthy enough environment in the process of development demonstrate flexibility in a range of situations with their ego strength and resilience, whereas anxiously resistant, anxiously avoidant, and anxiously ambivalent patients present with vulnerability and dependency. Depending on this characteristic (vulnerable or resilient), painful memories of the past can be dissociated from in a healthy or unhealthy manner. For example, Farina, as a resilient patient, denied her perceptions, dissociating her attention by turning away into a withdrawn, dream-like state of mind, or focusing on a small perceptual detail, which she used as a mediation enabling her to concentrate her attention on it without registering what was actually happening. Dissociation, in her case, was healthy and operative, and provided her with better psychic space. In contrast to Daniel's mourning, or lack of it, Farina's explicit violence in positioning the other as a target of nostalgic blaming enabled her to perceive her unresolved grief in melancholic mourning. This formed the foundation for endless mourning, recognizing the traces of her lost other that resided within her ego, leading her as a mourner away from the aggression of melancholy towards a pronouncement of enduring attachments that no work of mourning could split. Farina's pattern is in line with Freud's (1923b) idea on mourning, which provides an important framework for thinking about the traces of her lost other that creates her ego character and function and, therefore, her resilience. The type of therapeutic interventions and transference interpretations with Farina allowed us to shed light on possible theoretical difficulties:

- the difference between negation and dissociating (healthily) from reality;
- the way she dissociated and disavowed her melancholic mourning, as an ineffective attempt to attain the representation of being;
- limitation of her lost object and her subject that tends to hamper the essential process of symbolization for the use of phantasy.

Freud (1918b), in the case of the Wolf Man, speaks of a rejection of reality and distinguishes this from repression in that the rejected representation has not in any way been removed from consciousness. The meaning remains as if it is suspended and no longer open to deceit. In relation to Farina, identification of her psychic mechanism that seems to be at work raises questions of what in particular would generate such a dissociation and disavowal and what is to be augmented by precipitating a plausible negation and contradiction contained by consciousness.

The Rat Man's case (Freud, 1909d), to some extent, is similar to Daniel's losses, and his obsessive symptoms and thoughts were traced to his deep ambivalence about his sexuality and his uncertainty about his father, which he was not able to face. The Rat Man presented obsessional thoughts about torture stemming from something he had heard about from a military officer, having to do with rats eating away one's body. He was preoccupied that it might happen to someone dear to him, specifically his father, or the woman he admired. Freud theorized that this and similar thoughts were produced by conflicts consisting of the combination of loving and aggressive impulses the Rat Man had in relating to these people. The Rat Man was defending himself against his own secret thoughts and the wishes regarding his father's death and his subsequently inheriting all of his money. He would then phantasize that his father had died leaving him nothing. He had also developed the phantasy of marrying Freud's daughter, so that Freud would become rich as well after his father's death. These symptoms were keeping the Rat Man from needing to make difficult decisions in his life, and destroying the anxiety that would be involved in experiencing his angry and aggressive impulses directly.

Freud (1909c) composed and constructed stories and explanations to make sense of a group of circumstances he felt to be related to each other, and in some way related to symptoms that seem incomprehensible. He made sense of the significant symptoms and provided interpretations as explanations for the patient's particular behaviours, feelings, and thoughts difficult for him to understand.

Daniel, like the Rat Man, developed suicidal thoughts after the death of his father and, later, his mother. In considering and working through these losses, similar to the Rat Man, Daniel developed the ability to form verbal associations and symbolic meanings. Freud (1909d) says the Rat Man's feelings began with sexual experiences in infancy, in particular harsh punishment for childhood masturbation, and the vicissitudes of sexual curiosity. He elaborated the terms rationalization, doubt, and displacement, which are similar to defences that Daniel used, including dissociation, against some of the unthinkable experiences that he had endured.

Due to the dreadful, repressive environment in which Daniel was living prior to coming to London, his intrapsychic structure was deficient. Initially, it was not clear whether the emergence of his false character organization with deficiency was related to developmental personality formation, or his later traumatic experiences, or both. With traumatic experiences from his early childhood, Daniel's distortion of objects, pointing to his inherent difficulty in the search for relatedness, was one of the important concepts: not only what the enemy had been for him, but what he wanted the enemy to be. Greenberg and Mitchell (1983) suggested that

> although cognitive development is not independent of affective factors and psychodynamic struggles, early primitive forms of cognition are unavoidable and universal. . . . Early forms of perception and cognition, lacking a sense of time, space, and object

constancy, contribute to the painful intensity of the struggles within early object relations. For the relational model theories one need not fall back on drives to account for distortions of interpersonal reality. [p. 406]

Daniel's false self was adopted in a vulnerable state of his mind, against the unthinkable, and at the exploitation of his true self. Due to psychological ill health and, therefore, unhealthy dissociation (which was unconscious), there was no part-taking in search of an opportunity for the exploration, recognition, and integration of denied, dissociated, and disavowed or remaining aspects of his personality, or the avowal of his emergent parts. In the absence of those, his false self continued to be constructed. This was constructed in response to the fear of death, both of himself and of others.

I assumed that Daniel's unconscious displacement of the emerging false self and his unhealthy dissociation was related to his interpersonal conditions of the earliest object relations. In this context, his false self as a collection of dissociative behaviours, thoughts, and feelings was motivated by vulnerability, and his need to cling to his object. So, his false self and dissociative functions were defences against his separation anxiety, his fear of abandonment, and his fear of death and annihilation. This is not just the result of external trauma in his adult life, and it must be rooted in earlier trauma that left him unable to integrate his whole self-object representations, which is the basis of resilience. Daniel's capacity for spontaneity, autonomy, self-assertion, creativity, and resilience was blocked and lost in his false self, which was created to survive his unresolved internal conflicts and external atrocities, hence its effect on his internal being. Therefore, his mourning could not be just about the loss of his object, but was about both fear of annihilation and the loss of himself and other. And when he was in a paranoid state, he would even lose his false self, so that neither a true nor a false self existed, and he would be in a total psychic numbness, with no sense of self and no psychic space or capacity to think.

What was especially helpful in making sense of his psychical pain was the clarity and emphasis on different angles of his losses. This is different from the paranoid–schizoid positions (the fear of annihilation, total destruction of the self), and the depressive position (fear of the loss of the other and the self). There was the loss of the object and, as a result, the grief that Daniel's psyche internally went through: hence, no distinction of how other the lost other is and, where he himself is. The concept of projective identification of mourning was helpful to see that the loss of his loved object was equal to a disruption of himself, which is usually temporary in ordinary mourning. However, for Daniel, this has not been temporary, as his process of mourning was blocked. So, in the process of therapy, where he has not been totally fragmented, by having a listening other he was able to feel contained, and that enabled us to work towards restoring and reclaiming part of Daniel's lost self that had prevented him going through consolatory mourning, and unconsciously had been projected on to his lost other without recognizing that.

Other defences, such as isolation and undoing, were used by Daniel, and occasionally by other patients, such as Abdul, as acts of unhealthy dissociation, which are one of the features distinguishing hysterical neurosis from obsessesional neurosis. In obsession and compulsion, undoing brings opportunities to reverse hostile wishes that have been perpetrated by the doing. The attempt to undo is not just an attempt to make up for some error, but aims to attack the reality of the original hostile thought or wish, and recreate the past as though such intentions had never existed: hence, unhealthy dissociations. Internalization and incorporation as subordinate introjections were used by Daniel. This was also used by Zara (in a vignette in Part I) in the process through which she built her inner representational world, by taking in and modifying her external world. Intellectualization and rationalization also were among Zara's main defences, and contributed to her unhealthy dissociation. She had a tendency to cover a range of sub-defences, including thinking instead of experiencing with feelings, and paying undue attention to the abstract in order to avoid an issue, which led to undoing as well as rationalization. This offered logical belief explanations for irrational and dissociative behaviours that had been prompted by her unconscious.

Farina, in contrast to vulnerable patients such as Abdul or Zara, has a clearer sense of self from the beginning. This was due to the fact that she came to therapy with some level of resilience and, therefore, had some ability to dissociate more healthily, although she also presented unhealthy dissociation in many instances, specifically with those memories unbearable to her. In the process, through transference and dream interpretations, she learnt to build on her healthy dissociation, which was clearly reflected in the transference relationship.

As opposed to Daniel's presentation, Farina was aware that the impulses and thoughts that she projected in transference were inside her, but she attributed their presence to some outside influence. Initially, her dissociated impulses were experienced only outside her, without awareness that they were inside her and belonged to her own psyche. Thus, projecting her unresolved anger, of which she was unaware, to others and in transference, and understanding herself as a kind and harmless woman that others misunderstood, changed in the process as she gained insight about her dissociated awareness of the collapse of her hopes for motherly love experienced in projection.

The existence of Farina's resilience was evident within her inter-subjectivity, and in how the nature of her trauma varied as a partial function of the relational and historical context in which it occurred. Her experience of trauma led to her annihilation, embedded in her distinctive experience, and noticeably differed from the way Daniel dissociated. Her pattern of dissociation in response to extreme external trauma (being imprisoned and tortured) differed from her internal trauma during her childhood and adolescence (her sense of isolation), which she halted by becoming part of a group whose aims were to do something good and involving herself in political activity; this was a manifestation of dealing with her annihilation through not dissociating from her experiences. So, the difference between people's traumatic experiences that lead to annihilation and unhealthy dissociation, and those leading to healthy dissociation in the context of the patient's psychic space and psychological functioning amounted to a three-fold attack on the normal world, itself protected by the healthy dissociation that had sustained Farina throughout her life. By becoming involved with an opposition group, she had lost the supportive social framework of her family; she had been violently assaulted by the environment in losing her partner. In view of these losses, she possessed an ability to understand her enormous need for help if she was not to collapse psychologically.

The trauma that threatened Farina's way of making sense of herself and her life attacked sustaining connections to her fundamental feelings, but the trauma could be dissociated, thus diluting its threat to her existing organizations of experience, leaving sustaining connection to a more stable sense of self intact by healthily dissociating from the memory of the traumatic event she had endured. Farina's healthy dissociation was possible due to her level of resilience. Her annihilation experiences originated when her world of normality fell apart. The specific triggering event preceding Farina's vulnerability was related to her past in response to her absent (psychologically) m/other.

Work with Farina brought many challenges, both theoretical and technical. One of the challenges for me was to think about whether she was capable of discovering in transference an object with good qualities if she had not experienced this in her infancy. Although it was unclear in her presenting history, I was doubtful whether Farina's recall of her childhood was accurate. She must have been provided with some good object in her infancy in which she could place her psychological strength, her healthy dissociation, her level of insightfulness, and her resilience. My hunch was that in her early life there must have been some love and trust, in order to build her resilient capacity, otherwise she would not have come and asked for help the way she did, and if it was not for her resilient quality, she would perhaps have pursued a psychotic path alone in isolation rather than seeking psychoanalytic therapy. I assumed that her m/other as a good object must have been available to her before the age of four, which she could recall in her memory.

Another challenge was that, from our initial meeting, Farina seemed to focus and put emphasis on her traumatic experience, which was external (persecution, imprisonment, torture, excursions, and many losses, as well as the dilemmas and difficulties of resettlement and integration in London as her new social environment). I decided that I would initially have to deal with the memory of external traumas in her adulthood, then trace the movement and conflict within the transference, hoping to bring alive her feelings within a relationship, which clearly had been deeply defended against or only momentarily experienced. This working model was my initial and not very confident plan, but it proved to be right and helpful, as it enabled Farina to obtain firmer roots in the transference. I was not a totally new object, but, to a great extent, a strengthened object, because emotionally deeper feelings had been worked through in the transference. On reflection, I am saying that it was the right decision, as Farina evidently and very quickly regained some of her lost resilience. The type of psychic movement demonstrated in Farina, whose warmth and ability to value good things were there to some extent, but very blocked off, due to the trauma she has endured, enabled those innate qualities, over time, to come alive in the process, as her emotions were freed and strengthened. The representation of her objects had changed and shifted accordingly as she had become able to associate with some of her experiences that initially she was not able to deal with.

The important psychoanalytic technique in the process was the usefulness of transference, countertransference, and dream interpretations, relating to her past, which was helpful for Farina to reconstruct them. Although I was almost sure of the necessity for this, at times I was doubtful and unable to find a comfortable way of doing it. The particular and consistent difficulty was the possibility of sexual abuse by her father, which had not been made clear by Farina, but manifested in her war with me and her re-enactment in the transference. Although this was an important issue, I had to consider that Farina had decided to dissociate herself from it. So, it was important for me to keep in mind not to make these links if the linking disrupted what we were able to achieve and what was going on in the sessions. I also was concerned about using confrontational interpretations of Farina's dissociation with this part of her past, and was thinking that pushing the issue would lead to a kind of destruction and could potentially either lead her to stop therapy, or therapy could become merely explanatory and educational conversations. So, I decided that I should wait until Farina was ready and had adequate strength to get in touch with a deeper level of her experiences that could induce guilt and shame for her. In transference, it was clear to see the nature of her defences, as well as the level of psychic organization within which she was operating, so gradually it became reasonably easy for me to come to a decision to make transference interpretations which would not be too challenging for her state of mind and her psychic space at the time.

To summarize, in this work I used

- transference and countertransference as windows of evidence;
- interpretation and association with the content of dreams that were brought to the sessions by patients;
- association of dreams in relation to psychic space, the sense of self, and the ability to have and relate to a listening other in transference.

Combinations of these brought significant changes from inappropriate affects to appropriate affects, enhancing the patient's abilities and resilience in dealing with anxiety, depression, and overall state of mind, and changes in the level of dissociation from unhealthy to healthy, and then to associations. Going back to the two cases (Farina and Daniel), this was exactly what helped Farina to reclaim her resilience that had been lost as opposed to colluding with a victim role and staying vulnerable, as Daniel was more drawn to do. In comparison to Daniel as a vulnerable patient, I could see that there was a relative absence of unconscious interference in Farina's healthy dissociation of experiences that were unbearable to her at times. Although Farina had unpleasant experiences in her past, she clearly had a containing and good enough environment, in her positive developmental past that provided her with a milieu in which she could develop a sense of self, fostering resilience and the ability to dissociate healthily, and a good level of psychic space in which to function. This made her level of movement and progress in therapy much faster than that of Daniel, who was more vulnerable, with fragmented mind to begin with. One of the most significant things in Farina's case was her ability to use transference from the start as the key tool for psychoanalytic evidence. However, it is important to note that Farina's trauma (external) would, at times, be re-enacted in the transference, and needed specific space to be dealt with.

Understanding trauma in the context of environmental impingement was a way to understand the complex lack of psychic space and its relation to Daniel's and other patients' past and present. With this understanding, it was possible to see that these can be a combination of feelings of love and affection with violent, aggressive, hating, and envious states. What was also quite relevant was the fact that Daniel's and other vulnerable patients', for example, Abdul's (a vignette in Part I) state of mind was further

impinged upon due to the loss of their familiar cultural environment. This is important because it provides dimensions that are also
integral to a fuller understanding of the possible effect of retraumatization, and, indeed, its effect on the sense of self.

I hypothesized that part of Daniel, and, indeed, Abdul, had been
stuck in melancholic mourning (which is not central to this study),
unable to mourn the losses and to move on. In contrast to the feelings of love that could make it possible for him to mourn, Daniel's
melancholic grief has ambivalent feelings of love and hate for his
m/other. Daniel loved his m/other less for his m/other's unique-
ness and separateness, and more for m/other's ability to lessen his
own confusion: that is, to represent and reflect the part of himself
that he had invested in the m/other. This meant his loved ones
were irreplaceable and, therefore, it was very difficult for him to
distinguish precisely how other they are. Daniel's psychic function
in this regard fits the model of the narcissistic subject, where the
loss of a loved object is understood as a disruption of himself. This,
in turn, provides him with the stimulation to give up the lost object
by believing that love for his m/other fundamentally derived from
self-love, involving less grief for the passing of his unique m/other,
which open up some psychic space for him to think and process
towards restoring a certain economy of himself. By doing so in therapy, Daniel was reclaiming his lost self that had been projected on
to his m/other, a part necessary in the construction of his sense of
self as a reasonably autonomous and resilient being. Losing his
loved one, therefore, threatened to annihilate Daniel's imaginary
psychic integrity. He held on to his lost object, as, for him, acknowledging his loss would force him to grieve and recognize the full
extent of what he had lost, namely, himself, his coherent identity,
and his resilience. So, mourning for Daniel, and indeed many other
patients like him, is not just about the loss of the object, it is also
about the loss of the self or at least part of the self; it is about both
fear of annihilation of the self and fear of the loss of the other.

Here, I will present my impressions of the differences between
Farina as a resilient patient and Daniel as a vulnerable one.

A brief summary of Farina's characteristics is listed below.

- She came to therapy with her vulnerabilities, seeking help to
  improve. Most of the analytic segments I reviewed for this

study, therefore, contained sequences of disruption and repair, but the fact that she referred herself when she was functioning reasonably and had a clear sense of self was the sign of her resilience.

- The repair phase of these cycles was sustained by my active effort to re-engage Farina with her past through interpretations that successfully provided her with insight. However, an affirmative interaction was usually a prerequisite for interpretation in our encounter that resulted in effective outcome of interpretations. At times, these interactions alone were associated with change.

- From the beginning, Farina accepted me as her listening other. However, as she was idealizing me initially, it was necessary for me to acknowledge my limitations or my lack of precise understanding of her situation, as well as strive to make up for failures in our therapeutic connection. These breakdowns originated in me or Farina, and, at times, in both of us. They reflected a temporary lack of psychic space or the sense of self and the pathology of each of us.

- She often helped me to recognize and begin to address her disturbance, hence, she saw me as responsible for sustaining the repair.

- Much of the observed change in Farina occurred during the period of repair through interpretations of transference–countertransference and dreams. The change in Farina occurred during the ensuing period of our mutual collaboration.

- The critical moment in many of the clinical segments I reviewed and presented involved recognition on my part of both successes and failures as Farina's listening other. Farina behaved in ways that served her defensive and transferential needs. However, attempting to explore and interpret these motivations at first often furthered her alienation. In contrast, when I could be aware that I was wrong and assume responsibility, engagement and change were often reinitiated immediately.

To summarize, Farina

1. Entered analysis with hope.
2. As our relationship deepened, complications invariably arose

and Farina, on occasion, experienced me as failing her in some way as I made errors. As the result of these encounters, a hostile transference developed which helped Farina to get in touch with her deep anger and not defensively to detach and dissociate herself.

3. The loss of rapport with Farina was disconcerting and clashed with my introjective perception that I should understand Farina and the nature of her analytic interaction, which at the time resulted in my disorientation in the process.

4. The information I had about Farina that I worked with in the analysis could at times be speculative and incomplete. None the less, I committed myself to a course of action or a trial interpretation aimed at repairing the disruption. This process often involved me acknowledging my part in creating the difficulties in interpretation, which usually was helpful for Farina to gain more confidence and a stronger sense of self as well as relating to me as her listening other more confidently. This led to a productive interpretation characterizing the transference and countertransference that always helped to re-establish our analytic process as reciprocal and collaborative.

5. Farina's characteristics I observed to be identifiable as resilient.

With Daniel, in contrast to Farina, if I failed to recognize what he was presenting, he would refuse to engage and stopped work even when I could see my own contribution to the situation and acknowledge it with the hope of reinvolving Daniel. He would not respond to my acknowledgement or any interpretation of his lack of engagement. Daniel could see how my countertransference played into our standoff, but he was not able to let go of it as he felt injured and rejected. In these analytic situations, Daniel would refuse to look at himself as he experienced me as his therapist not to be available and accessible. He perceived me as fallible and afraid of any scrutiny that I was asking from him. On my request, on many occasions he would tell me, "Because you have the author-ity and see yourself as superior and want me to go away, far away, but you can't say it openly." I would discuss with him that in his mind the atmosphere of safety that we created together for his personal good had been lost and I needed to work hard with him to recreate it again. This process and exchange was repeated on many occasions. To summarize Daniel's characteristics and his improvement in the context of object relations,

1. I, as his listening other, was a medium and means for his expression through whom externalizations of aspects of his internal objects and his sense of self could be experienced, modified, and reinternalized.

2. By means of transference as encircling the projection and reintrojection of Daniel's introject, the process led to a modification of Daniel's sense of self system via the mechanism of identification, enabling him to associate and dissociate more healthily through the dialectical exchange occurring in transference and between many levels of his personality and his internal and external world.

3. Change in Daniel occurred through the interfacing of two subjectivities. It involved his encounter with me as his listening other as separate from him and as a centre of his subjective reality as well as his object. As a result of this process, he developed more psychic space, so that the unhealthy, dissociated aspects of him and his traumatic memories became reintegrated into his personality, resulting in some quality of resilience, enabling him to dissociate healthily when he was not able to bear the pain.

4. Daniel's association was changed with projective and introjective processes, and, as his cognitive functioning was changing, he became more able to develop a sense of self and, therefore, more psychic space. I had to work with Daniel through a transformational process, progressively arriving at less unhealthy dissociations that enabled constructions of his past, and this further developed his sense of self so that his projected concept of me as his therapist was continually revised as he compared it with me in reality.

5. As therapist–patient, we reached a stage in which our relationship constituted a holding environment in which Daniel could symbolize his earlier developmental phases. As he lived out these earlier experiences in analysis, he learnt to employ healthy dissociations.

6. As our work progressed further, although slowly, I became Daniel's new developmental object, who was able to

empathize with him and facilitate his growth in reciprocity through being his listening other as the key to his engagement in non-confrontational but corrective interpretations where I could actively facilitate the involvement. My reason for not using any confrontational interpretations was based on my observation that Daniel was improving very slowly and he needed to feel the presence of another human being striving to be helpful his listening other. Our relationship reached a reciprocity in assisting each other towards repairing his disturbances that he accepted. To my surprise, as our relationship developed some level of trust and containment for him, he showed gratitude that usually I was, as his therapist, leading the process which helped his integration.

I claim that the essential factor of unhealthy dissociation is the aetiology of developmental defects and that arrests lie in early developmental trauma. Thus, the lack of early object relationships and the lack of empathic mirroring and responsiveness, and opportunities for idealization, are the primary aetiological factors in accounting for vulnerability and lack of resilience. Developmental failures related to trauma and deficiencies in early care, due to extreme inconsistencies and frequent exposure of the child to affectively unbearable neglect, abuse, and aggressive commotion, is the foundation of vulnerability in adulthood, and, therefore, inability to cope with trauma in adult life.

Daniel's case answered and acted in response to my research question, and confirmed one of the hypotheses that the essential factor of unhealthy dissociation is the aetiology of developmental defects caused by the trauma of arrests in early development. Thus, the lack of early object relationships and the lack of empathic mirroring and responsiveness and opportunities for idealization are the primary aetiological factors in accounting for vulnerability and lack of resilience.

CHAPTER TWELVE

Conclusion

M y findings in working with severely traumatized people suggest that psychoanalytic treatment provides an empirical basis for outcome-relevant treatment formulations with chronic post trauma symptoms and dissociations. In addition to formulations based upon reprocessing of dissociative behaviour in the process, psychoanalytic techniques help therapists to pay attention to the potentially overwhelming phenomenological and physiological differences between the traumatic defects in different people due to their past experiences. The disturbing experience in which the sense of self becomes lost, complicated by the loss of psychic space and deregulation of primitive affects, can lead to unhealthy dissociation.

In the assessment and treatment of traumatized patients who present with features of unhealthy dissociation, it is vital that there is a listening other to establish a sense of holding, containing, and safety in which the patient can experience his or her own body, thoughts, feelings, and relating, and gain a better sense of self, psychic space, and some level of resilience. Object relations theory and practice permit the patient to get in touch with overwhelming impulses and self-defeating interpersonal styles, and provide an opportunity for patients to reconstruct the past through having a therapist who provides a listening other, which is the foundation for a holding and containing environment, focusing on the object relational deficits, through transference interpretations.

The main question in this research is: *what is it in the personality of traumatized people that makes some resilient to their traumatic experiences, but leaves others vulnerable to psychological collapse* (for example, development of PTSD)? As it is not something that lies in the objective external event, what is it about the personality that enables, or disables, resilience? This opens the door for a new theory central to this work on dissociation. Although this study has several limitations, such as the sample size, which was relatively small, and the setting, which was a single treatment programme, it did respond to and answer what it is in the personality that makes some people more resilient to their traumatic experiences, but leaves others vulnerable to psychological collapse, by identifying and discussing the four factors (the psychic space, listening other, sense of self, and healthy dissociation) being characteristic in resilient people and lacked by vulnerable people. I have identified these factors throughout the analysis of trauma, the discussion on the development of PTSD, and the analysis of therapeutic intervention with traumatized patients. Answering the question, this study provides reassessments of long-term outcomes. However, given the potentially complex, multi-variate relationships among personal characteristics (e.g., language, and other cultural factors such as ethnicity, beliefs, age, and trauma history), a larger and more varied sample and a longitudinal assessment of pre- and post treatment clinical interventions and outcome is worthy of future study. If the assumption that dissociation is the result of the disruption of the usually integrated functions of consciousness, memory, identity, or sensitivity to the environment and a solid sense of self, this study has been able to show how, through the act of healthy dissociation, some people survive massive trauma and human rights' violations.

Although the focus has been on my work as a single clinician, it adds values of independent and blind reliability for intervention. The input, output, and outcome of the clinical interventions described in vignettes in the first part and in case studies in the second part confirmed that progress is made (1) through transference and countertransference and its monitoring, both regularly and at periodic intervals, (2) by further reflection within the psychoanalytic dyad, (3) by means of supervision and consultation, and (4) later literature review. The outcome confirmed that childhood trauma history specifically determined the patients' vulnerability and hypersensitivity to trauma in adulthood that, in the clinical setting, resulted in the separation of dissociations into the categories of healthy and unhealthy, which is measurable for precision or variability of resilience and vulnerability and the patterns of dissociation to adequately test the relation to treatment outcome by monitoring the transference–countertransference.

My findings suggest that psychoanalytically informed psychotherapy is a basis for identifying problems known and yet unknown to the patient through the patient's responses to transference interpretations, using myself, the therapist as a listening other, and helping patients' development of the sense of self, which may have been altered or lost as a result of trauma. I identified that a traumatized patient's lack of response to the treatment is evidence of unhealthy dissociation and temporary emotional impairment that can be healed through therapeutic interaction and interplay in the transference–countertransference. Rehabilitation of this type of chronic trauma, therefore, involves a method to reverse environmental damage that has resulted in longstanding and pervasive symptomatic strengthening and, concomitantly, problems arising that are likely to be exacerbated by the lack of having a listening other and impulse control of the unconscious–conscious, which affects the gaining or regaining of a sense of self and impairs the person's ability for self-organization, and the lack of essential psychic space for relatedness to the available listening others in therapy, which results in unhealthy dissociation in vulnerable patients, which is linked with the early trauma in childhood. Thus, psychoanalytic treatment for traumatized patients is enhanced by the clinician's recognition of the effects of the traumatic experience for which, although early childhood trauma may serve as a marker, the trauma endured in adult life appears to best serve as a conceptual framework for clinical intervention as a starting point with both resilient and vulnerable patients.

Because of the unpleasant experiences and circumstances that many traumatized people have endured, their intrapsychic structure may be deficient. There may not be a clear sense of self or any psychic space, for reasons of both developmental personality formation and later external trauma, meaning that the emergence of a false character organization is likely, which is reflective and the result of the social environment. So, there is no capacity to play to begin with. If there is no participation for such a person in searching for an opportunity for the exploration, recognition, and integration of disavowed or discarded aspects of the personality, and for the affirmation of emergent parts, then the false self continues to construct further. This is in line with Stern's (1985) "unformulated experience", Stolorow and Atwood's (1992) "pre-reflective unconsciousness", Bollas's (1987) "unthought known", "projective identification" (Bion, 1967; Hinshelwood, 1983, 1994a, 1999; Joseph, 1987; Rosenfeld, 1971, 1983; Sandler, 1990; Segal, 1973; Spillius, 1992); "enactment" (Jacobs, 1986, 1991; McDougall 1985, 1986; McLaughlin 1992); "basic fault" (Balint, 1968), and "self as an object and the other" (Cassimatis, 1984; Searles, 1959, 1965, 1986).

These are indications that personality development throughout life, from infancy to adulthood, occurs as the result of complex dialectical developmental forces. The development of an increasingly differentiated, integrated, resilient, and mature sense of self is contingent upon establishing satisfying interpersonal relationships. Equally, the development of mature, reciprocal, and satisfying interpersonal relationships depends on the growth of mature self-definition and resilience. Relatedness, or attachment to the developmental line, enables people to note more clearly the dialectical developmental transaction between relatedness and self-definition. Psychoanalysis posits the idea that aggression is not behavioural, but instinctual, and not social but psychological. Obviously, it is vital that humanity finds more mature, less primitive ways of dealing with individual and collective hatred and aggression, and better use of psychoanalytic intervention is one way.

Sometimes, when a trauma is too unspeakable, the individual psyche responds by simply denying the existence of such experience. Mind and body act together to expel painful experiences, especially in a vulnerable situation. Pain, as an alien substance, like an antigen, stimulates dissociation as a reaction that will counteract the pain, much as an antibody would. But, though the act of dissociating from trauma keeps the person from feeling overwhelmed, it also may prevent the person from feeling anything. When one can no longer feel, there are no great sorrows or joy, no keen disappointments or pleasures, no exciting surprises or discoveries. The immune reaction of repressive pain creates a state of neutrality, a sense of existing behind a wall, where life seems to be going on beyond one's reach, somewhere out there. The recovery of well-being depends on the person's resilience.

What is specifically helpful in understanding this type of psychical pain is the clarity and emphasis on different angles of losses. There is a difference between the paranoid–schizoid positions, the fear of annihilation, total destruction of the self, and the depressive position that is the loss of the other and the self. There is also the loss of the object and, as a result, the grief that the psyche internally goes through: hence, no distinction of how other the lost other is, and who and where the self is. The concept of projective identification of mourning was helpful in seeing that the loss of a love object is equal to a disruption of the sense of self, which is usually temporary in ordinary mourning, but has not been temporary, and has, for many, blocked the process of mourning and, indeed, without therapeutic interventions, may pass this delay in mourning on to future generations. So, in therapy, if the sense of self has not been totally fragmented, there is a need for containing, restoring, and reclaiming part of the lost self that, in not being able to go through consolatory mourning, has been projected on to the lost other. This is important for reclaiming an autonomous and resilient self.

I conclude that the drive model and the relational model are complete and comprehensive theories to account for human experience. The grounds upon which they rest constitute two compatible visions of life and the basic nature of human experience. The foundation of both theories indicates that the good object comes from ego strength, that is, resilience. History has shown that people do survive trauma and atrocities, but the question is, what has happened to them and what type of people have they become after surviving? Here, resilience factors and different types of dissociation (healthy and unhealthy) become important concepts of continuity. It is helpful and important to distinguish and differentiate the severe psychological injury of people whose environment was impinged upon in their earlier developmental process from the many others who possess resilient qualities due to their early, healthy enough environment. The former may be impaired for life. The latter have their environment impinged upon by the state superego and not a parental one, so there is some level of resilience and self containment there to begin with that temporarily have been lost due to the external environment in adulthood. The use of projective identification in object relations theory, as a method of control of the object and unmanageable feelings, is important in assessing resilience, or lack of it, and the patterns of dissociations which are used in the treatments of patients presented in this study. Resilient people can use projection and introjection, and are able to use a kind of dissociation as a defence in order to survive and feel protected even when they are in pain. In contrast, vulnerable people use unhealthy dissociation and autistic withdrawal as defence strategies and to disconnect from the world and real relationships, bearing in mind that there is a fine line between being resilient and oppressing one's feelings because of the cultural environment or one's isolation and helplessness. Nevertheless, focusing on people's resilience in dealing with their vulnerability is a working model that is easily adaptable.

Dissociating (both healthily and unhealthily) from trauma keeps the person from feeling overwhelmed and tearing apart; however, it is possible to keep the person from feeling anything, and this difference distinguishes healthy and healthy dissociation. The recovery from trauma towards well-being depends on people's ability to gain resilience. However, in the circumstances in which many people are traumatized, which are beyond any normality, as discussed by patients such as Farina in this study, healthy dissociation can well be used to survive by a person with a resilient quality, with the aim of removing an aspect of the external world and its effect on one's internal world from their consciousness. When working with a person who has experienced trauma, it is important to focus on individual resilience and vulnerability as well as the person's collective cultural characteristics. Denial, disavowal, and sometimes even his pattern of dissociation, I consider to be aspects of a patient's developing resilience. These patterns were also seen in Zara's case, and, to a much lesser extent, in Abdul's defences, used to deal with external reality and enable repudiation or affective control of their response to a specific aspect of the external world. These patients use of denial in the process of therapy progressed to the form of splitting, in which there was cognitive acceptance of a painful event while the associated painful emotions were rejected. Reaction formation and identification with the aggressor, along with unhealthy dissociation, were some of Daniel's main defences, which were used by him before he could reach a more mature defence, such as healthy dissociation and sublimation. In cases such as Daniel's, this is because there has been no clear sense of self for him to mourn the loss of his loved one. There has been no self for relatedness and self-definition. The struggle would, in these types of trauma, take place in the interpersonal and inter-subjective relational medium, and, therefore, become lost and replaced by various defences, indeed, dissociation (both healthy and unhealthy), to construct a sense of self in response to external demands. Thus, ego organization of a patient such as Daniel, the purpose of which is to serve adaptation to the new environment, may become fragmented. Repeated compliance with such demands, associated with a withdrawal from self-generated spontaneity, which could lead to an increased stifling of impulses for spontaneous expression, thereby culminates in the development of a false self.

In this long-term study (seventeen years), I attempted to use methods required to examine the efficacy of psychoanalytic treatment while recognizing a level of commitment to newly developed methods and data derived directly from the clinical material within the psychoanalytically orientated psychotherapy treatment of traumatized patients. The aim was to reflect, analyse, and evaluate the clinical processes and relate them to various indicators and manifestations of outcomes. Hence, the different types of dissociation (healthy and unhealthy) and their relation to resilience is identified as an important gap in the psychoanalytic literature, and, therefore, in psychoanalytic treatments. My starting point is with Freud's ideas of trauma, including mourning and melancholia, transference, and interpretation of dreams as basic psychoanalytic methods of data collection. A body of cases presented in the form of vignettes and case studies aims to develop the possible methods that utilize the benefits of psychoanalytical intervention, while taking into consideration the socio-political and other environmental factors. The methodology for assessing psychoanalytic and psychotherapeutic processes, and clinically relevant dimensions of psychoanalytic processes in the cases presented in this study have been reliably assessed by outside observers (supervisors, both clinical and academic) to determine fully their validity and reliability.

The outcome that is derived from these methodological assessments and treatments establishes the differences and similarity in the treatment of a resilient patient and a vulnerable one in a clinically meaningful way and evaluates the qualities of a treatment, through transference–countertransference and the patient–therapist interaction, that have important predictive effects, in every step in the process looking for the psychic space, sense of self, or lack of them, the listening other, or lack of them, healthy dissociations, and resilience. The study, therefore, is designed to sanction valid estimates of the relationships between specific dimensions of psychoanalysis (object relationship), focusing on the above four characteristics and the outcome in treatment of traumatized patients. The data collected considered evidence that is a distinctive attribute of psychoanalytic therapeutic processes and outcome.

The multiple vignettes and case studies in the study determine the validation in psychoanalysis that can provide insights into the mechanism of an individual patient's changes, and allows a better assessment of how an observed change resulted from treatment, and whether there are similarities between patients' presentations and characteristics of changes beyond a single case. The flexibility of the single case study produces lucid and comprehensible features of causal links that can be compared and contrasted with other cases, while the observable fact phenomena and occurrences can be examined in detail as and when they occur in each individual patient. Furthermore, the distinct information about individual patients that is central to the person's psychopathology can be identified and worked with. This is a shortcoming in a population study, in which the distinct information about individual patients that is central to the person's psychopathology can be neglected or be lost due to the population studies.

The combination of vignettes and case studies and outcome has enabled me to assert that resilience has its positive roots in an early environment, as well as vulnerability and its negative effects of colluding in the victim role and suffering resulting in aggression and difficulties in functioning. Evidence in vignettes and case studies indicates that victimization and suffering, if overcome in therapy, can lead people to ordinary life. The relation between resilience and vulnerability is that trauma for a resilient person results in post trauma growth, as opposed to that of a vulnerable person, which results in post trauma stress and victimhood. The qualities of resilience include having a sense of self to recognize the need for help. Seeking therapy as a restorative measure is an important characteristic of a resilient individual, which helps to strengthen the self, as well as creating positive relations with others. The outcome of cases presented demonstrates the compatibility of psychoanalytic assessment and treatment as a useful therapeutic approach for people who have endured trauma. The factor structure of psychoanalytic intervention with different traumatized patients refers to the construct validity of the psychoanalytic treatment interculturally and with contextual factors.

There are, however, some questions arising from this study that I hope can be used for future research, investigation, and explorations, such as:

• when working with this type of patients, do therapists need to be resilient? And, if so, how, when, and by what mechanism should the resilience or lack of it in therapists be measured?;

• do all types of therapeutic approach need to be aware not only of what patients bring, but also what therapists may bring and project to patients?;

• what is the extent and degree of defensiveness that is characteristic of conflict behaviour that represents personal and emotional needs of individuals to hate an enemy in order to keep the conflicted selves together?;

• to what extent does the group, community, or state's superego play a role in the individual mind of the traumatized person and where do the social responsibilities lie?;

• to what extent does a traumatized person have the capacity for splitting and projecting, which can play a part in how one sees and feels about others, and, through the process of projective identification, how one can make others feel? Is psychoanalytic treatment just the intuition of the therapists, or is there anything more objective? And in what sense is clinical material empirical evidence and data, rather than an illustration of a pre-decided theory?

REFERENCES

Ahumada, J. L. (1994). What is a clinical fact? Clinical psychoanalysis as inductive method. *International Journal of Psychoanalysis*, 75: 949–962.

American Psychiatric Association (1994). *Diagnostic and Statistical Manual of Mental Disorders* (4th edn) (*DSM-IV*). Washington, DC: American Psychiatric Association.

Andrews, G. (2001). Should depression be managed as a chronic disease? *British Medical Journal*, 322: 419–421.

Andrews, G., Sanderson, K., Corry, J., & Lapsley, H. (2000). Using epidemiological data to model efficiency in reducing the burden of depression. *Journal of Mental Health Policy and Economics*, 3: 175–186.

Balint, M. (1968). *The Basic Fault*. London: Tavistock Publications.

Barker, P. (1991). *Regeneration*. London: Viking Press.

Bergmann, M. (1993). Reflections on the history of psychoanalysis. *Journal of the American Psychoanalytic Association*, 41: 929–955.

Bion, W. R. (1959). Attacks on linking. *International Journal of Psychoanalysis*, 40(5–6): 308–315.

Bion, W. R. (1967). *Second Thoughts*. London: William Heinemann.

Blatt, S. J., & Blass, R. B. (1996). Relatedness and self-definition: a dialectic model of personality development. In: G. G. Noam & K. W. Fischer (Eds.), *Development and Vulnerability in Close Relationships* (pp. 309–338). Mahwah, NJ: Lawrence Erlbaum.

Blum, H. (1980). The value of reconstruction in adult psychoanalysis. *International Journal of Psychoanalysis*, 61: 39–54.

Blum, H. (1994). *Reconstruction in Psychoanalysis: Childhood Revisited and Recreated.* New York: International University Press.

Blum, H. (2000). The reconstruction of reminiscence. *Journal of American Psychoanalytic Association*, 47: 1125–1144.

Bollas, C. (1987). *The Shadow of The Object.* New York: Columbia University Press.

Bowlby, J. (1969). *Attachment and Loss, Volume 1.* New York: Basic Books.

Bowlby, J. (1973). *Attachment and Loss: Separation, Anxiety and Anger, Volume 2.* New York: Basic Books.

Bowlby, J. (1980). *Attachment and Loss: Loss, Separation and Depression, Volume 3.* New York: Basic Books.

Braithwaite, R. B. (1953). Object relations as a predictor of treatment outcome with chronic posttraumatic stress disorder. In: *Scientific Explanation: A Study of the Function of Theory, Probability and Law in Science.* Cambridge: Cambridge University Press.

Brenner, O. C., & Vinacke, W. E. (1979). Accommodative and exploitative behavior of males versus females and managers versus non-managers as measured by the Test of Strategy. *Social Psychology Quarterly*, 42: 289–293.

Cassimatis, E. G. (1984). The false self. *International Review of Psycho-Analysis*, 11: 69–77.

Charcot, J. M. (1878). *Lectures on Localization in Diseases of the Brain, Delivered at the Faculté de Médecine, Paris, 1875*, Bourneville (Ed.), E. P. Fowler (Trans.). New York: William Wood.

Charcot, J. M. (1879). *Lectures on the Diseases of the Nervous System, Delivered at La Salpêtrière*, George Sigerson (Trans.). Philadelphia, PA: Henry C. Lea.

Colby, K. M. (1960). Experiment on the effects of an observer's presence on the imago system during psychoanalytic free-association. *Behavioral Science*, 5(3): 216–232.

Coltart, N. (1988). *How to Survive as a Psychotherapist.* London: Sheldon.

Cooper, A. M. (1993). Discussion: on empirical research. *Journal of the American Psychoanalytic Association*, 41: 381–391.

Creamer, M., Burgess, P., & McFarlane, A. C. (2002). Post-traumatic stress disorder. *General Psychiatry*, 59: 242–248.

Davidson, J., & Colket, J. T. (1997). The eight-item treatment-outcome post-traumatic stress disorder scale: a brief measure to assess treatment outcome in post-traumatic stress disorder. *International Clinical Psychopharmacology*, 12: 41–45.

Davies, R. (1998). [Review of] *What Do Psychoanalysts Want? The Problem of Aims in Psychoanalytic Theory*, by Joseph Sandler and Anna Ursula Dreher, Routledge, £37.50 (hb), £13.99 (pb), pp. 141. *Psychoanalytic Psychotherapy*, 12: 81–83.

Delpit, L. (1996). The politics of teaching literate discourse. In: W. Ayers & P. Ford (Eds.), *City Kids, City Teachers: Reports From the Front Row* (pp. 3–10). New York: New Press.

Eagle, M. (1995). The developmental perspectives of attachment and psychoanalytic theory. In: S. Goldberg, R. Muir, & J. Kerr (Eds.), *Attachment Theory: Social, Developmental, and Clinical Perspectives* (pp. 123–150. Hillsdale, NJ: Analytic Press.

Eagle, M. N. (2003). The postmodern turn in psychoanalysis. A critique. *Psychoanalytic Psychology*, 20: 411–424.

Edelson, M. (1986). *Hypothesis and Evidence in Psychoanalysis*. Chicago, IL: University of Chicago Press.

Eissler, K. R. (1950). The Chicago Institute of Psychoanalysis and the sixth period of the development of psychoanalytic technique. *Journal of General Psychology*, 42: 103–159.

Elliott, A., & Frosh, S. (1995). *Psychoanalysis in Contexts: Paths Between Theory and Modern Culture*. London: Routledge.

Erikson, E. (1950). *Childhood and Society*. New York: Norton.

Everly, G. S., & Mitchell, J. T. (2000). The debriefing 'controversy' and crisis intervention: a review of the lexical and substantive issues. *International Journal of Emergency Mental Health*, 2: 211–225.

Ezriel, H. (1950). A psycho-analytic approach to group treatment. *British Journal of Medical Psychology*, 23: 59–74.

Ezriel, H. (1956). Experimentation within the psycho-analytic session. *British Journal for the Philosophy of Science*, 7: 29–48.

Fenichel, O. (1945). *The Psychoanalytic Theory of Neuroses*. New York: W. W. Norton.

Figlio, K. (1982). How does illness mediate social relations? Workmen's compensation and medical–legal practices, 1890–1940. In: A. Treacher & P. Wright (Eds.), *The Problem of Medical Knowledge: Examining the Social Construction of Medicine* (pp. 174–224). Edinburgh: Edinburgh University Press.

First, M. B., Spitzer, R. L., Gibbon, M., Williams, J. B. W., Davies, M., Borus, J., Howes, M. J., Kane, J., Pope, H. G. & Rounsaville, B. (1995). The structured clinical interview for DSM-III-R personality disorders (SCID-II), Part I: Description. *Journal of Personality Disorders*, 9(2): 92–104.

Foa, E. B., & Tolin, D. F. (2000). Comparison of PTSD symptom scale-interview version and the clinician-administered PTSD scale. *Journal of Traumatic Stress, 13*: 181–191.

Foa, E. B., Riggs, D. S., Dancu, C. V., & Rothbaum, B. O. (1993). Reliability and validity of a brief instrument for assessing post-traumatic stress disorder. *Journal of Traumatic Stress, 6*: 459–473.

Foa, E. B., Davidson, J. R. T., Frances, A., & Ross, R. (1999). Expert consensus treatment guidelines for posttraumatic stress disorder. *Journal of Clinical Psychiatry, 60*: 69–76.

Foa, E. B., Hearst-Ikeda, D., & Perry, K. J. (1995). Evaluation of a brief cognitive–behavioral program for the prevention of chronic PTSD in recent assault victims. *Journal of Consulting and Clinical Psychology, 63*: 948–955.

Fonagy, P. (2001). *Attachment Theory and Psychoanalysis*. New York: Other Press.

Fonagy, P. (2002). Evidenced based medicine and its justifications. In: M. Leuzinger-Bohleber & M. Target (Eds.), *Outcomes of Psychoanalytic Treatment* (pp. 53–59). London: Whurr.

Fonagy, P. (2002). Genetics, developmental psychopathology and psychoanalytic theory: the case for ending our (not so) splendid isolation. *Psychoanalytic Inquiry, 23*(2): 218–247.

Fonagy, P., & Target, M. (1996). Playing with reality. I: Theory of mind and the normal development of the psychic reality. *International Journal of Psychoanalysis, 77*: 217–234.

Fonagy, P., & Target, M. (1997). Attachment and reflective function: their role in self-organization. *Development and Psychopathology, 9*: 679–700.

Fonagy, P., Gergely, G., Jurist, J. L., & Target, M. (2002). *Affect Regulation, Mentalization and the Development of the Self*. New York: Other Press.

Ford, J. D., Fisher, P., & Larson, L. (1997). Object relations as a predictors of treatment outcome with chronic PTSD. *Journal of Consulting and Clinical Psychology, 65*(4): 547–559.

Frances, A., & Dunn, P. (1975). The attachment–autonomy conflict in agoraphobia. *International Journal of Psychoanalysis, 56*: 435–439.

Freud, S. (1892). Sketches for the 'preliminary communication' of 1893. (C) On the theory of hysterical attacks. *S.E., 1*: 51–54. London: Hogarth.

Freud, S. (1895a). On the grounds for detaching a particular syndrome from neurasthenia under the description "anxiety neurosis". *S.E., 3*: 87–118. London: Hogarth.

Freud, S. (1895f). A reply to criticisms of my paper on anxiety neurosis. *S.E.*, *3*: 121–140. London: Hogarth.

Freud, S. (1896a). Heredity and the aetiology of the neuroses. *S.E.*, *3*: 141–156. London: Hogarth.

Freud, S. (1899a). Screen memories. *S.E.*, *3*: 301–322. London: Hogarth.

Freud, S. (1900a). *The Interpretation of Dreams*. *S.E.*, *4–5*. London: Hogarth.

Freud, S. (1905d). *Three Essays on the Theory of Sexuality*. *S.E.*, *7*: 125–245. London: Hogarth.

Freud, S. (1905e). *Fragment of an Analysis of a Case of Hysteria*. *S.E.*, *7*: 3–124. London: Hogarth.

Freud, S. (1909c). Family romances. *S.E.*, *9*: 235–244. London: Hogarth.

Freud, S. (1909d). *Notes Upon a Case of Obsessional Neurosis*. *S.E.*,

Freud, S. (1910a). Five lectures on psycho-analysis. *S.E.*, *11*: 3–55. London: Hogarth.

Freud, S. (1913f). The theme of three caskets. *S.E.*, *12*: 289–302. London: Hogarth.

Freud, S. (1913j). The claims of psycho-analysis to scientific interest. *S.E.*, *13*: 165–192. London: Hogarth.

Freud, S. (1914g). Remembering, repeating and working through. *S.E.*, *12*: 145–156. London: Hogarth.

Freud, S. (1915b). Thoughts for the times on war and death. *S.E.*, *14*: 275–300. London: Hogarth.

Freud, S. (1915c). Instincts and their vicissitudes. *S.E.*, *14*: 111–140. London: Hogarth.

Freud, S. (1915d). Repression. *S.E.*, *14*: 143–158. London: Hogarth.

Freud, S. (1915e). The unconscious. S.E., 14: 159–205. London: Hogarth.

Freud, S. (1916a). On transience. *S.E.*, *14*: 303–308. London: Hogarth.

Freud, S. (1917e). Mourning and melancholia. *S.E.*, *14*: 243–258. London: Hogarth.

Freud, S. (1918b). *From the History of an Infantile Neurosis. S.E.*, *17*: 1–123. London: Hogarth.

Freud, S. (1919d). Introduction to psycho-analysis and the war neuroses. *S.E.*, *17*: 205–211. London: Hogarth.

Freud, S. (1920g). *Beyond the Pleasure Principle. S.E.*, *18*: 7–64. London: Hogarth.

Freud, S. (1923b). *The Ego and the Id. S.E.*, *19*: 12–66. London: Hogarth.

Freud, S. (1924c). The economic problem of masochism. *S.E.*, *19*: 155–170. London: Hogarth.

Freud, S. (1924e). The loss of reality in neurosis and psychosis. *S.E.*, *19*: 183–190. London: Hogarth.

Freud, S. (1926d). *Inhibitions, Symptoms and Anxiety. S.E., 20:* 87–157. London: Hogarth.

Freud, S. (1936). An open letter to Romain Rolland on the occasion of his seventieth birthday. www.pep-web.org/document.php, accessed on 16 April, 2010.

Freud, S. (1937c). Analysis terminable and interminable. *S.E., 23:* 211–253. London: Hogarth.

Freud, S., & Breuer, J. (1895a). *Studies on Hysteria. S E., 2.* London: Hogarth.

Freyd, J. J. (1996). *Betrayal Trauma: The Logic of Forgetting Childhood Abuse.* Cambridge, MA: Harvard University Press.

Garland, C. (1998). *Understanding Trauma: A Psychoanalytical Approach.* London: Tavistock.

Garmezy, N. (1970). Process and reactive schizophrenia: some conceptions and issues. *Schizophrenia Bulletin, 2:* 30–74.

Garmezy, N. (1971). Vulnerability research and the issue of primary prevention. *The American Journal of Orthopsychiatry, 41*(1): 101–116.

Garmezy, N. (1981). Children under stress: perspectives on antecedents and correlates of vulnerability and resistance to psychopathology. In: A. I. Rabin, J. Arnoff, A. M. Barclay, & R. A. Zucker (Eds.), *Further Explorations in Personality* (pp. 196–269). New York: John Wiley.

Garmezy, N. (1991). Resiliency and vulnerability to adverse developmental outcomes associated with poverty. *American Behavioural Scientist, 34:* 416–430.

Garmezy, N. (1993). Children in poverty: resilience despite risk. *Psychiatry, 56:* 127–136.

Garmezy, N., Masten, A. S., & Tellegen, A. (1984). The study of stress and competence in children: a building block for developmental psychopathology. *Child Development, 55:* 97–111.

Gelpin, E., Bonne, O., Peri, T., Brandes, D., & Shalev, A. Y. (1996). Treatment of recent trauma survivors with benzodiazepines: a prospective study. *Journal of Clinical Psychiatry, 57:* 390–394.

Gordon, K. (1995). The self-concept and motivational patterns of resilient African American high school students. *Journal of Black Psychology, 21:* 239–255.

Green, A. (2000). *Fabric of Affect in the Psychoanalytic Discourse.* London: Routledge.

Greenacre, P. (1956). Re-evaluation of the process of working through. *International Journal of Psychoanalysis, 37:* 439–444. New York: International University Press.

Greenberg, J. R. (1986). Theoretical models and the analyst's neutrality. *Contemporary Psychoanalysis, 22*: 87–106.

Greenberg, J. R., & Mitchell, S. A. (1983). *Object Relations in Psychoanalytic Theory*. Cambridge, MA: Harvard University Press.

Grotstein, J. (1978). Inner space: its dimensions and its coordinates. *International Journal of Psychoanalysis, 59*: 55–61.

Grünbaum, A. (1984). *The Foundations of Psychoanalysis: A Philosophical Critique*. Berkeley, CA: University of California Press.

Heimann, P. (1950). On countertransference. *International Journal of Psychoanalysis, 31*: 81–84.

Herbert, J. D., & Sageman, M. (2004). First do no harm: emerging guidelines for the treatment of posttraumatic reactions. In: G. M. Rosen (Ed.), *Posttraumatic Stress Disorder: Issues and Controversies* (pp. 213–232). New York: Wiley.

Herman, J. L. (1992). *Trauma and Recovery: From Domestic Abuse to Political Terror*. New York: Basic Books.

Higgins, G. (1994). *Resilient Adults: Overcoming a Cruel Past*. San Francisco, CA: Jossey-Bass.

Hinshelwood, R. D. (1983). Projective identification and Marx's concept of man. *International Journal of Psychoanalysis, 10*: 221–226.

Hinshelwood, R. D. (1991). *A Dictionary of Kleinian Thought*. London: Free Association Books.

Hinshelwood, R. D. (1994a). *Clinical Klein: From Theory to Practice*. New York: Basic Books.

Hinshelwood, R. D. (1994b). Attacks on the reflective space. In: V. Shermer & M. Pines (Eds.), *Ring of Fire: Primitive Object Relations and Affects in Group Psychotherapy* (pp. 86–106). London: Routledge.

Hinshelwood, R. D. (1995). Psychoanalysis in Britain: points of cultural access, 1893–1918. *International Journal of Psychoanalysis, 76*: 135–151.

Hinshelwood, R. D. (1997). *Therapy or Coercion*. London: Karnac.

Hinshelwood, R. D. (1999). Countertransference. *International Journal of Psychoanalysis, 80*: 797–818.

Hinshelwood, R. D. (2002). Symptoms or relationships? Comment on Jeremy Holmes' 'All you need is CBT'. *British Medical Journal, 324*: 288–294.

Holmes, J. (1993). *John Bowlby and Attachment Theory*. London: Routledge.

Isaacs, S. (1952). The nature and function of phantasy. In: *Developments in Psycho-analysis*. London: Karnac.

Jacobs, T. J. (1986). On countertransference enactments. *Journal of American Psychoanalytic Associciation, 34*: 289–307.

Jacobs, T. J. (1991). *The Use of the Self*. Madison, CT: International Universities Press.

Janet, P. (1892–1907). *The Major Symptoms of Hysteria* (2nd edn). New York: Macmillan, 1920.

Johnson, J. G., Cohen, P., Brown, J., Smailes, E. M., & Bernstein, D. P. (1999). Childhood maltreatment increases risk for personality disorders during early adulthood. *Archives of General Psychiatry, 56*: 600–606.

Joseph, B. (1987). Projective identification: clinical aspects. In: J. Sandler (Ed.), *Projection, Identification, and Projective Identification* (pp. 65–74). London: Karnac.

Kernberg, O. (1975). *The Subjective Experience of Emptiness in Borderline Conditions and Pathological Narcissism* (pp. 213–224). New York: Jason Aronson.

Kernberg, O. F. (1976). *Object Relation Theory and Clinical Psychoanalysis*. New York: Jason Aronson.

Kernberg, O. F. (1979). Some implications of object relations theory for psychoanalytic technique. *Journal of American Psychoanalytic Association, 27*: 207–239.

Kernberg, O. F. (1983). Object relation theory and character analysis. *Journal of American Psychoanalytic Association, 31*: 247–271.

Kernberg, O. F. (1993). Discussion: empirical research in psychoanalysis. *Journal of the American Psychoanalytic Association, 41*: 369–380.

Kessler, R. C., Sonnega, A., & Bromet, E. (1995). Posttraumatic stress disorder in the national comorbidity survey. *Archives of General Psychiatry, 52*: 1048–1060.

Khan, M. M. R. (1974). *The Use and Abuse of Dream in the Privacy of the Self*. London: Hogarth.

Klein, M. (1923). The development of a child. *International Journal of Psychoanalysis, 4*: 419–474.

Klein, M. (1929). Personification in the play of children. *International Journal of Psycho-Analysis, 10*:193–204.

Klein, M. (1930). The importance of symbol-formation in the development of the ego *International Journal of Psycho-Analysis, 11*: 24–39.

Klein, M. (1935). A contribution to the psychogenesis of manic–depressive states. *International Journal of Psychoanalysis, 16*: 145–174.

Klein, M. (1940). Mourning and its relation to manic-depressive states. *International Journal of Psycho-Analysis, 21*: 125–153.

Klein, M. (1946). Notes on some schizoid mechanisms. *International Journal of Psychoanalysis, 16*: 145–174.

Klein, M. (1975). *Envy and Gratitude and Other Works, 1946–1963*. *International Psycho-Analysis Library, 104*.

Kleinman, A., & Good, B. (Eds.) (1985). *Culture and Depression: Studies in the Anthropology and Cross-cultural Psychiatry of Affect and Disorder*. Berkeley, CA: University of California Press.

Kleinman, A., Das, V., & Lock, M. (1997). *Social Suffering*. Oxford: Oxford University Press.

Kohn, A. (1993). Choices for children: Why and how to let students decide. *Phi Delta Kappan, 75*(1): 8–16.

Kohut, W. (1971). *The Analysis of the Self*. New York: International Universities Press.

Kohut, W. (1972). Thoughts on narcissism and narcissistic rage. *Psychoanalytic Study of the Child, 27*: 360–400.

Kohut, W. (1977). *The Restoration of the Self*. New York: International Universities Press.

Laing, R. D. (1959). *The Divided Self*. London: Penguin Books.

Laplanche, J. (1999). *Essays on Otherness*. New York: Routledge.

Laplanche, J., & Pontalis, J. B. (1973). *The Language of Psycho-Analysis*, D. Nicholson Smith (Trans.). London: Hogarth.

Lerner, M. J. K. (1980). *The Belief in a Just World*. New York: Plenum Press.

Lewin, B. D. (1954). Sleep, narcissistic neurosis, and the analytic situation. *Psychoanalytic Quarterly, 23*: 487–510.

Lichtenberg, J. (1983). Subjectivism as moral weakness projected. *Philosophical Quarterly, 33*(133): 378–385.

Lichtenberg, J. (1989). *Psychoanalysis and Motivation*. Hillsdale, NJ: Analytic Press.

Lifton, R. (1994). *The Protean Self: Human Resilience in an Age of Fragmentation*. New York: Basic Books.

Litz, B. T., Gray, M. J., Bryant, R. A., & Adler, A. B. (2002). Early intervention for trauma: current status and future directions. *Clinical Psychology: Science and Practice, 9*: 112–134.

Mace, C. (1995). *The Art and Science of Assessment in Psychotherapy*. London: Routledge.

Macy, R. D., Behar, L., Paulson, R., Delman, J., Schmid, L., & Smith, S. F. (2004). Community-based acute posttraumatic stress management: a description and evaluation of a psychosocial-intervention continuum. *Harvard Review of Psychiatry, 12*: 217–228.

Mahler, M., Pine, F., & Bergman, A. (1975). *The Psychological Birth of the Human Infant: Symbiosis and Individuation*. New York: Basic Books.

Marmar, C. R., Weiss, D. S., & Metzler, T. J. (1997). The Peritraumatic Dissociative Experiences Questionnaire. In: J. P. Wilson & T. M.

Keane (Eds.), *Assessing Psychological Trauma and PTSD* (pp. 413–428). New York: Guilford Press.

Mayou, R. A., Ehlers, A., & Hobbs, M. (2000). Psychological debriefing for road traffic victims: three-year follow up of a randomised control. *British Journal of Psychiatry, 176*: 589–593.

McDougall, J. (1985). *Theatres of the Mind: Illusion and Truth on the Psychoanalytic Stage.* New York: Basic Books.

McDougall, J. (1986). *Theatres of the Body: A Psychoanalytic Approach to Psychosomatic Illness.* New York: Norton.

McLaughlin, J. (1992). Clinical and theoretical aspects of enactment. *Journal of American Psychoanalitic Association, 39*: 595–614.

Meier, D. (1995). *The Power of Their Ideas: Lessons for America From a Small School in Harlem.* Boston, MA: Beacon Press.

Mill, J. S. (1852). *Principles of Political Economy, With Some of Their Applications to Social Philosophy.* Oxford: Oxford University Press.

Milner, M. (1969). *The Hands of the Living God.* London: Hogarth.

New Oxford English Dictionary (2001). Oxford: Oxford University Press.

Ortlepp, K., & Friedman, M. (2002). Prevalence and correlates of secondary traumatic stress in workplace lay trauma counselors. *Journal of Traumatic Stress, 15*: 213–222.

Parson, E. R. (1986). Transference and post-traumatic stress: combat veterans' transference to the Veterans Administration Medical Center. *Journal of the American Academy of Psychoanalysis, 14*: 349–375.

Popper, K. (1974). Replies to my critics. In: P. A. Schilpp (Ed.), *The Philosophy of Karl Popper, Volume 2.* LaSalle, IL: Open Court.

Pynoos, R. S., & Eth, S. (1986). Witness to violence: the child interview. *Journal of the American Academy Child Psychiatry, 25*: 306–319.

Quine, W. O. (1961). *From a Logical Point of View.* Cambridge, MA: Harvard University Press.

Reich, A. (1960). Pathologic forms of self-esteem regulation. *Psychoanalytic Study of the Child, 15*: 215–232.

Rivers, W. H. R. (1918). Psychiatry and the war. *Science, New Series, 49*(1268): 367–369.

Rosenfeld, H. A. (1971). A clinical approach to the psychoanalytic theory of the life and death instincts: an investigation into the aggressive aspects of narcissism. *International Journal of Psychoanalysis, 52*: 169–178.

Rosenfeld, H. A. (1983). Primitive object relations and mechanisms. *International Journal of Psychoanalysis, 64*: 261–267.

Roth, S., Newman, E., Pelcovitz, D., Van der Kolk, B., Mandel, F. S. (1997). Complex PTSD in victims exposed to sexual and physical abuse: results from the DSM-IV field trial for posttraumatic stress disorder. *Journal of Traumatic Stress*, 10(4): 539–555.

Russell, B. (1948). *Human Knowledge: Its Scope and Limits*. London: Routledge, 1992.

Rutter, M. (1995). Psychosocial adversity: risk, resilience, and recovery. *Southern African Journal of Child and Adolescent Psychiatry*, 7(2): 75–88.

Rutter, M., Maughan, B., Mortimore, P., Ouston, J., & Smith, A. (1979). *Fifteen Thousand Hours*. Cambridge: Harvard University Press.

Sandler, J. (1983). Reflections on some relations between psychoanalytic concepts and psychoanalytic practice. *International Journal of Psychoanalysis*, 64: 35–45.

Sandler, J. (1990). On internal object relations. *Journal of the American Psychoanalytic Association*, 38: 859–880.

Sandler, J., & Rosenblatt, B. (1962). The concept of the representational world. *The Psychoanalytical Study of the Child*, 17: 128–148. New York: International Universities Press.

Sandler, J., & Sandler, A.-M. (1992). Psychoanalytic technique and theory of psychic change. *Bulletin of the Anna Freud Centre*, 15: 35–51.

Saul, L. J. (1940). Utilization of early current dreams in formulating psychoanalytic cases. *Psychoanalytic Quarterly*, 9: 453–469.

Schafer, R. (1968). *Aspects of Internalization*. New York: International Universities Press.

Schore, A. (1997). A century after Freud's Project: is a rapprochement between psychoanalysis and neurobiology at hand? *Journal of the American Psychoanalytic Association*, 45(3): 807–840.

Searles, H. F. (1959). The effort to drive the other person crazy. In: *Collected Papers on Schizophrenia and Related Subjects* (pp. 521–555). New York: International Universities Press.

Searles, H. F. (1965). Review of the self as the object world. *International Journal of Psychoanalysis*, 46: 529–532.

Searles, H. F. (1986). *My Work with Borderline Patients*. Northvale, NJ: Jason Aronson.

Segal, H. (1973). *Introduction to the Work of Melanie Klein*. London: Hogarth.

Seligman, M. (1995). *The Optimistic Child*. Boston: Houghton Mifflin.

Sinason, V. (1993). *Understanding Your Handicapped Child*. London: Rosendale Press.

Sinason, V. (1994). *Treating Survivors of Satanist Abuse*. London: Routledge.

Sinason, V. (1996). From abused to abuser. In: C. Cordess & M. Cox (Eds.), *Forensic Psychotherapy: Crime, Psychodynamics and the Offender* (Vol. 2) *Mainly Practice* (pp. 371–382). London: Jessica Kingsley.

Sinason, V. (2002). *Attachment, Trauma and Multiplicity: Working With Dissociative Identity Disorder*. Hove: Brunner-Routledge.

Sinason, V. (2003). Valerie Sinason talks to Graeme Galton. *Free Association, 10*(4): 56.

Sinason, V. (2004). Disability as trauma and the impact of trauma on disability. Unpublished PhD thesis, St Georges Hospital, University of London.

Sinason, V. (2006). No sex please—we're British psychodynamic practitioners. In. G. Galton (Ed.), *Touch Papers: Dialogues on Touch in the Psychoanalytic Space* (pp. 46–60).

Sinason, V. (Ed.) (2010). *Attachment, Trauma and Multiplicity: Working with Dissociative Identity Disorder*. London: Routledge.

Spillius, E. (1992). Clinical experiences of projective identification. In: R. Anderson & H. Segal (Eds.), *Clinical Lectures on Klein and Bion* (pp. 59–73). London: Tavistock.

Spitz, R. A. (1945). Hospitalism: an inquiry into the genesis of psychiatric conditions in early childhood. *Psychoanalytic Study of the Child, 1*: 1–28. Reprinted in: R. N. Emde (Ed.), *Dialogues from Infancy* (pp. 53–74). New York: International Universities Press, 1983.

Steiner, J. (1993). *Psychic Retreats: Pathological Organisations in Psychotic, Neurotic and Borderline Patients*. London: Routledge.

Stekel, W. (1939). *Technique of Analytic Psychotherapy*. London: Bodley Head.

Stern, D. N. (1985). *The Interpersonal World of the Infant: A View from Psychoanalysis and Developmental Psychology*. New York: Basic Books.

Stolorow, R., & Atwood, G. (1992). *Contexts of Being: The Intersubjective Foundations of Psychological Life*. Hillsdale, NT: Analytic Press.

Sullivan, H. S. (1953). *Interpersonal Theory of Psychiatry*. New York: W. W. Norton.

Sullivan, H. S. (1962). *Schizophrenia as a Human Process*. New York: W. W. Norton.

Sullivan, H. S. (1964). *The Fusion of Psychiatry and Social Science*. New York: W. W. Norton.

Sundin, E. C., & Horowitz, M. J. (2002). Impact of event scale: psychometric properties. *British Journal of Psychiatry, 180*: 205–209.

Symington, N. (1986). *The Analytic Experience—Lectures from the Tavistock*. London: Free Association Books.

Tuckett, D. (1994). Developing a grounded hypothesis to understand a clinical process. *International Journal of Psychoanalysis*, 75:1159–1180.

Van der Hart, O., & Horst, R. (1989). The dissociation theory of Pierre Janet. *Journal of Traumatic Stress*, 2(4): 399–411.

Van Zelst, W. H., de Beurs, E., Beekman, A. T., Deeg, D. J., & van Dyck, (2003). Prevalence and risk factors of posttraumatic stress disorder in older adults. *Psychotherapy Psychosomatics*, 72: 333–342.

Von Wright, G. H. (1957). *The Logical Problem of Induction*. New York: Macmillan.

Weathers, F., Litz, B. T., Herman, D. S., Huska, J. A., & Keane, T. M. (1993). The PTSD Checklist (PCL): reliability, validity, and diagnostic utility. Paper presented to the 9th Annual Conference of the International Society of Traumatic Stress Disorder, San Antonio, Texas.

Werner, E. E. (1984). Research in review. *Young Children*, 39(9): 68–72.

Werner, E. E. (1989). Children of the garden island. *Scientific American*, 260: 106–111.

Werner, E. E. (1992). The children of Kauai—resiliency and recovery in adolescence and adulthood. *Journal of Adolescent Health*, 13: 262–268.

Werner, E. E. (1993). *Risk, Resilience, and Recovery: Perspectives From the Kauai Longitudinal Study*. Cambridge: Cambridge University Press, 1993.

Werner, E. E. (1994). Overcoming the odds. *Journal of Developmental and Behavioral Pediatrics*, 15: 131–136.

Werner, E. E. (1995). Resilience in development. Current directions in psychological science. *American Psychological Society*, 4(3): 81–85.

Werner, E. E. (1996). How kids become resilient: observations and cautions. *Resiliency in Action*, 1(1): 18–28.

Werner, E. E., & Smith, R. S. (1982). *Vulnerable But Invincible: A Longitudinal Study of Resilient Children and Youth*. New York: McGraw-Hill.

Werner, E. E., & Smith, R. S. (1992). *Overcoming the Odds: High-risk Children from Birth to Adulthood*. New York: Cornell University Press.

Whewell, W. (1858). Novum Organum Renovatum. In: R. E. Butts (Ed.), *William Whewell: Theory of Scientific Method*. Indianapolis, IN: Hackett, 1989.

Winnicott, D. W. (1947). Hate in the counter-transference. *International Journal of Psychoanalysis*, 30: 69–74.

Winnicott, D. W. (1951). Transitional objects and transitional phenomena. *International Journal of Psychoanalysis*, 34: 89–97.

Winnicott, D. W. (1958). *Collected Papers: Through Paediatrics to Psycho-Analysis*. London: Tavistock.

Winnicott, D. W. (1960). Ego distortions in terms of true and false self. *The Maturational Processes and the Facilitating Environment*. New York: International Universities Press, 1965.

Winnicott, D. W. (1965). *The Maturational Processes and the Facilitating Environment*. London: Hogarth Press.

Winnicott, D. W. (1971). The use of an object and relating through identification. In: *Playing and Reality* (pp. 101–111). London: Tavistock.

Winnicott, D. W. (1974). Fear of breakdown. *International Journal of Psychoanaysis*, 1: 103–107.

World Health Organization (WHO) (1992). *International Classification of Mental and Behavioural Disorders* (10th edn) (*ICD-10*). Geneva: WHO.

World Health Organization (WHO) (1995). *The World Health Report*. Geneva: WHO.

INDEX

Klein, M., 10, 17, 114, 135, 159, 221,
    254–255, 264, 298–299
    Erna, 255
Kleinman, A., xxv, 126, 299
Kohn, A., 7, 299
Kohut, W., 39, 135, 299

Laing, R. D., 13, 299
Laplanche, J., 8, 21, 31, 59, 299
Lapsley, H., 121, 291
Larson, L., 106, 294
Lerner, M. J. K., xiii, 299
Lewin, B. D., 136, 299
libido, 8, 15, 21, 70, 120, 155, 223,
    261
Lichtenberg, J., 33, 136, 299
life
    adult, 10, 13, 22, 58, 63, 72, 74, 89,
        104, 106, 111, 113, 134, 139,
        147, 158, 160–161, 163–164,
        178, 182, 189, 204, 270, 280,
        283
    daily, xiii, 46, 110, 143, 150
    real, 32
Lifton, R., 8, 299
listening other, xv, xviii–xix, xxii,
    xxiv, xxvii, 4, 8, 11, 13, 18, 20,
    22, 32, 34, 42–43, 45, 47, 50–51,
    53–54, 72–73, 77, 79, 81–82,
    85–86, 93, 96, 98–99, 102,
    105–106, 108–110, 112–113,
    126–128, 131, 134, 140–141,
    146–147, 162–163, 169, 175–178,
    190, 196–199, 203–209, 211,
    213–214, 220, 227–228, 230–231,
    235, 237–238, 245, 248–252, 254,
    262, 265, 271, 275, 277–283, 288
Litz, B. T., 71, 123, 299, 303
Lock, M., xxv, 126, 299
loss of the
    object, 10, 20, 271, 276, 285
    other, 10, 271, 276, 285
    self, 12, 20, 63, 271, 276, 285
    sense of self, 10–11, 21

Mace, C., 32, 299
Macy, R. D., 71, 299
Mahler, M., 136, 299
Mandel, F. S., 105, 130, 301
Marmar, C. R., 123, 299–300
masochism, 41, 47, 170, 178, 199,
    201–202, 209, 211, 215, 220–224,
    247
    sado-, 40, 45, 170, 220
Masten, A. S., xxiv, 4, 6, 296
masturbation, 130, 220, 231, 238,
    240–241, 245, 248, 263, 269
Maughan, B., 7, 301
Mayou, R. A., 71, 300
McDougall, J., 14, 284, 300
McFarlane, A. C., 121, 292
McLaughlin, J., 14, 284, 300
Meier, D., 7, 300
melancholia, 9, 20–21, 267–268, 276,
    287
memory
    traumatic, xxv–xxvi, 15, 75, 86,
        150, 153, 182, 185, 190, 203,
        246, 262, 265, 279
    unbearable, xxi, 130, 144, 146,
        149, 160, 173, 205, 211
Metzler, T. J., 123, 299–300
Mill, J. S., 33, 300
Milner, M., 19, 257–259, 300
Mitchell, J. T., 62, 71, 293
Mitchell, S. A., 9, 269, 297
Mortimore, P., 7, 301
mother
    bad, 168
    biological, 41, 44
    –child relationship, 114, 261
    good, 170–171, 175, 201
    grand-, 41–42, 226, 229
    mourning, 10–11, 20–22, 63, 81, 150,
        190, 201, 203, 261–264, 267–268,
        270–271, 276, 285, 287

narcissism, 35, 39, 65, 109, 138, 178,
    190, 245–246, 263, 276